# A German Paradise in Texas

*The Fate of German Emigrants to Texas in the 1840's*

A German Paradise in Texas

The Fate of German Emigrants to Texas in the 1840's

©2019 Stephen A. Engelking
ISBN 978-3-949197-73-4

Based on the German Novel:
*Deutsche*
*suchen den Garten der Welt*
*Das Schicksal deutscher Auswanderer in Texas vor 100 Jahren*
*nach Berichten erzählt von Fritz Scheffel (1889-1942)*

This edition is set in *Book Antiqua*
and includes notes and illustrations

Texianer Verlag
Tuningen
Germany
www.texianer.com

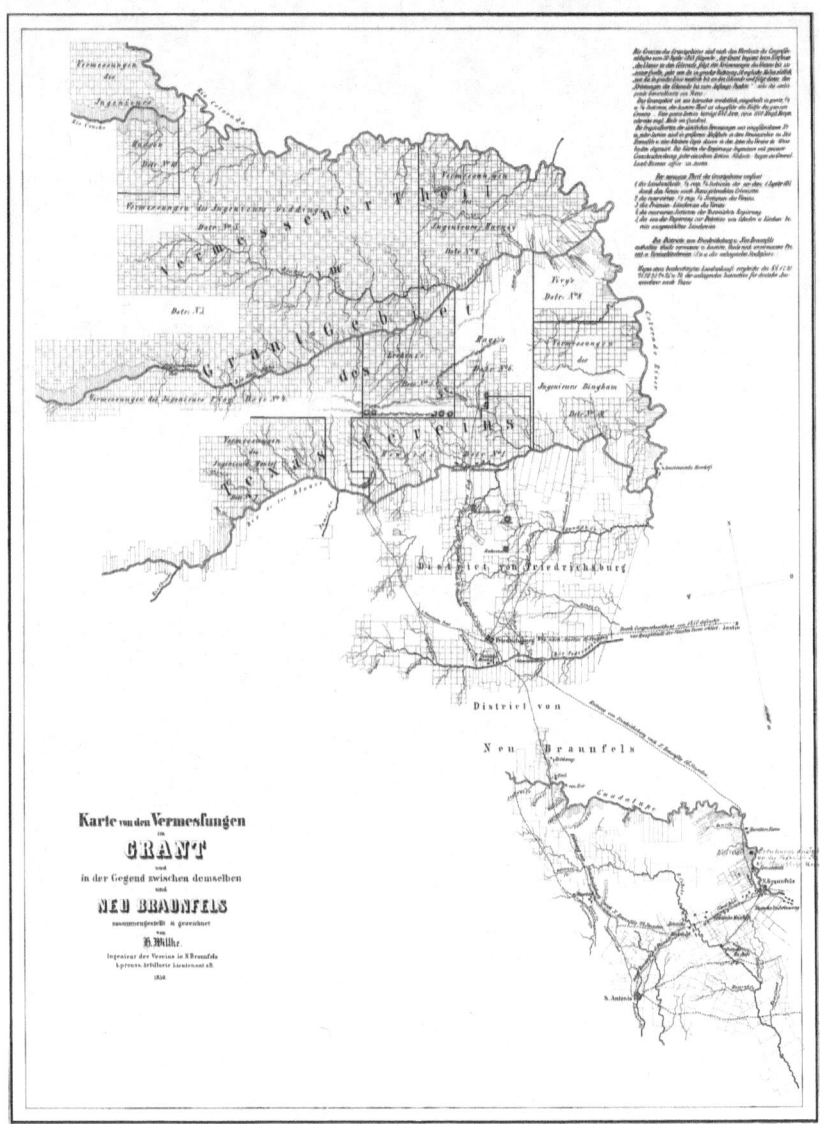

*Fig. 1: Survey Map drawn by H. Wilke*

## Preface

After discovering a copy of the German novel, *Deutsche suchen den Garten der Welt – Das Schicksal deutscher Auswanderer in Texas vor 100 Jahren nach Berichten erzählt von Fritz Scheffel*, I was so fascinated by the way the author related the story of the German Texas pioneers that I decided to republish the book in German in order to make it available to German readers once again. The book was originally published in 1937 and is written in a style and with elements of the German nationalistic culture of the time. It seems that the novel had almost been forgotten and hardly appears in any information about Scheffel. I have not been able to discover why Scheffel was interested in this theme.

Fritz Scheffel was born in Roda (now Stadroda) on July 6, 1889. The small town of less than seven thousand inhabitants is located in Thuringia on the River Roda. This undoubtedly colored some of the characters and scenes in his novel, especially the political overtones which were certainly influenced by the fact that he was sacked from his teaching post in 1933 for political reasons (the reader should note the story about the school teacher who suffers the same fate in this book).

The fact that Faust was born in the same town in 1480 may also have been a covert inspiration for him to become an author and storyteller, the profession Scheffel took up after he left teaching. During his writing career he wrote a number of books including textbooks on technical matters and a number of historical and biographical novels. He died in Weimar on February 19, 1942.

In the meantime, there are unfortunately hardly any German speaking Texans left and the descendants of those pioneers have no access to this literary and historical work which, whilst it is a good story, it is very close to the real history of Texas of the 1840's and has the potential to bring history alive to them.

At this point I would like to mention that I am also a descendant of Texas pioneers, a Son of the Republic of Texas and a member of the ancient Prussian Sack Family. My ancestors actually emigrated from Germany to Texas in the 1830's, settling in the area of Cat Spring in Austin County previous to the emigrations related in this book. Their story is partially published in *The Engelking Letters* which I co-published with Flora von Roeder and the interested reader will also find information about that settlement in the book I co-authored with Jim Woodrick, *The Millheim and Cat Spring Pioneers — German Immigrants Building a New Life in Texas*. I have been living in Germany for over forty years and have regular contact and make frequent visits to my many relatives in Texas. Common to many Texans, all of us have German ancestry and owe what we are very much to those pioneers who so bravely opened a new world for us.

Members of the family of my ancestors actually would have come into contact and helped some of the characters we find mentioned in this novel therefore it is of special interest to me.

It was for these reasons that I decided to set about translating the novel into English which has turned out to be a time-consuming and somewhat daunting task. Scheffel's prose is very much a child of his time and his style does not work well in English for the modern American reader. There are also passages which would not be politically correct today and might come under the Censor's hammer! I have written with the intention of not wishing to hurt anyone's feelings or sensibilities.

I therefore decided to re-write the book into English rather than leave it as a pure translation. However, I have tried to retain the original flavor and the storyline of the novel whilst attempting to make reading acceptable for the average American today. I hope I have been successful in achieving this — only time and readers' comments will tell.

Included are some notes and illustrations mainly from public domain sources. No doubt there are many other pieces of information which would interest many readers and I would suggest the use of a browser and Wikipedia if there is a desire to follow up any of the characters and places mentioned. Most of the titles I have anglicized as well as most Texan place names. I have retained the title *Herr* rather than *Mr* because I felt that this retained more of the character of the telling. German uses so-called Umlauts — vowels with two dots over the top and I have converted *ö* to *oe*, *ä* to *ae* and *ü* to *ue* respectively as well as the *ß* to *ss* according to standard convention. The reader who is unfamiliar with German need not take the trouble to try and pronounce these letters correctly and a simple *o, a* or *u* will suffice. I also decided to keep the name *Adelsverein*[1] for the Nobility Society in Mainz, as this word is know to many in Texas.

I hope you will enjoy reading this book as much as I have writing it.

*Stephen Engelking, December 2019.*

# I

"So, ain't I right? Always the same old story that's been going on for two years now — meeting after meeting. I'm beginning to wonder if their Lordships will ever be finished. They talk and talk and there's no end to it, whilst we in the kitchen have to sort out the mess. Ain't I right, Lovage?"

Lovage, Silver Polisher, Stoker, Lamp Lighter and General Dogsbody, servants in Prince Carl's Leiningen Castle[2] in Mainz all nodded in agreement.

That's just how it is Herr Haeberle, and every time the food that has been cooked for their lordships burns. That delicious food! What a disgrace after our skillful cook, Herr Haeberle, has taken so much trouble. There are eight courses today, starters and desert on top.

Lovage felt under his apron strap for his watch: "It'll happen at two, Herr Haeberle, don't you think, at two o'clock? It was ordered for twelve."

The kitchen door flew open. "Yes Lisett, what's up then?" both men called at once.

The kitchen maid flopped onto the bench.

"My dear God, what a shock I had, the way that lad up there looked at me!" She pressed both hands to her heart.

"Lad, did you say, what lad?" Haeberle let the lid fall onto the bulbous soup pan and lifted his fine, long soupspoon as if he were going to strike. Lovage's eyes nearly popped out of her head.

"Upstairs in the hallway in front of the Saloon where their Lordships are gathered, a strange lad is striding back and forth. Huh, he looks like a spider! Yellow and thin with a black goatee beard and eyes as if they want to burn through you! The way he looked at me, I thought it must be the Devil himself. So..." Her eyes widened and stared at Lovage, who recoiled.

*Fig. 2: Carl Friedrich Wilhelm Emich Fürst zu Leiningen*

Somewhat calmer she then said, "But he didn't limp, I could see that for sure. He strode up and down as if someone had wound him up! What on earth do the fine sirs want with such a rascal?"

She sniffed. Haeberle pulled around on his high, white cook's hat, drops of perspiration emerging on his forehead.

"Keeping this to ourselves…" A cloud of hissing steam came out of the pan, spitting fat, shooting, scorching and dancing between saucepans and frying pans on the hot cooker hob.

Haeberle did not finish his sentence and hastily got to work deftly moving vessels backwards and forwards in the midst of the spitting and steaming as a greasy cloud climbed to the ceiling, floating over the heads of the three.

"So I was right. It's going to be afternoon again just like last time", Haeberle claimed as if nothing had happened.

"And what is with that lad upstairs who frightened Lisett so? Perhaps he's one of those from yonder America, from Texas. Clerk Kagelmann, who's my friend and is always the minute taker when they need one, said to me, 'Ludwig', he said, 'that's an important matter what they're doing there, in fact a matter of life and death for the whole of Germany.'"

The kitchen door opened quietly. The three moved around and laughed. "Greetings dear Colleague", said Lovage and bowed deeply in front of His Importance, the Count's Valet Sebastian Schmoller. He surveyed the situation sitting next to Lisett on the kitchen bench, saying and gesturing with a raised hand, "Carry on." Then he complained, "The wine's going to be warm again 'cos the ice has melted. I don't have any more and therefore decline all responsibility. Today seems to be an especially important day up there. I stood a while in the Yellow Saloon and looked through the keyhole. They talked and talked whilst Kagelmann was having to write until his fingers shook. Yet I've the impression that they actually want to come to a conclusion today."

He raised his eyebrows and flicked a speck of dust from the lapel of his livery. "It's certainly about time!"

"Just what I reckon", interrupted Haeberle. "Didn't I say it'd work out today? Just like my friend Kagelmann said to me in confidence. The Adelsverein (Nobility Society) of Mainz, so called by their lordships since summer '42, wants to finalize things today whatever happens. People in those parts of Germany where too many people are living should go—go to Texas in America. This is what their Lordships are hoping to achieve."

Haeberle leant against the massive kitchen table, laid a finger on his nose and tried to reiterate the thoughts of his friend Kagelmann.

"He said we've had peace in Germany for too long. Each year there are three hundred thousand more people so just where is that going to lead us? Many people have hardly enough to eat and who is going to feed everyone in ten or twenty years time? They'll be piled on top of each other like bugs amongst the flowers but the world is so big and has so much space. Population growth brings hunger and misery, unrest and discontent will grow. Revolution and civil war will break out while the masses 'll be ruined. Therefore they just have to go before it's too late. Germany will be rid of its surplus people and there are quite a few who we've secretly wished good riddance to for a long time."

"You're right, Herr Haeberle", Schmoller stated thoughtfully, his finger raised in the air. "As far as I'm concerned, those folks should get out and as many as possible—it's getting too tight for comfort in our homeland."

Lovage nodded and Haeberle continued to report, "Only so many can live and be fed off the land we've got. The Earth ain't going to grow with the number of people. The more there are the less there is for each and everyone. If the surplus leave, that means better times for all of those who stay back home and if a lot of poor people could be moved out then there would be peace and quiet again for those who do own something. They should take any with them who would like to search for their luck in the world."

He bowed and said quietly, "And I can understand as well, that there are a lot of people who are fed up. Taxes, police and clerics—there are more today than any sensible person can bear. My brother-in-law Christian, who is landlord of 'The Lion', told me that we're living as if we're in prison. Whichever way you try to go there are obstacles. One watchdog stands over the next and if you do manage to earn a few bucks, then they find some way to get 'em off you.

"You have to tighten your belt one hole at a time. Make a squeak and they'll have you by the scruff of your neck. The state is like a millstone around your neck and the poor folks are always the ones to carry the can. Take a look at this poor Germany. If only it was united and everyone would stick together!

"Of the thirty-nine state rulers, each one struts around in his own state like a cockerel on a manure heap. Each has its own taxes and levies, its army, its police, its minister, lords and civil servants. Thousands of hands that do nothing productive grab out to someone who works and rip out their earnings from their fingers."

"No offense Herr Haeberle", interrupted the opinionated Schmoller, surprised, "this seems to me not to be the place to badger so dangerously and your brother-in-law, landlord of 'Die Loewe', is well known for his wild talking. The well-being of our rulers is our bread and if that wasn't the case, we wouldn't be standing here. It wouldn't hurt that landlord brother-in-law of yours if he went off with all those going to Texas or, as far as I am concerned, anywhere else for that matter."

Haeberle was just about to deal a trump against Schmoller when the bell above the kitchen door rang loud and shrill. Heads moved apart and Lovage, smoothing her hair and apron leaped away.

---

As Lovage rushed up the slowly climbing stairs to the first floor she glimpsed the stranger stiffly striding by. Lisset was right—he certainly could give you a fright.

Quietly mumbling to himself, he strode along the red carpet-runner. Lovage bowed out of the way and let the scary one pass by, at which point he swiftly turned to the right and disappeared behind the many doors that opened onto the hallway.

The stranger was called Baron Bourgeois d'Orvanne[3] who had been staying in Mainz for several days. The "Mainz Society for the Protection of German Immigrants in Texas (*Adelsverein*)" had invited him to conclusive negotiations in the official apartment of the Castle Commander. Some time previously he had made the princes and noblemen an offer of a large area of land in Texas and the Adelsverein was not finding it easy to make a purchase decision, which is what Herr Bougeois d'Orvanne wished to achieve.

During an initial discussion, the Duke of Gotha[4] had examined him thoroughly, saying openly that the man had not made a good impression on him.

"I don't like this person", he had whispered into his neighbor, Prince von Solms-Braunfels'[5] ear already during the first round of negotiations who, knowing how to calm him down whispered back, "Your Highness, maybe it is the strangeness and weirdness of this man that is upsetting you. He doesn't need to be bad just because he looks different."

The Duke of Gotha was not the only one who felt uncomfortable about the stranger from Texas. The cunning imposter Bourgeois noted the undercurrents that were forming into a hidden resistance against him but his superior knowledge of human nature had taught him to remain calm and control himself.

He was able to defend himself against any objections raised by the use of emphasized objectivity, determined to achieve his goal in whatever way he could and by any means necessary. He thought to himself, "What are these little potentates in comparison to my experience? They'll have to give in to me and buy the grant on the upper Medina."

He smiled despite the insecurity of his position, once again demonstrating a clear assuredness to their Lordships. In his talk before the assembly he knew how to give the appearance of one with genuine humanity, calculating and careful as never before in his life. Their Lordships would become his victims and the sale had to take place that would free him of all those worries that had been harrowing him for a long time. They had now been negotiating for two days and still had not arrived at a conclusion.

Bourgeois d'Orvanne stepped back and forth in irritable unrest along the red runner, ready at any moment to step in front of the assembly and sign the sales contract. He had travelled to Europe with what was left of his money, setting all he had on one card.

*Fig. 3: Sam Houston in 1861*

The magic that the word "Texas" breathed across to Europe in those years had attracted him like so many other joyriders. He belonged to those who never sow but always reap and in the course of time had gathered exceptional know-how with land fraud, for which the unclear and little organized conditions in Texas offering him rich possibilities. Many settlers who had come into his hands mentioned his name with fear and trepidation as tears and unhappiness were left in the track of his activities. He loved the big, dangerous life and threw that which had been swindled pitilessly to the wind.

Now, with one massive bang, he would be free at once from his debts and enjoy his greedy hunger for life. The ground under his feet in Texas had become really hot so the trip to Europe had come at just the right time. Hands-on Texan justice did not mess about with the likes of him and there were enough trees and nooses to go around for sure.

The country had freed itself from Mexico in 1836 through bloody battles and become independent. Free Indians still lived in the wide-open prairies in its inner parts. The phrase "Garden of the World" remained a byword since the time of the Spaniards who had referred to the country as such. It lay empty, open and waiting behind the Gulf of Mexico. Gently and softly it rose out of the warm sea and climbed slowly over swamps and quagmires to the heights in the West. Green and bushy, in gentle flat waves, the horizon lost itself at the edge of a sky retreating further and further into the distance as it wandered for weeks on end in front of any rider who dared to penetrate the rippling flood of grass of the prairie. "The Rolling Country" lay between the swamps at the coast, in which decay and fever fomented, and the stunning mountains in the West.

All that which North America expressed in the way of excessiveness and insecurity disappeared without trace amongst those green waves. Coming up from the sea via New Orleans and Galveston the white man from Europe carefully felt his way up the river valleys, wretched towns charting the route as he made his way. Every heap of paltry log cabins was called a town having given itself a pompous name.

The primal force of beginning something and the disquiet of the boundless distance was the force that drove those arriving, from one place to the next. The "Yellow Curse" the fever was called that in its unmerciful nature drove many away from the spot where, full of hope, they wished to start a new life. Uncountable numbers died or fell in the war-screeching cries of the Comanches and were scalped with their bones left to bleach in the prairie.

Nevertheless, the current of immigrants did not cease as antlike they crawled up from the coast. No one knew how large that country actually was or how many people it accommodated nor where its boundaries in the West were. There was no exact answer to these questions and on the maps one could just see a large white space, many, many days of travel hence. A few Indian trails, two or three old trodden tracks from the Spanish era meandered small and covert through the endless expanse of the waves of the sea of grass through rustling oak forests, losing themselves in the gorges and unknown mountains.

Fig. 4: The Stamp of the „Mainz Adelsvereins"

The quantity of game in the Indian hunting grounds seemed inexhaustible and the land was waited eagerly for the plough. The young state started to plan the distribution of the territory. Sitting at a desk with ruler and protractor, the lazy, the land hungry and the greedy set off for Texas. The message being sent over seemed to be too tempting as the desire to emigrate swept like an epidemic across whole areas, depopulating them in the process.

The fear of falling into impoverishment and pauperization lay like a dark cloud over Germany and anybody who was poor was also dangerous.

"Poverty is like a smoldering fire in a filled barn. It has to be stamped out. Therefore away with the poor and expendable", said the complainer. Without a plan, a goal or a clear perspective many travelled across the great ocean whilst many died, forsaken and disappointed.

Bourgeois d'Orvanne suddenly stopped in his tracks. An indignant cacophony of men's voices forced its way out to him from behind the high double doors of the Saloon. He felt as if he was sitting on a knife's edge, as their Lordships still did not seem to be in agreement at all. After years of deliberation, the task that their Lordships had set themselves, of managing the German emigration from a single point and to settle the emigrants according to a plan, seemed to be becoming more and more difficult to carry out the nearer it got to the planning stage.

Today, on March 25, 1844, the prepared work was to be brought to a conclusion. After irksome turmoil, setbacks and mistakes, the Adelsverein had managed to get a business connection to an influential Texan (the majority taking Bourgeois d'Orvanne to be such). They believed that he really had control of an area of country that could become a home for thousands. Duke Adolf von Nassau, who was leading the negotiations, made every effort possible to bring the purchase to a conclusion.

Bourgeois d'Orvanne got moving again, his heart feeling as if it were drawn together wondering what would happen if the sale did not go through. He looked at the time and saw that he had been striding up and down the corridor for some three hours now.

"In Germany you learn to wait", he mumbled angrily to himself. "Won't you just let me get a word in edgewise? You need to understand that land ownership in Texas, contrary to bureaucratic Germany where a piece of land the size of your palm has to be registered, does not require the slightest proof."

The president of Texas, Samuel Houston[6], generously handed out land lots during one night on the bottle. Bourgeois d'Orvanne had harvested a fantastically large grant from that blessing, over which he had no more than a note on a scrap of paper from the president. What put him under pressure as a new property owner was the requirement to settle the area by July 31, 1844. On the piece of paper in question it stated that, should he not meet that date, then ownership of the land would fall back to the government.

This he did not disclose to the Adelsverein, musing that their Lordships could see how they sorted that out with the Texan government after they had failed to meet the deadline. By then it would no longer be his worry anymore.

However, it was not that far yet and they were still negotiating whilst Bourgeois d'Orvanne continued to stride up and down the red carpet-runner.

---

The Duke of Meiningen[7] leaned, standing up over the table, gaining the ear of all with his strong voice. The general chatter went silent.

"Everything has to be done to ensure peace in the country. Should the ambitions of obsessed do-gooders collapse, the blight of communism should not poison all and everything, as Pastor Weidig in Hessen[8] preached. In other words, the overthrow of the social status quo that is slowly creeping up on us has to be countered and there is only one radical means — emigration.

"I'd like to call to mind the words of the insurrectionist George Büchner[9] of Darmstadt that he spread to the masses: 'Peace to the hovels! War on the palaces!'

"It remains even today the unrelenting war cry of certain circles and it seems to me as if its influence is becoming stronger. Let us encourage emigration! However, one may not allow it to run wild, it needs to be ordered and controlled. In that we are all unanimous. Those who look at the movements in the country folk from their desk may think that prisons, workhouses, police and military are enough to keep down the excesses of these social effects.

"But believe me, a new time is coming upon us whose final consequences no-one can avoid to notice. The era of the steam engine is coming and it will transform the world. Workshops will be made desolate and the trades will fall into poverty. Unemployment will permanently hit large portions of the population. On top of this, we had a whole series of failed harvests in the last few years with farmers and workers falling into debt. In Hessen this is particularly bad.

*Fig. 5: Friedrich Ludwig Weidig*

"The last strength in an otherwise healthy people is collapsing in impotence, hopelessness and exasperation. Foreign profiteers are sucking their bones dry. And who is the victim of this situation? – They become a burden to the state and the communities. In the end they put aside all their inhibitions and commit crimes, brutalize and become an increasing threat to human society.

"Such appearances cannot be solved with petty measures. Therefore we want to bring together and coordinate this blind chaotic emigration. We owe that to the people. It is good but little has been done to lift their self-confidence and common sense. Those who have lost their faith in their habitat and mother country go without a plan into a country that they have been told flows with milk and honey. This must stop.

"It is my opinion that we should go for it. If this large area of land in Texas is only half as big as what Herr Bourgeois d'Orvanne promises, then we can help thousands. The measures that the emigration committee of our society has been preparing for two years, to carry out a cohesive emigration, would be fulfilled by this purchase contract. Time is running out. I beg you gentlemen to now come to a conclusion."

Fig. 6: Carl Prinz zu Solms-Braunfels (1812-1875)

The Duke looked down the long table and sat down.

"Thank God! At last the saving word", called the Prince von Solms-Braunfels, following the words of the Duke of Meiningen with bright, penetrating voice amongst the mumblings.

"Say yes at last gentlemen! Who would like to seal the numerous advantages that this project offers. Any number could maintain their German culture in the new homeland through cohesive settlement. German towns and villages shall grow along the river banks and line the roads."

He stood up. His eyes glowed. "And the thousand over there across the sea will manage that for which our strength in the mother country is not sufficient — a cohesive German state! I see New Germany coming to fruition in Texas! And the blessing that the fertile earth gives should be brought by German ships to us to relieve our shortages. The surplus of our production of goods and trading will then flow there as recompense."

After these excitedly spoken sentences he paused and allowed his radiant eyes to roam over the men. "Aren't we at a turning point? Germany across the sea is calling and wants to happen! We are ready. Let us conclude the purchase! The work can begin at once. I am burning to at last take action, after all the years of planning and discussing."

"If only it was all so easy!" Prince Friedrich of Prussia interrupted young Solms' hotly spoken words with an air of reservation. "Then it could be achieved with enthusiasm alone. But I feel conscious of the heavy responsibility that we are taking on. Should the undertaking fail, then, through this land purchase, we are signing the death warrant of many on the spot. If Bourgeois d'Orvanne is a scoundrel, then the world will poke a finger at us and make us a laughing stock. When we sent Count Boos Waldeck[10] over to Texas two years ago, so that he could look around and get a feel of the place, what we heard was not very encouraging. His reports were sparing until we didn't hear a word at all. He stayed there and established his own farm and didn't manage to obtain a large tract from the state for our settlement intentions. That which the Count did not manage, this exotic gentleman is now supposing to provide. Be careful gentlemen! What does this man possess in the way of clear ownership titles? Laughingly little. A note that the President of Texas is supposed to have signed plus a vague map on which a large area on the Medina River is drawn with a pencil. Is the signature genuine? What does the empty map tell us? The point was made beforehand that the man is from old French nobility and therefore would not dare to swindle us but is his nobility genuine?"

Prince Friedrich of Prussia thoughtfully ran his fingers through his beard and screwed up his eyes, "One needs to dig down to the roots of the ongoing pauperism, Prussia will perhaps try to move excess town populations into the distant country areas of the East. Fifty years would not be enough to compensate for the disarray that Napoleon caused in Germany. It is not so bad here as it is in Hessen and Thüringen yet. Emigration will become an obsession if one does not want to restrict it and it should not be pushed. It is shaking the people like a fever. However, will it be free of its nightmares if one offers it a better place to sleep? I warn you! Crises pass by. One shouldn't irresponsibly support the romantic nostalgia of dreamers. Is it possible for a state to remain healthy if it operates such a depopulation policy?

"Shouldn't we rather put a gag on the press, who with their gossip are causing even more confusion? Recently I read this sentence in a South German newspaper: 'Whereas in Europe the drones take advantage of all privileges, in America even the bees get a chance!' Such impressions get through. Hard working yet poor citizens that cannot cope with the burden of taxes, healthy but over-indebted farmers and innovative thinking craftsmen will be thrown out. We will be left with the scum of the streets, the reprobate prison candidates and the eternally lazy. One doesn't cure the damage with measures against those who are only the victims. I warn you once again!"

He took a break and allowed his serious eyes to run across the assembled party. Prince Moritz von Nassau laughed and said, "His Highness is obviously referring to the terms of the Texas government whereby only morally acceptable and non-convicted persons are allowed to immigrate? That is no cause for concern. Everyone we help to get over the big pond will be given a perfect certificate of good conduct. The angels we send over will be landing pure and sin-free."

Squeezing his fingers together so that the bones cracked, "The state is not a charity institution", he continued derisively, "and those who don't like it should go. And those we don't like we'll help get there. There have been so many careful words talked about these things and I would like to speak them out clearly once and for all. We need to reckon this out properly — if the cost of supporting certain subjects in penitentiaries, prisons and workhouses is higher than the settlement costs, then it would be outrageous to keep those beneficiaries of the state here. Away with them! One might mix quite a few in every transportation. Away with all those who live off the state without offering anything in return. Go for it and buy the land from Herr Bourgeois d'Orvanne. We have to elect a directorate for the work in Texas. Then good, we'll take the man on board and give him a paid position. Then we have him in our hands and can make him liable if he has swindled us."

The suggestion of Prince Moritz von Nassau was found acceptable by the majority of the their Lordships. They agreed to buy the grant and to give Bourgeois d'Orvanne a post in the directorate. Prince von Solms-Braunfels was to be the Commissioner-General.

The managing directorship in Mainz, the seat of the Adelsverein, was awarded to Count Carl von Castell[11]. Prince Solms and the Frenchman were to travel to Texas with the utmost haste in order to prepare for the accommodation of the first transport. They would have to reach the settlement area before the onset of winter so that the sowing in the coming spring would not be delayed.

Bourgeois d'Orvanne was called into the saloon. The slightly built man entered the room, creeping like a cat and a wave of homely joy covered his face once he had taken in the assembled with his penetrating glance, "They've fallen for it", he rejoiced warmly within.

He bowed. The chairman began, "Baron, the high assembly have decided that they will take up your offer."

D'Orvanne bowed deeply and laid his right hand on his heart. "Ten thousand dollars, half the purchase price, will be transferred through the bankers L.H. Flersheim in Mainz after the contract has been signed. The rest you will receive through Commissioner-General Prince von Solms-Braunfels in Texas after the final takeover of the grants."

The Frenchman became a shade paler. He felt a strangling sensation surging up his throat behind his white, firmly sitting neckband as he swallowed.

"Ten thousand?" shot through his head. "Only half? Then the rest is lost because, latest in Texas, they will know that they have bought puff and wind." A dry cough forced itself from his throat but he immediately pulled himself together.

"Zank you very much, Zank you very much", he rasped with a gravelly voice, dropping his eyelids. Nobody noticed the disappointment that rang out from these words inside the Frenchman's tanned head or sensed anything from the hefty thought processes with which he tried to master the situation.

Count Castell continued, "The money will only be paid out to you when you are willing to take up the post of Second Commissioner in Texas."

Bourgeois d'Orvanne ran his finger behind his neck band, feeling like one being hanged and wondering if he was hearing right. Now he would have to change his plans because he had intended to disappear from Mainz as soon as possible after receiving the money but his smiling countenance did not give away what was going on inside his head.

"Zank you very much, a great 'onor, zank you very much", rasped his voice and he bowed again several times.

"You accept our terms and will act as advisor to his Highness Prince von Solms-Braunfels and travel back to Texas immediately, accompanying the expedition to the grant and working together with the best of your ability for our undertaking. In return we wish to award you an appropriate salary and various securities that are contained in the sales contract and that you will be able to see before signing it."

Bourgeois d'Orvanne had by now pulled himself together. A confirming smile swept over his tanned face. Their Lordships interpreted it as a recognition of their clever offer. The Frenchman thereby expressed a rather fine superiority though, as new ways with which he could avoid the unexpected difficulties revealed themselves to him. Now he would be returning to Texas as representative of the Mainz Adelsverein. Who would dare to lay hands on him under these circumstances?

"Oh, I will make a zery good work to the Society, you be very content about me. I am 'appy for zis carrière fameuse." he exclaimed, swinging his right arm in a long-winded gesture, appearing to express the greatest satisfaction.

The sales contract was passed to him and his eyes hastily flew across the pages.

As he already knew the main points, he could not care less about the details. His brain worked feverishly because he had to get enough of a head start to achieve his goal, despite all the disturbing conditions of the contract. He suddenly remembered the rule that all contracts made in Germany had no validity in Texas. Thus he grasped for the pen with an exuberant lofty movement of the hand and set his name broadly under the contract. An important stage in the development of the Mainz Adelsverein was thus brought to a conclusion.

"And yet he is still a rascal", said Duke Ernst von Gotha to himself, having not taken his eyes off the Frenchman for one second.

That was on March 25, 1844.

---

"You know, Koechert, I'm really surprised by the cold openness with which you make your confessions—as if you had nothing to lose!"

Church Councillor Koser pressed his forehead on the window and turned his back on the Candidate Teacher Hermann Koechert[12] from Stedtfeld near Eisenach. The young teacher stood in the door and was confronted by the slender form of the man of the frock in the dusky study room in which thin clouds of pipe smoke were clinging to the corners. On the other side of the windowpane one shower was chasing the next on this changeable April day.

Koser turned around. For a moment the profile of his face stood before the window pane, drawn and sullen. "I'm waiting for a word of apology from you, Herr Candidate. Have you nothing to say to me?"

"No, nothing", answered Koechert. The tension stood between the two men like a string stretched to breaking point.

"Good, then I'll repeat once again the points of your confession that I'll refer to the government." he said, staring at Koechert severely.

"You stated to the mayor of your school town, as he confronted you about regularly attending church that the dear God would not even bother to count the number of trouser bottoms that have been worn through on church pews and that you believe that he looks at the heart of a person and the whole man, saying that Christendom is more than just a Sunday habit in a frock coat. Do you have anything in the way of an excuse to add to this point?"

"No."

"Additionally, you declared to the same gentleman, as you discussed the moral decay of our time, 'Bad thoughts come more often from an empty stomach than from a depraved heart. Most times a good meal would be of more use than the best Sunday sermon.' Did you say that?"

"Yes"

"Furthermore you tried to apply the immature ideas about the so-called 'Theory of Emanation'[13] in your lessons. You pointed to the development of the human and animal being in the course of time. That happened repeatedly and I have the evidence to prove it."

Koser stood before the young man. He looked at him openly into his screwed up eyes.

"Don't you realize that you have thus transgressed against a world completed by God from the Beginning, in that you have tried to unhinge his mighty work of creation?" His high-pitched voice trembled with the last words.

Koechert stayed calm. "Yes, I know that. Nevertheless, it does not reduce the greatness and glory in any way. I just had trouble interpreting what is actually a very beautiful story from the Old Testament. The writer who invented it would not be angry with me if today I sought after a different way to find out how the world came to be."

Koser went off the deep end. His voice cracked. He clawed his scrawny fingers into the teacher's frock revers and tried to shake the young man. Yet he stood firm like a post.

"Outrageous halfwit!" he hissed. "Misuse of vague perceptions at a time of foment when immaturity takes up things uncritically, leading to useless self destruction."

He stared at Koechert with piercing eyes. "Young man, there is still time to turn back. Regret your words and promise to change for the better, returning to the safe haven of our faith!"

Koechert pushed away the hand of the cleric from his frock revers and said cooly, "I can't take even one step backwards. I've struggled my way through too many nights to arrive at this realization."

"Shut up!" shouted Koser disgusted. "God will punish you in his anger. The Church will not budge one millimeter from its fundamentals. Now I know exactly who you are and also understand how you could get to the point where you could speak in front of your colleagues about, and read from, the writings of that, spat out of hell person from Hessen, Georg Buechner. Thank God! There are still some decent men with rock hard faith. Why did you do it? The times are bad enough without you adding to it. It is seething amongst the people. Somewhere decisions come to maturity. The romantic desire of young people for a unified Germany, empire and of peoples coming together confuse the heads of those not prepared. You are in the service of the Grand Duke and the rest is none of your business. That's the way it is Herr Koechert and from now on you won't need to reckon with a secure position in the civil service."

Koechert let the torrent of words go over his head. The Church Councilor moved a few steps back to his desk, picked up a note with pointed fingers and gazed maliciously at the teacher: "And with this the crown is set on your treasonable goings-on."

He waved the note like a flag through the air. "Justice has played into my hands!"

His scrawny fingers held the crumpled paper far away, reading with perceptible disgust, "For Scripture says that what God has united, man should not tear asunder and that the Almighty, who can make a paradise out of the wasteland, can also turn a land of misery into a paradise, as our dearest Germany was, un-

til its princes lacerated and wounded it..." And so on.

"The German people are one body and you are members of this body. When the Lord gives you a sign through men, by which he leads the people out of servitude to freedom, then arise and the whole body will stand up with you. Lord, break the rod of our taskmasters and let your Kingdom come to us, the Kingdom of Justice! Amen."

Koser pinched his thin lips firmly together and looked at Koechert with contempt. "You wrote that?" he asked, emphasizing every word.

"Yes, copied", answered Koechert dryly.

"How do you mean, copied?"—Koser's eyes blinked mistrustfully.

"These sentences come from a pamphlet by the Hessian naturalist George Buechner. The man died in 1837 and knew the deepest feelings of the people. His words will remain alive among all who long for freedom and justice and I reckon myself to them. Germany should become free, great and united. The tyrants—"

"Windbag! Stop the mischief!" Koser stomped his foot and threw the note on the floorboards. "Man, do you know that you are a traitor? An agitator against the order set by God! God has made the state as it is. And that's why no one shall touch it without impunity!"

He took a deep breath and tugged at his meager beard. "See, I have you completely in my hands and I can destroy you if I want." he gasped, taking a few more breaths. "Can you not find a single word from which I could assume your conversion?"

"Do what you think you have to do," Koechert answered firmly.

Church Councilor Koser reflected. Something held him back to say what was on his tongue. He had wanted to bring the teacher to his knees and humiliate him yet he had not managed to succeed so far. Koechert was not allowing himself to be pushed away just one tiny bit from his position.

"Koechert," he began after a pause, "you are a heated, unclear person and I'm sorry but I want to give you time to think. Think again. If you pause for a moment and find your way back to law and order, then what has just gone on shall stay between us and have no further consequences for you."

He wanted to shake his hand.

Koechert's pale face lifted slightly. It appeared unnaturally white in that gloomy room. He took a step forward, ignoring the cleric's hand.

"Thank you, Herr Church Councilor. But let things run the way they have to go. I do not need time to think and I'm ready to carry the consequences. Nothing will ever be achieved for Germany if we haul in our sails and turn from the road at the first signs of danger just for the sake of personal gain."

Sweat appeared on the cleric's forehead. He turned and looked out of the window again as rain showers whipped against the windows.

"Can I go?" asked Hermann Koechert simply.

The Church Councilor turned around, hurried up to him, staring at him with piercing eyes. "You unhappy person! I'm sorry for the girl you got engaged to a few weeks ago but I'll give you some good advice: There is no room for people of your type in Germany. Emigrate! You belong to the superfluous people who do not get their money's worth here. Go over to Texas as far as I'm concerned! There, the State has founded Cloud-Cuckoo-Land and maybe you can become something there."

He chuckled and leaned over his desk and pulled out a newspaper under a stack of files. He tore off the right half, folded it up and handed it to the Candidate Teacher, Hermann Koechert from Stedtfeld. "That's something for you—let God's will be fulfilled."

He pointed with his hand to the door. The teacher walked out without saying farewell.

The storm tore the heavy front door out of his hand as he rushed out, slammed it shut and drove him out into the rain-drenched streets. Koechert felt the newspaper in his left hand, slipped it into his coat pocket and threw up his collar.

The excitement he had just held down with all his strength was now aflame in him. Thoughts rushed into his mind. "Emigration," he recalled Koser saying as he was now wondering where Texas even was. At first the word was nothing but an empty sound, filled with the feeling of space and strangeness. Koechert was breathing hard and he felt cast out and lonely. Shivering, he thought that it was all over with his schoolmaster career, speculating what would come of him. "Emigration", Koser had said. The word stuck in his brain. He knew some who had turned their backs on their homeland in recent years — Farmers, workers, artisans, scholars, many, many who were tired of it all.

The thought had not come to him up to now and he had wanted to fight in order to win but now he was already off track. A splash of rainwater fell onto his hat from a gutter and sprayed upon his burning face. He pulled out his handkerchief and dried himself off. "Why were they gone?" he asked himself. The shadow of Metternich[14] still hung almost like a nightmare upon all free spirits. Thought-snoopers stood around everywhere eagerly catching every open word of man, all sighs and every curse, in order to play all the insecure into the hands of the all-powerful police. In fortresses and prisons sat those who had pronounced those things that oppressed all. Minds were narrowed by church intolerance.

Like a legion of troops it was drawn from the German states, gathering in the port cities to crumble and blow like dust into the whole world. Letters came from afar telling expectedly of marvels. They lied and exaggerated because it was so hard to admit the disappointment and misfortune that remained with them. Perhaps the wishful thinking of those far away gave them everything that they had dared to hope and wish for and this belief was stronger than all that reason could provide. Thus this was quietly sneaking into Hermann Koechert's thinking although he just was not yet aware of it. Avoiding a new shower, he stepped under a door archway

"Is that still a life at all? Do you really make progress with openness and honesty? Aren't the selfish and the flexible more successful?"

In the distress of his heart, he found no clear answer to these questions. He felt as if he were looking himself in the face. He had to laugh bitterly at what he saw—a deranged schoolmaster, with a head full of noble thoughts in a miserably botched reality.

"Sort it out," his brother had said angrily to him in the morning, before he made his way to Eisenach. "You can't carry on like this and until you are sure of your office, marrying is also out of the question." Now everything was over.

The brother was also worried for his own part because he knew that Hermann could come before him any day and demand his inheritance. This question remained unspoken between the brothers. One of them was silent because he knew the was bringing the worries about the farm with him, and the other was tormented by incessant anxiety, fearing that the money might now be required of him.

The sun, shining in the puddles and rivulets, lingered for a moment among the clouds as Koechert stepped out into the street, spreading his arms and inhaling the clean air.

He thought to himself, "The money? I'll have to have it and the sooner the better. It can't be helped and he'll have to suffer the consequences. I want to make a new life for myself, free and independent, with Luise!" He stopped. "Yes, with Luise!"

The shivering man, flushing hot, remembered how she had spoken to him as he told her about being relieved from his post, "And if I have to, I'll go to the end of the world with you." A new gust of wind mixed with rain and snow was blowing up the alley and it grabbed Koechert, driving him past the houses. The whimsical, ornate sign over the door to the "Klosterkeller" rocked creaking in the wind as Koechert sprung up the three steps in front of the tavern to get away from the storm. He settled himself down at a table that was standing, lonely and remote, next to the heavy, green tiled stove in the twilight of the paneled dining room. A few men sat in eager conversation around the regulars' table under the window and as Koechert entered the room, their heads spun around as if they were waiting for someone.

He asked the landlady for a jug of light beer.

"It should be in there at last," said Master Plumber Sauermilch deliberately.

"Where on earth is the Vice President?" asked Master Saddler Bachmann. "I've become very confused about what they are writing in the papers and saying everywhere. You just want to know what's actually going on. 'Annegret', I said to my significant other before I left, 'you don't have to wait with lunch for me today, I have to go and get some things done.'"

He laughed grimly as outside, the clock on the church tower on the marketplace struck ten.

"What do you want to do if the women are watching behind you counting each beer grog like hunting dogs and nagging all the time? What's better than being a bachelor like you, Herr Assessor, you don't have to steal away from home for a morning pint as well as enjoying a well-deserved retirement to boot? Hello, you poor craftsman, I say to myself every morning. Has it something to do with retirement, pension and…?"

The door flew open and Deputy Head Schaefer came in, his long pipe in his left hand and his right hand swinging a newspaper.

"I was late," he said, a little short of breath. "But it could not be otherwise with this weather, the postman came much later than usual."

The men squeezed up together and made space for him.

"Well, now we finally know what's up. The society had to come up with a clear concept and here it is!" He struck the spread out Frankfurt Post Newspaper.

"So first things first: The Mainz Adelsverein for the Protection of German Emigrants has acquired an area of six hundred square miles in Texas, that is, eleven hundred and ten square kilometers where they want to accommodate German settlers. In this way they are hoping to arrive at a better outcome by keeping it all together as a well-ordered area to create a new home country over there. Six hundred and forty acres will be allocated to each family.

"Unmarried men over the age of seventeen will get three hundred and twenty acres.

"Each lot should be kept together in one piece. Fifteen acres around each house has to be fenced.

"Before departure, the emigrant will be guaranteed his land in writing. He will receive it as a gift on arrival. Once he has lived there for three years, the land will finally become his property. Before the expiration of this time, all profits accrue to him without limitation.

"The Society shall provide good, spacious ships for the crossing as well as cheap and healthy food for which there will be a small charge. Society agents will be ready to receive the arrivals at the landing places. There will also be harnessed wagons waiting to carry the luggage free of charge to the place of the settlement. Likewise, the Society will ensure provisions during the land journey."

Deputy Head Schaefer sniffed a bit during his hasty speech as everyone gasped in amazement.

"The truth is," said the market pharmacist, "it'd be better to be young again and do it, but I doubt there's much left to get out of us"

The hastily thrown sentences of the Deputy Headmaster had struck home with Hermann Koechert like stones. Springing to his feet, he listened as if they were meant just for him.

Schaefer coughed, lit his pipe and continued, "Every family will be given its own log cabin on the spot. The association will build storehouses and provide food, tools, seeds and plants in the enclosed settlements. Upon arrival, plow oxen, horses, cows, pigs and sheep will be made available for settlers. All this will be sold to the arrivals at a much lower price than on the American market. If the hard working emigrants have no money, then the association will make an advance to be repaid from the profits of the first harvests. The products resulting from agriculture can be sold to the Society warehouses at the discretion of the settlers."

"That's what I call organization", said Assessor Weibezahl slowly. "Well, men, as I have always said, our princes and lords are not as bad as most people today like to think—I mean the craftsmen as such." He looked around the group with a sneer. "Where do you find so much goodwill, sacrifice, wisdom and nationalism in one place? Their Lordships know what they want—I mean, such a plan could really help Germany. Cheers, Herr Candidate!"

He raised his glass and turning to Koechert he said, "In the heat of the moment I hadn't yet noticed you. We are emigrating and Texas is the journey. Only on paper at first but don't you feel like doing that too?"

"Yes, yes, I would quite…"

The idea had cast such a spell on him that Koechert got stuck in the middle of the sentence. The word "Texas" had come to his ears for the second time today. He had absorbed every word that came across from the regulars' table. The thought rushed over him in waves, "Was he not young and healthy? Luise would go."

The Deputy Head continued, "The Society will provide for the religious and moral education of children as well as building churches and schools. Doctors, pharmacists and hospitals will ensure the health of the emigrants. In May, His Highness Prince von Solms-Braunfels and Herr Bourgeois d'Orvanne will precede in order to make the necessary arrangements for the arrival and accommodation of the settlers there. The first transport is due to leave this September. The costs, including all expenses, amount to six hundred guilders for families from the Rheinland and the half for unmarried persons. In addition, lists with donations that can be used to enable emigration for families without means, are being drawn up all over Germany. The Society is publishing the names of the benefactors in the most widely read papers. The company L. H. Flersheim in Mainz is the Society's bankers. From the money from those emigrants paying in full, three percent is being deducted for poor settlers. The announcement is being issued in Mainz on April 9, 1844. Today we have the fifteenth. Now we can get on with it."

"That will take off," said the market pharmacist.

"Six hundred guilders that I've meanwhile calculated comes to three hundred and forty-two taler that is quite a bit of money. Who has so much money on the side?" asked Bachmann thoughtfully.

"A lot of money will flow out of Germany and so again, the whole thing only benefits those who already have money."

"Wait a minute, here it is stated differently," the Deputy Head commented. "The required deposit can be dispensed with in special cases. So there is the possibility of bringing over even destitute people. There are sure to be plenty who will want to make use of that."

"I have not seen so much money in one pile in my lifetime" said Tailor Sussdorf, lost in thought and wiping his thumb on the edge of his beer jug and taking a long sip.

"But Master, that all costs money. Listen, my dear friends, to what is exactly going to be provided for."

The Deputy Head moved his glasses to the tip of his nose and continued reading: "The Society calculates sixty guilders for the crossing and the food, for land transport from the Matagorda Bay to the colony on wagons and in tents, ten guilders and for a residential building, sixty guilders. The money is to be paid before the trip to the bank in Mainz. In the harbor each family gets back fifty guilders and a single person ten guilders for additional expenses.

"I reckon the journey across the sea will take sixty to ninety days. That's really quite a lot of money. The cash is safer in the hands of the Society than if each one were to keep it in their pockets. And then I also believe that the collection of donations will bring a lot in. The state and communities now have the opportunity to get rid of many a problem child."

The regulars' table started to fill up. More and more men pushed into the discussion. Smoke smoldered from pipes and artisan's fists lay heavily upon the table.

Bookseller Jakobi had brought a world map and pointing his finger described the journey, as he knew a lot about the distant land. Everyone joined his journey over to Texas, saw the blue sea and penetrated into the green tide of the prairies.

Time passed as a change came over Hermann Koechert. A great longing began to burn in him as if all the past had fallen away as he rose from the shambles of the morning like one being newborn to the light. As if he were already on the swaying ship, he closed his eyes as if the sun were dazzling him. He had his arm around Luise and the sails billowed above them whilst the ship went quietly west on its way to Texas.

On his way home to Stedtfeld in the afternoon, Koechert found the newspaper in his pocket that the cleric had pressed into his hand. It was the same page of the Frankfurter Post Newspaper that the Deputy Headmaster had read out in the "Klosterkeller".

## II

Germany was being warmed by festive May weather after an April full of storms, rain and cold. The sky above the earth shone blue and transparent above the earth like thin glass. Life was busily stirring in the harbor of Bremen. Barrels and bales were being unloaded from the holds of high-masted sailing ships, chains clanked and winches shrieked. Stevedores carried loads across staggering jetties from land to ships and from ships to land. Wagons and carts rumbled along the harbor streets, warehouses opening up their gates like giant mouths to receive them. Ships brought in the abundance of the earth and shipping out what Germany could dispense with, which was not a lot. The hollow bellies of the ships swallowed the superfluous people that was their main cargo, the belongings of the emigrants lying piled up high upon the harbor walls.

They themselves squatted or stood around, a colorful image of costumes and a diverse tangle of German dialects catching eye and ear. If it had been possible to look into the hearts of men and women, one would have seen many things that were shamefully concealed and restrained from the outside world.

Some had overcome and felt strong in their ability to focus their thoughts onto the new destination whilst others suffered in desperation without words. There was no turning back and it was only here in the harbor that they had come to realize the finality of their decision. The cloudy waters of the Weser struck upon the mighty ashlars of the quay walls that marked the way into the sea and into the far away places none of them knew. Germany lay behind them now. Some, in the last hours before departure, felt as if they had lost all their strength as it all slowly dawned upon them, whilst their limbs obediently obeyed a dark urge that was stronger than any single hardship that no one wanted to let others see. Nevertheless, often the rough backs of hands would wipe furtively over eyes flooded and obscured by a wave of hot tears.

The children, eyes popping out of their heads, enjoyed the new and unfamiliar. They romped about between crates and boxes continually asking questions, happy in the fullness of everything that here assailed them. Careworn mothers, helped by young girls with cheeks pale or glowing with excitement, tried to keep the fluttering swarms together. Some sat dreamily on a bale of bedclothes whilst the men hid their inner restlessness by incessantly arranging something—here tightening a rope, or there, reorganizing belongings anew.

Noise and pipe smoke emanated from the taverns at the harbor. Some, with the aid of beer and schnapps, stupefied their groaning hearts or incessantly amplified the joy, now and for all time, of having escaped all the things that tied them down. Looking out upon the water and listening to the confusion of languages from the foreign sailors, Bremen no longer seemed part of Germany any more.

A bustle of emigrants crowded in front of a proud three-master sailing ship moored at the quayside that displayed "Aurora" in tall gold letters on its bow, now preparing for departure to New Orleans that would begin its journey downstream with the ebb. All cargo having been stowed and the preparations for departure completed, by noon the last emigrants had disappeared into the steerage.

Captain Feistel ran impatiently back and forth between cabin and chartroom, looking over at the shore as if he were waiting for someone. "That's what comes of it," he growled at Butenschoen, the first helmsman, "when you get involved with the high and mighty. The steerage is jam-packed, the people were on time and, as far as I am concerned, we could set off. We are now only waiting for His Highness, the prince," he proclaimed, spitting a quid of chewing tobacco in a high arc overboard.

A strange procession broke out of one of the harbor streets across the way. A carriage was driving slowly towards the ship and behind it ran a troop of men dressed in flamboyant uniforms. Then a few carts rumbled into the open air laden sky-high with luggage.

"Man, helmsman, get on with it! Is that pageant perhaps our prince?" The captain laughed so raucously that he almost choked. "This looks as if it could be good — they look like lion tamers in a circus."

Meanwhile the carriage had drawn up to the gangway having been trailed by curious people from the city. The foredeck emptied as people crowded along the ship's side to enjoy the strange spectacle.

His Highness, Prince Solms von Braunfels rose stiffly and self-confidently from the carriage. He was followed by a strained and somewhat sheepish Baron Bourgeois d'Orvanne. The prince was taller than the curious spectators surrounding him. A huge, white slouch hat with a bobbing turkey feather, stuck behind a heavy, silver clasp, sat upon his head. The gray jerkin with enclosed plain buttons tightly and restrictively cramped the slender body. The legs were in loose, black velvet pants and the soft leather boots, heavy wheel spurs ringing above the heels, ranged high up to above the knees. Warlike brown eyes flashed under the brim of the hat and the prince's left hand clutched the handle of a massive cavalry sable, two pistol holsters hanging threateningly on the broad, black leather belt. He was also adorned with cartridges in a belt across the chest and shoulders, daggers and all kinds of defensive devices.

The eight guardsmen that he was taking with him to Texas were similarly equipped but instead of the usual tight jacket, they wore comfortable shirts and huge carbines to compliment their over-abundant armament.

The procession caught the attention of the people of Bremen, even though they were used to many things. A small cannon stood on the second baggage cart whilst one wondered what could be packed in the accompanying quantity of crates, suitcases, and bales.

Bourgeois d'Orvanne was, of course, overlooked in such surroundings. Impressive with a black swallowtail coat, tight, dark trousers pulled scarily taut by leather straps and his silky-glossy top hat, he looked like a distinguished dandy. His one and only suitcase was invisible under the mountains of luggage.

Butenschoen, the helmsman, stood beside the captain. "That's Rinaldo Rinaldini with his gang of robbers," he laughed, "and with him some yellow rascal. I wonder what they think about Texas?" "Be quiet, he's coming", whispered the captain. He went up to the prince and led him into the cabin that he was to share with Bourgeois d'Orvanne. The guardsmen were assigned a free corner in the steerage.

After that the pilot came aboard and the ship was cleared with a paddle steamer tugging in front, the journey could now begin.

The emigrants stood man-to-man watching the city disappear out of sight.

Then the prince's soldiers began to sing a song that one of them had composed. Every verse ran out with the refrain:

> *Then come what may come,*
> *Yet we serve our prince true,*
> *We valiant brave Texans.*

"Premature praise," sneered the pilot at the wheel.

As the prince sat down to dinner with Bourgeois d'Orvanne and the captain that evening, he said thoughtfully, "I hope, sir, that this is one of the last human charges to be shipped off without leadership to America. When we in the Society are that far, everything random and blind must have been finally eliminated and the German emigrants will feel safe in our care. They should transplant their German-ness abroad whilst we will watch over their well-being with everything in the best of hands. The Baron", he continued, nodding in the Frenchman's direction, "will assist us with his considerable experience. Organizing will be taking place back home during the weeks of our journey as we want to make sure that everything is ready when the first ships of the Society arrive in Texas at the end of the year. I want to take advantage of the idleness of the crossing to make use of the Baron's valuable knowledge about settlement for this good enterprise. Cheers my lords, let us toast! Long live New Germany in Texas!"

He looked at the other two with gleaming eyes. Bourgeois d'Orvanne's hand trembled as he raised his glass and the ship felt more like a prison to him. From the very first hour of departure his thoughts had begun to work feverishly as to how he would extricate himself from the great adventure.

In Bremerhaven, fresh water and post was also taken aboard whereupon the tug remained behind with the pilot guiding the "Aurora" out through the difficult waters of the Lower Weser into the North Sea. The home country finally disappeared into a thin streak in the far distance, wind grabbing the sails, thrusting the ship into the open sea.

One morning at the end of May a flicker of light above the water was blinding to the eyes as a number of voices shouted, "Ship ahoy, Ship ahoy".

It emerged slowly on the horizon standing out like a white feather against the blue sky under the weight of its full sails and Butenschoen took course towards it. After some hours, both ships had come within calling distance.

"That's the barque 'Franziska' heading for Bremen under Captain Stuerje," said Feistel. He stood with the prince and Bourgeois d'Orvanne on the roof of the chart room. The people from the steerage stared over the side and there were only a few people aboard the "Franziska".

The ships were approaching ever closer. With time, people of both ships began to recognize one another. A short, stocky man in a light linen suit was leaning next to Captain Stuerje, waving his broad hat and shouting in German, "Fellow countrymen, greetings to the new homeland!" as all kinds of shouts flew over from the "Aurora". Without anyone noticing, Bourgeois d'Orvanne suddenly turned around as he had recognized someone calling across who had probably recognized him too because at that moment a curse flew. Yet no one understood him, the words being lost in the noise of the bow wave.

"Did you also see the down-trodden character who was standing on the chart room of the 'Aurora'?" asked the man in the linen suit of the captain on the "Franziska".

"Of course, Consul, one couldn't miss him, when a man beneath the thirtieth degree of latitude wearing a frock coat and top hat sails past bound southwest. He looked just like the 'Wandering Jew'[15]."

The Franziska landed at the wharf in Bremen in the second week of June. The man in the white linen suit seemed to be in a great hurry because he traveled to Mainz by the fastest means

*Fig. 7: St Louis in 1846, Painted by Henry Lewis*

and allowed himself be announced to the Count of Leiningen at his castle.

Sebastian Schmoller, the valet of His Highness, took the stranger's card. It read, "Carl Fisher[16], Consul of the Free Hanseatic City of Bremen, New Orleans".

"Lead the gentleman into the Yellow Salon," ordered the count.

"Excuse me, Excellency," said Fisher, after a deep bow and with a sweep of his hat, "that I intrude on you without any advance warning. I have just come from Texas and have, I believe, something extremely important to communicate." His eyes focused tightly on the Count's.

"And what would that be?"

"Have you been dealing with a certain Baron Bourgeois d'Orvanne lately?"

"Certainly, sir! The Mainz Adelsverein bought an extensive land area in Texas from him at favorable conditions, upon which German emigrants are to be settled. The Baron was paid half of the purchase price, the other he will be getting in Texas.

In addition, he is a member of the directorate and receives a monthly salary in advance..."

"Well, then," the consul went on, "you've fallen into the swindler's trap! I came too late." His tension eased as he collapsed, his arms sinking over the back of his chair.

The count turned pale, leaned forward and asked in alarm, "Why? Swindler? Explain yourself, Consul."

"Before I go into any details, first of all the most important thing: Bourgeois d'Orvanne is a well-prepared rascal for whom the ground in Texas got too hot. He has a land concession that falls back to the state on the first of July this year if the area has not been populated by at least six hundred families. Were you aware of that, Count?"

"No, no, that was never mentioned in the negotiations with the Society but neither can it be so, no, Consul, how are you going to prove that? Anyway, we have a binding contract with the man!"

"That doesn't mean a thing and, because he lives from fraud, contracts are nothing to him whilst money — he needs money for his wild life. And he manages somehow to get hold of it by any means. I would love to have heard the people rocking with laughter when he got your money paid out to him."

"What about our contract then?"

"It has no value at all if the Texan government has not authenticated it. Since this will hardly be the case, you can't hope for a thing!"

Count von Leiningen rose abruptly from his chair and struck his fist on the table. "Miserable rogue! What can be done?"

"Nothing Count, nothing at all. You will have to write off this item and start all over again. You've paid dearly to learn the hard way!"

"How do you mean that?"

"It will take many weeks before it's possible to track down the swindler. Consider the journey — you have to reckon with sixty to ninety days, which gives the man an extraordinary advantage. Even supposing you would really catch him, then you would not have furthered the cause of the Society one millimeter."

The count fell back into his chair, his eyes fixed helplessly on the floral patterns of the rug. "I must call a meeting of the Society immediately—urgently! But what is going to happen next? The prince is on his way so what will he do?"

He wrung his hands in despair, "Advertising has started and newspapers and agents have already got to work. Help and advise us Consul! The world will laugh at us," he groaned.

"A beastly situation. The money is lost, the activity cannot be stopped and neither do we have any land! It doesn't help if the Society members are now going to get at each other's throats. I can already hear the mischievous laughter of the Duke of Gotha. He warned about the scoundrel!" For a while it remained silent between the two men.

"I feel like smashing everything to pieces", the Count blurted out, biting his teeth into his lower lip.

Fisher got up and bowed. "If you would allow me, Your Highness, I would like to make a proposal that could really help the Society. What I have to say does not need to concern the public and the work can be continued just as before whilst you will really be helped, really…"

"Be brief Consul, I am at the end of my tether."

Fisher opened his suitcase and pulled out a bundle of papers. "Here, I have brought you a new contract! My grant is located on the upper San Saba and is noted on this map! Here! The land is extremely suitable for settlement, having fertile river valleys, endless green plains as well as mineral deposits in the mountains."

Count von Leiningen eyed the speaker with narrowed eyes. "Just like Bourgeois d'Orvanne began his speech, the devil should have him!"

"I can understand your Highness's suspicions," said Fisher shyly. "But here, please!" He gave the Count a bundle of papers.

"These are the documents—my contract of sale, here the settlement conditions, as well as a power of attorney to enter into negotiations with the Mainz Adelsverein with the consent of the Texas government. Each paper duly signed and sealed and the purchase price is low compared to the profit that you will extract from this area. You will get out of this dead end in one fell swoop. You have three years to survey, divide and settle the land and the only condition imposed upon you is to introduce six hundred families during this time. That you will manage whatever happens. In addition, there will be space for at least six thousand families.

"The Government also assures that it will extend the settlement period by half a year if necessary. Texan President Samuel Houston has already signed both the terms and the draft treaty. If the Society could decide in favor, then the validity of all arrangements would certainly be binding."

While the count examined the papers, Fisher continued, "I come from Kassel where my father was a teacher and I emigrated at a young age. I learned of the intentions of your Society on the Nassau farm at the beginning of this year—by the way, my compliments, Count—you are on the right track! I was also told that the impostor Bourgeois d'Orvanne had traveled to Mainz. That could not be a good thing for sure. I hurried after him but was not able to stop the disaster happening. We passed each other South of the Azores and the wretch recognized me and probably understood immediately why I was traveling to Europe."

There were several extremely turbulent days in Mainz at the end of June. After their Lordships had sufficiently calmed down, the pressure of circumstances forced them to make a contract with Fisher. They bought his grant and immediately paid him a hundred Prussian gold sovereigns. He was to receive fourteen thousand guilders on July 5, the remainder of two thousand guilders to be paid on the first day of September 1845 in New Orleans.

The Society would receive two-thirds of the company's profits and Fisher one-third. The implementation of the settlement in Texas was to be handed over to a committee of six persons, five appointed from the members of the Society and the sixth was Fisher. The managing director position was to be kept by the prince Solms-Braunfels.

In the meantime, he was traveling unawares through the labyrinth of the Bahamas towards fulfillment of his great task, a favorable wind driving the "Aurora" onwards. The fairytale island of Cuba appeared, the Gulf of Mexico laying behind in a wistful expanse of water and a clear, blue sky.

Guided by the pilot, going with the tide, the ship finally wound up the Mississippi, landing in New Orleans on one of the last days of June 1844. The city was almost empty because the inhabitants, as far as their circumstances permitted, had chosen healthier areas as the fever spread in the lowlands.

At last released from the agonizing cramped conditions of the ship, the German emigrants landed and already after a few days were scattered to the four winds.

The Prince moved into the Grande Hotel awaiting the onward journey to Galveston. On the morning after the first night in America he noticed with horror that Bourgeois d'Orvanne had disappeared without paying his hotel bill.

---

Up and down the streets, in shops and offices, at markets, weddings and children's baptisms, in taverns, workshops and parlors, everywhere there was talk of the activities of the Mainz Adelsverein.

Its agents passed through villages and towns like flocks of sparrows, telling people about the distant land about that which they most wanted to hear and it must have sounded like fairy tales to them. Yearnings infused the thinking of the population like colorful veils as very many of them began gently to pull up their roots from the homeland, setting all their hopes and wishes on the journey to Texas.

The power of advertising was most influential for the poorest who were asking if the creation of a better future now lay in their own hands. Mothers glowed with the visualization of a new children's paradise whilst fathers, clenching their fists, strengthened their will to create a habitat for the family. The word "Texas" captured their thoughts in the promise of great things to come.

The donation lists that the Society had issued filled up. The rich brought sacrifices that bought them a sense of security and donations flowed together from all over Germany into the Bank House Flersheim in Mainz.

Anyone who decided to emigrate was looked upon as a hero in his street or village and his confidence would give strength to the weaker, inhibiting the devouring unrest in the hearts of the undecided.

In some areas, the belief in Texas grew into a movement that seized all classes of the people. A bitter time of adversity was all over Germany. In Fulda at that time, wild rye and rapeseed meal was being baked into the bread of the poor. The small Hessian town of Hunfeld had twenty-one hundred inhabitants of which seven hundred had to be supported on public welfare. With the approval of the authorities they had split themselves into three groups, each headed by a gendarme, and twice a week they would go begging in accordance with an official plan, once inside the city and once in the nearby villages. These people heard the tidings about Texas as if it were a gospel.

The Hessian village of Meimbressen in the district of Hofgeismar offered itself to the state with all its possessions, both movable and immovable property, because the whole community wanted to emigrate together to Texas. Eighty families had cemented the belief of a new life in a new world.

The situation was similar in the village of Pferdsdorf near Buedingen, which unanimously backed the leadership of its pastor and mayor. The community property that could be taken with them was thirty thousand guilders as well as the property of each individual. However, all the reasoning the authorities put forward in an attempt to hold the two hundred and fifty people on their soil proved to be fruitless.

"Herr Bailiff, let it be," said the very tall, haggard Mayor of Pferdsdorf in the council office in Buedingen. His clenched fists lay on a broad pile of papers that covered the whole table. "Let it be. Every word is futile. What know what they want. If we wait for the government to agree with us, then it is going to be too late. So we will take everyone with us, every single one, Herr Bailiff. We're going to rebuild Pferdsdorf in Texas and then you can visit us in the moonlight, Herr Bailiff, together with all the other bloodsuckers. Then we'll keep what we have made and woe to the one over there who demands more from us than he deserves."

The mayor's hard chin moved forward whilst his right hand swept aside a pile of paper. "That's God's will, Herr Bailiff. We want to witness his kingdom already in this world. We'll put the plow in the ground over there for God's sake. There must be one thing and one thing only—God's will and the works of man."

In Darmstadt the Post brought an application to the Ministry from the fourteen-hundred-inhabitant municipality of Egelsbach. All the family fathers wanted to emigrate to Texas and signed it off without exception. "Should the High Government ask us why, let them reflect on what has been done to us and our forefathers in the last hundred years." This sentence formed the conclusion of the explicitly clear document.

Then there was the market town of Großzimmern, a poor little nest. "It just can't be that we let the people starve to death," said the mayor in a local council meeting, wiping his burning brow. "We seven-hundred local poor are those without a penny to our names, we! More than half of the population lives from the community coffers. If we sell what we have left in the way of properties, meadows, fields and forests, then it may be possible to cover the costs of emigrating to Texas. Neighbors, it has now come to the point where we have to deport our own people. The state is shoving its fingers into its ears, saying that the cry of distress, which it does not hear, isn't there anymore. Fifty-thousand guilders are needed and I know no other way out." He looked around the circle of councilors. Dull, with their thoughts occupied, they sat at the table and stared straight ahead whilst within them the word "Texas" glowed like a promise of heaven.

Brains and hearts were being penetrated by the message of the Mainz Adelsverein. In Osterode, a town in Masuria, the pubs were filled, craftsmen stepped out of the workshops onto the street, and farming people forsook their work. A decades-old load of worries was searching for expression as it rolled along the rows of houses in torrents of protest. They wondered if there were any alternative to emigrating, all sense of reason seeming to have been submerged.

"We have to grab our chance," one droned, "as soon as possible before the land in Texas has already been distributed. Come on, decide! Leave the junk here where it stands and off to Texas!"

And what one said was soon believed by everybody. Day and night, anxiety ate into those thus roused because they could end up being the last one and thus too late to get anything. Applications to the district administrator piled up. House and yard were sold dirt-cheap and the very last penny was scraped together from wherever. The district administrator, wanting to calm things down insisted, "The government grants which you want can not be procured as fast as you expect," to a deputation that asked him about the state of affairs. "Also, I cannot issue the passports before all the other formalities are completed. We haven't yet sorted things out with the Society. Such things don't happen over night. Don't forget there are more than twenty applications for exemption from military service and before that is decided, none of those due to be called up can get away from here and there are heavy penalties for desertion. Be reasonable because I won't be pushed, not even for your sakes! You can be sure that I am aware of my responsibility—do you understand?"

Yet they did not understand him. Only a person with evil intent could speak like that. The people gathered in front of the district office and besieged it. A hail of paving stones and clubs flew towards the district administrator when he called for people to be calm. No single windowpane was left whole and the crowd wanted to storm the building. Clerks and gendarmes entrenched themselves on the ground floor whilst doors were broken open, shutters torn down, wood splintered and stones clattered. Some young men had already laid ladders to climb down from the roof into the inside.

It was high time for a squadron of dragoons to burst into the square with loaded carbines. The crowd turned around and tried to push the soldiers back but the dragoons finally had to open fire and a real battle took place with losses on both sides. By the evening the square had been cleared and the troops were able to march away.

The local councilor of Kleinschmalkalden in the Thuringian Forest struggled for three days with the letter that he had to write in reply to a request from the Ducal Judiciary of Gotha. Starting over and over again, he tore up the paper four times, starting each time from the beginning again but at last he was finally finished. Full of momentum, underneath he inscribed: "Most worthy Ducal Judiciary, I remain, with the utmost respect, your humble local councilor of Kleinschmalkalden." Satisfied, he read the whole thing through once more:

"... I have to report that Dittmer with his family that consists of four uneducated children and the fifth that the wife will soon expect to give birth to, find themselves in the most oppressive poverty. Since most of the poor local inhabitants cannot afford the high prices and because collecting wood from the forest only lasts a few weeks, fallen wood, from which many a poor family once nourished itself, can no longer be sold and there is none left. So he has no other choice if he wants to prevent his family from starving to death but to damage the manorial woodlands, poaching and trapping, when, after repeated repentance, he will end up in the penitentiary.

"A great many from here, who are without food or earnings and in extreme poverty and are to the detriment of the Most Gracious Lords, could emigrate to Texas. But from where should they get the travel money and clothes?"

He sealed the letter and gave it in at the post office, leaving the poor people in Kleinschmalkalden to hope for many weeks.

However, the government in Gotha had other concerns: "If people have lived so far, they will continue to live. One should not make it too easy for them by clearing away all hardships the minute they cry. Those incapable of coping with life will rot of their own accord and are useless. Majesty, I think we should first make use of the emigration fund diverted from the treasury to get rid of all the stuff that populates our prisons and workhouses. The increase is frightening in the number of vagabond women who, laden with any number of children, are making the roads unsafe. I could imagine that, in the case of predominantly male immigration, there will be a shortage of women in Texas." The Minister of State von Wangenheim smiled. "Would that not be a task for us?"

The duke considered and said, "It won't be so easy, Your Excellency. You know that every individual who wants to emigrate must present a police certificate of good conduct when registering in Mainz..."

"Allow me Your Highness, please note that this is my least concern," the Minister said, squinting. "Those we set out on the way will have papers which are in order."

Thus the emigration to Texas in Gotha was prepared through the state.

Yet, at the same time, artists, scholars, officers, merchants, lawyers and doctors listened to the enticing advertising of the Society. There were some who doubted that things would get better in Germany and many felt as if they had lost their right to breathe whilst Texas promised enough space and emptiness with which to occupy oneself and one's existence.

"Anyone who sells his pants can buy a principality over there." Such rumors spread like wildfire across the country.

An unscrupulous seller of souls started to send people to Texas on his own account and brought his victims down the Rhine to Rotterdam where he left them to their own devices. Devastated and ill, they spent months in the harbor without money and food and no ship would pick them up because the funds for the return journey were not at hand. So they lived from begging and many starved and died. Finally, the Dutch government intervened and deported them over the German border whereupon some one hundred and fifty of them were housed temporarily in the Brauweiler penitentiary.

Fake letters depicting Texas as a paradise passed from hand to hand. Texas communities emerged in Hesse gathering in each other's houses in turn to sing Texas songs to choral melodies with religious fervor:

> *There is a spirit in ev'ry place*
> *Around in German fatherland;*
> *On every house, on every gate*
> *You hear him knocking with his hand.*
> *Want to see him? It is a farmer*
> *A disgruntled farming man!*
> *Indeed, he's fed up with his life!*
> *He wants to leave. He speaks to you:*
> *Who's joining me?*

On Sunday, the pastor preached from the pulpit in a small village on the Vogelsberg mountain: "The European world is sinking and it is not worth much more but the Lord God is standing on the green shores of Texas calling all his good and righteous children." The ladies wore Texas-style hats—big, wide-bodied swingers with a long turkey feather. The registrations piled up in the office of the Society in Mainz. Money ran in an uninterrupted stream into Flersheim.

"I can't stand another winter," said Cantor Carl Blumberg to his wife. "Two years in a row of flood and bad harvest. What should we use to feed the children?"

The woman cried.

The cantor considered his situation on the way from Kokozko to the district town of Kulm,. Seven underage children lived together with their parents in the two rooms of the house that had been left from the flooding of the Vistula River. He could not even think about schooling because the schoolroom with everything in it had been washed away by the water. His fields lay silted and sandy under the oppressing sky. Tired and battered, the haggard man crept down the sodden dirt road to Kulm where the district administrator had invited him. Wondering if the government had given him the support he had asked for, he bowed to the district administrator.

"Unfortunately, I have to inform you that your request has been rejected." The district councilor drummed his fingers on the bare desk. "Look, Blumberg, as bitter as it has hit you, you're just one of many. It is not possible for the state to help everyone. Bite your lips and wait for better times ahead." He twirled the tips of his Blucher mustache through his fingers. "That's life, Blumberg—no paradise nor a bed of roses—it goes up and down, so let's hope for the best. Pray, Blumberg, God will help you more than the state can."

Then the canton found himself standing back on the street numb and with a heavy heart. In the pub "Zur guten Einkehr" he found a newspaper with an advertisement from the Mainz Adelsverein and that was to determine his fate.

---

After weeks of intensive arguing and severe bitterness, the decommissioned teaching candidate Hermann Koechert from

Stedtfeld finally managed to get his brother so far that he agreed to pay him his inheritance but it took a lot of effort to raise the money. Eight hundred taler was a lot of cash.

At last they came to an agreement with a man named Isaac Gruenstein in Eisenach. He took over the demand with a cash payout of six hundred taler and five percent interest on the remainder. Only with a heavy heart did the brother sign and the whole table was covered by the time the moneylender had put the coins in rows.

"The father's blessing builds houses for the children," he said as he counted. Now the way to Texas for Koechert was free.

In the evening he sat together in the gazebo with his bride, the daughter of the linen weaver Steinbrück. The night was mild and full of mysterious life. Holding the girl tightly he said, "I knew it, after all, your father had to say yes but if there had been no other way, I would have absconded you from the house by stealth."

"And I would have gone with you," she whispered, kissing him, "to the end of the world — tell me something about Texas!"

Hermann Koechert pulled her head very close to his. With colorful words he wove illuminating pictures of the distant land. In his sentences the word "freedom" was repeated time and time again as he talked hotly, and she felt secure in the power that emanated from him.

"Oh, Luise," he said with less certainty, "does it really have to happen this way? Shouldn't the homeland be like a mother who cherishes everyone with the same love in her heart? How many may be thinking of Texas this night! I have read many a book where it jumped out of the pages at me, where Germans started afresh everywhere in the world, sacrificed themselves and paved the way for culture. Many did it because they had to be true to themselves and it was the sense that there was just no alternative which finally drove them away."

The girl did not hear the last words as she slept in her beloved's arms.

When, after many searches and enquiries Bourgeois d'Orvanne's escape could no longer be doubted, the prince realized how much he had been counting on the assistance of the Frenchman. A hundred times over during the voyage he had repeatedly heard the same idiom from him, "Oh, I'll paint quick vezy good situation for immigrants. I know government, many delegates know me. Why ze questions? Why speeches? Words, words! Your 'ighness can rely on me. Texas my zecond 'ome. I love ze country, and ze country love me."

With such words he avoided the prince's questions that became more and more urgent as they got closer to the mainland. Often Solms would drop his cards in the middle of the game and suddenly ask Bourgeois d'Orvanne such a question. Then the Frenchman would be startled and sidetrack, wondering if the prince had escaped the fact that he was intentionally playing false cards and that he had emptied a number of ducats from his pocket.

For many hours Solms sat over the map and drew roads from the shore into the country. He wanted to build railways with wooden rails and the trains pulled by horses. He mused what the cities that were going to be founded should be called and had put together lists of names, many of which had been discarded and new ones added. Forts had to be built to protect against the Indians and wagons, horses, wagoners, oxen, food, tools, seeds, weapons, medicines—often the abundance of what seemed needed oppressing him as notebooks were filled.

He wondered what speeches would he have to hold before the authorities and during state visits and at night he would pace up and down the deck under the southern sky compiling great words. "Herr President will certainly appreciate the settlement and the honor it bestows upon the land of Texas. Our ships are carrying thousands of the best from the German homeland across the sea. They want to build a new home here and, with everything they have and want to be, will be an extremely valuable addition to your state…"

After Bourgeois d'Orvanne's escape, all of this had passed behind a shadow and what was now to be done was less clear.

The prince wandered the sun-scorched streets of New Orleans dressed in full military regalia yet perhaps his sense of security was melting away. However, had he have known that the grant was also lost....

White, meal-fine dust whirled around his boots with every step and he startled as a few blacks came towards him.

"That's the south," it passed through his mind. "Cotton, Negro slaves, yellow fever, corn, sugarcane, swamps and an unpredictable river."

That's what was stated in the books but he was not sure whether he was reading it right now or whether he was really there because the town was so quiet.

A voice called from afar, "Milk, Milk!" Solms stopped. A milk cart drawn by tired mules rumbled around the corner in a cloud of dust. The yellow, shiny bell clanged brightly as the coachman shouted, "Milk, Milk!!"

Solms looked up. He was almost grateful to the man for the noise but somehow the voice seemed familiar and he was sure that he recognized it. Quickly he ran after the cart.

"Milk! Milk!!"

The cart stopped and the carter dismounted whilst a few Negro women in brightly colored clothes emerged from the slumbering houses.

"My God, Herr von Patschkow, is it you?" cried the prince, grabbing the milkman by the arm. He turned around involuntarily, terrified, choking down a substantial curse.

"Your Highness is right, it is I, Baron Wilhelm von Patschkow from Lobsens. That is to say — it *was* me."

"How did you come to be here?"

"I could ask you the same question. Your Highness looks like as if you want to perform in a circus," he laughed, clapping a fist on the prince's shoulder.

"Yes, those were times in Berlin, Your Highness! Court ball, theater, parades and such other beautiful things."

He turned and pointed his hand towards his cart, laughing deeply and hollowly, "My nobility is now in the milk churn. Just a moment, I first need to get rid of the clientele."

He measured the milk out for the blacks, collected the money and then turned back to the prince. "The way I came here is actually quite straightforward. There was no way to hang on to the outfit at home — the moneylenders had devoured it. Then I became Royal Prussian Commissioner of Justice but did not furnish the sedentary attitude required of such a permanent profession. I came to Texas with the rest of my assets two years ago, bought an area where thousands at home would live and, with my last pennies and all my strength, I brought it to the point where I could hope for a good harvest. One day, during lunch break, the rogue from whom I had bought the farm suddenly appeared and told me to immediately leave the house and land.

"'Mother, put a cold wet cloth on the gentleman's forehead, 'he must've had a sunstroke,' I said to my wife. However, it didn't help. The rogue created by God in his wrath, knowing all the tricks, was in the right. We had to leave yet again. The purchase contract had been concluded on a Sunday and therefore it was worthless under the law of Texas.

"That was Baron Bourgeois d'Orvanne's trick with which he conned the green horns from Europe in dozens and sold his farms one time after another. Every time he could get more, because the beginners threw themselves into the task with all their strength, improving the acquired value in next to no time."

"Bourgeois d'Orvanne, did you say, wait a moment, and you know the man?"

"And don't I know him! For a while I could only look at trees from the point of view of being able to use them to hang the swindler, though I haven't caught him yet."

Now Solms told the baron milkman the deal made by the Adelsverein with the Frenchman. Patschkow often interrupted him with exceptionally rude curses. Finally, he gripped the prince's hand with pity.

"Do not give yourself any false hopes. The sooner you come to terms with the situation, the better it will be for you. There's no point crying over spilt milk but you need to immediately find a plan of action after the new situation has arisen. You've lost Bourgeois d'Orvanne's grant, that salt and chalky desert in the upper parts. You should be happy because there is not a button to be had there. I know the situation—hold your head up! Texas is big. Try to get another area from the government, which urgently needs money because of the impending war with Mexico, and they will surely do a deal with you. Nothing is impossible here as you can see with me. With my dairy business I earn five dollars a day and that's just why every Prussian Commissioner of Justice can envy me. I'm a free man to boot and that's truly priceless."

The prince remained silent, hard hit by fear and disappointment as he was, questioning whether not every thought that he had held for the undertaking so far had been in vain and all the great plans hammered out for nothing.

Now he felt ridiculous in his uniform. It was suddenly too tight and restricting as he wondered where they would go from here.

"Where does your Highness live?" asked the milkman, climbing under the sun canopy over his seat.

"At the Grande Hotel. How is Madame? What are the young lady daughters doing?" The prince knelt in a slight bow.

"The two girls do sewing and earn four dollars a day. My wife, yes God, my wife, she could not cope with the situation and I ended up taking her to a lunatic asylum. More of it tonight. I'm coming to the hotel."

The mules moved on and the bell clanged as the milk truck drove away. It could be heard in the distance for a long time together with the cry, "Milk, milk!"

For a few minutes the prince stared at the place where the milk truck had just stopped, the tracks still visible in the street dust. So that was the American reality.

Broken, he went back to the hotel, which was one of the few stone houses of the big trading city in the cotton state of Louisiana.

The heat paralyzed his thinking and he was thirsty, an unceasing thirst tormenting the prince and his men. The next steamer to go to Galveston was not leaving for three days so that was how long they would have to wait. Nevertheless, schnapps was cheap and the guardsmen let it run down their throats like water. A benevolent twilight embraced the men as they forgot the agony of the mosquitoes, the fear of the fever and the exhausting heat.

In the evening the baron came, "If our circumstances had permitted, I would have invited his Highness to come to us but that is not possible because, unfortunately, we are not in a position to receive guests."

It felt really good for the milkman to be able once again to use the language of his past.

The two talked about the Mainz Society's plans. "That's all a great and noble thought," said Herr von Patschkow, "but, but! What use is the most beautiful agriculture with the best yields to the people if there are no markets to sell and buy? That's what's missing. There are no roads or navigable rivers into the interior just a few wooden shacks called cities here and there. The rivers are clogged with driftwood and end at the sea in swamps and morass. Galveston is a nest the devil has dropped on a sand island. Well, you will see for yourself. I don't want to mislead you and anyway it's probably too late for that. Believe me, you can't look reality in the eye soberly enough."

There was something in the prince's heart that balked at the baron's words and he felt as if he was being skinned alive.

The door was ripped open and a man in high boots and a long pleated jacket stepped into the opening. A bulge in the hip area revealed a few heavy pistols in leather holsters hidden beneath, whilst a brass star shone with an 'S' in the middle of the right lapel.

"Aha, the sheriff," said the milkman, remaining seated.

The gaunt lawman scanned the room with a few glances and headed for the prince. "Ah, Mister Braunfels!" He grabbed his hand, shaking it with a squeeze as if all the bones in it were to be squeezed to pieces, whilst spitting a load of tobacco juice over the seated prince into a distant corner of the room.

Then he pulled up two chairs, sat down and stretched his long, skinny legs one over the other. "Nothing can be done, you came too late, Herr Braunfels. My people had caught him in a pub at the harbor whilst he was playing cards but the bird flew away. That guy can shoot, I tell you and one of the men has a nice bit of lead between his ribs now."

The sheriff rolled the chewing tobacco from one cheek to the other and shoved his hat onto the back of his neck. "One day we'll get him, that leather-colored rogue, right, Herr Patzko? After all he's your good friend, isn't he?" The crumpled face of the lawman from New Orleans squeezed itself into the folds of a smile as he put his hands on his pistol holsters. "But then, woe to him!"

After the sheriff had left, the prince and the baron sat for a while in silence, Solms feeling as if he had been undressed. "Herr Braunfels," the American had addressed him whilst painfully shaking his hand and he had kept his hat on his head. Asking himself if there was no respect for ancient nobility here, the prince felt deeply hurt.

Baron von Patschkow understood him and said consolingly, "This is America, your Highness — Chewing tobacco, pistols, whiskey and disrespect! Anyone who can't put up with is a done deal. Guns sit very loose in the holster in Texas and it is said that there are as many men as pistols and as many pistols as men."

The prince lay awake for a long time after he had crawled under his mosquito net to sleep. The marsh air, tasting disgustingly sweet, crushed one's chest whilst loneliness as heavy as lead spread over him in the muggy, hazy darkness. Tangled dream images drove the drowsy one from torment to torment whilst long trains of people, many looking at him with distorted faces, crawled past him. It was not until morning that he found a little sleep.

---

The Germans left New Orleans behind them like a nightmare as they stood on the steamer watching the whirring of the paddle wheels. The ship sailed extremely flat and lay like a bowl upon the water. The pilot carefully guided it down the Mississippi past shoals and driftwood islands. The boilers were heated with wood stacked up in huge piles on deck and steam hissed from poorly fitting valves and any openings it could find. It looked as though the airy vessel with its two decks had been wrapped frugally and playfully around the innards of the iron machine.

Negroes stoked the fires, Negroes served the passengers and the prince elegantly kept his distance, as he felt obliged so to do after his experiences in New Orleans. The river rolled murkily and clumsily toward the sea, the mud it carried dyeing it a dirty brown.

The coast slowly rose from the warm, blue water, treeless and sandy. Behind it somewhere lay the mainland full of mystery.

The guardsmen were disappointed with the sobriety of the area, which had now lingered past them for several days.

The first day of the journey from the sea had been enough to bring the prince back to himself after his shaking up in New Orleans. He looked to the future, thinking about the first measures he deemed necessary. First of all, an attempt had to be made to extend the concession for Bourgeois d'Orvanne's grant. That would certainly not be too difficult, given the strength of the reputation that he claimed as a representative of the Adelsverein and he would not be looking to save money. Once this had been achieved, an expedition into the settlement area had to set off immediately. Land was to be bought on the approach route to secure the train of immigrants through way stations that lay one day's journey apart. Then it was necessary to establish contact with the Germans who were already living in Texas and to win them over to relocating to the Society's area. With their experience they would form the core team of the undertaking. At the same time it was necessary to explore the conditions pertaining to whether and to what extent one could expand maritime trade with Germany.

The island of Galveston finally rose from the sea like a long, narrow line, lagoons of fallow and marshy water retreating into the interior. Nowhere was there a shimmer of green no matter how much the eyes of the travelers searched for it. He questioned whether this could then be the paradise that was promised to them.

The ship came to a halt at a group of three trees that seemed to float alien and solitary above the water. White weatherboard houses appeared behind it and church towers pointed sharply toward the sky. Then the ship docked.

It was July 1, 1844, the day of the Bourgeois d'Orvanne grant's expiration, when the prince went ashore.

Accommodation was found at a pub at the harbor and the landlord, a German, was a shoemaker and pastor besides.

"You have chosen a bad season," he said anxiously to the prince as a large part of the city is ravaged by the fever. I advise you to continue as soon as possible. We have no fresh water and there is only liquor, beer and wine. Some of the houses are empty because the people have either died or fled. The poorly buried corpses are contaminating the groundwater which already spurts out of the ground at two feet down."

"Nice outlook," growled one of the guardsmen and the men could not hide their disappointment even though they tried to pull themselves together. What they had experienced so far was unlikely to encourage them in the coming days and they started to ask where was this "Paradise on Earth" was to be found.

Galveston had been hurriedly and carelessly built on stake piles in order to support the insecure ground. The city had about three hundred and fifty wooden houses at that time and had stood for seven years, a pretty age for Texas. The docks, on scaffolding and a confused forest of piles, pushed a little way out into the sea to make it possible for ships to dock. Filth and decay accumulated under the bridges and footbridges and was the breeding grounds of the terrible fever that struck the city almost every summer. The "Yellow Jacob" would suddenly crawl out of the swamp, creeping along the houses and bludgeoning the people until it had satisfied its greed.

The German shoemaker, an experienced man who at first found the prince quite amiable, stated, "What you see here in Galveston is not Texas, and the people here aren't Texans. They have been swept up by the wrath of God. Only in the interior, far away from here, lies the land of your yearning. Many are called, but only a few are chosen and whoever wants to go there must first get through this."

At the dusk, the man was suddenly possessed and, climbing on a table, he began to preach. His eyes rolled as he pulled himself together and with a grave voice, in a mixture of English and German, hurled frightful imprecations at the perditious humans.

Then his teeth began to chatter as if he were freezing, his shaking face dropped and he began to beat himself with his arms and legs until sweat broke into streams. Finally he collapsed exhausted and fell asleep. A few blacks that had been standing by carried the cobbler out, recognizing such seizures and remarking that this was not a rarity here in the fever season.

The city lay upon the hot sand like a spider waiting for prey. There was every conceivable kind of exploitation to be found, from the crudest forms of fraud and swindling to the most sophisticated money exchange offices, banking houses, shops, red-light districts and land agents. Some who had come off the ship with a mind for enterprise ended up here as a victim to then use their experience to make others victims, until the fever seized and slowly consumed them. The city lived on poverty, hope and despair. The staid guardsmen were overcome by the horror, wondering if this was what the world was like when you looked it straight in the face. They rejoiced when the prince told them that they were going to go up the Galveston Bay into Buffalo Bayou in Houston the next day.

---

The Mainz Adelsverein actually got off pretty lightly and although Bourgeois d'Orvanne had cheated them out of about ten thousand dollars, the sum could be discreetly booked as a loss.

Consul Henry Fisher, as he named himself in English, had achieved his goal of getting rid of his grant and the contract won him considerable influence. Being a merchant, he saw the possibility of doing lucrative and secure business for years and with respect to Bourgeois d'Orvanne, he had eliminated a dangerous competitor. Money would roll in because an essential part of the immense material deliveries would have to pass through his hands. His pockets would be filled and he could involve himself in all kinds of business, which for him was supreme happiness.

The Texan from Kassel knew how to get the board members in Mainz on his side and to convince them of the success of the project through his confident demeanor, his knowledge of the country and clever argumentation, allowing them to retain their old sense of security.

"It is not at all clear which possibilities for exploitation can be opened up in the Society's new area. When I just think about the minerals—one thing's for sure—that already several hundred years ago, the Spaniards owned silver mines at the upper Colorado. They are within my grant and waiting to be reopened.

Remember, gentlemen, silver, pure, pure silver! Allow it to flow into Europe and you can stir up currencies."

It seems that nobody saw through the enterprising man wanting to become rich the American way, yet nobody was in a position to verify anything at the time, and most would have harshly rejected such mistrust because Fisher came like a savior appearing just at the right moment.

Texas fever in Germany continued to climb and in the autumn of 1844, registrations for passage on the first ships had to be closed, as they were fully booked. In December, the Society announced their divorce from Bourgeois d'Orvanne and the purchase of the Fisher Grant, a matter that was hardly noticed.

All of the Society's plans, as published in the "Collected Documents", were considered to be realizable. Only a few newspapers very bashfully dared to warn of their concern in public.

"Emigration is turning from a necessity into a mania, into a feverish crazy state of affairs from which, so to speak, the sick man after deceiving the sleeping guard, jumps out of bed and into the infirmary in order to escape into the fresh air looking for ideas to save him from his evil and frightening dreams", wrote a leading newspaper — yet nobody heard.

"Germans in America will feel the same way as their compatriots at home where ideas sprout like mushrooms, their thoughts rising sky high. Yet when it comes down to putting things into practice they often get stuck, running into the thorns and thistles of reality." Such sentences struck home by just about no one.

"I must warn about Texas," said the Württemberg State Minister von Gagern to the people's representatives. "Count Boos-Waldeck's verdict on Texas is wholly unfavorable." But the reputation of the Society was not to be shaken even by such a high authority.

Fisher returned with a fast-sailing ship back to Texas as second commissioner of the Society, as assistant to the prince and with extensive powers. His first task there would be to seek Solms and acquaint him with the changed circumstances, for it had to be ensured that the break with Bourgeois d'Orvanne caused as little sensation as possible in Texas as well.

A tiny paddle steamer carried the prince and his men up the Galveston Bay and through Buffalo Bayou to the city of Houston that the Texans had named after their president. It was young, consisting of a few dozen weatherboard huts and lay under the merciless sun as if it were dead. The few people still alive lived in dread because the fever was lurking everywhere.

There was no one with whom the prince could have negotiated in his affairs so he wondered how he could move on from here. One would sink in the marshes and there was neither way nor footbridge so he bought horses and the guardsmen regained courage and self esteem. The main luggage had been left back in Galveston, the traveling party only taking the bare essentials and confining itself in Houston again to what the horses could carry.

As they made their way through the hard, tall grass to the west it was as if the ground was floating beneath them. The land did not seem to possess solid ground at all, with the horses trembling in fear as their hooves sank into the black broth.

They often halted and the prince would spread out the map, trying to use the compass to determine the right direction. The next destination was San Felipe de Austin and upon arrival all they found were five or six miserable weatherboard huts.

The biggest one was a tavern where a Negro received the horses and tied them to the porch railing. Then the landlord brought in a few buckets of water with a gourd hanging on each as a ladle to allow the riders to wash themselves.

Later, food was served and they sat down at the chunky table on chairs covered with calfskin. There were fresh, warm corn cakes and fried bacon and the landlady placed herself at the top of the table with a large, tinny coffee pot beside her. Anybody wanting a drink had to move their cup across the table to her. Although more guests came, nobody took notice of the other whilst the Americans scoffed down their meal in barely ten minutes and everything was quickly cleared away. Anybody needing longer had their food almost ripped out of their mouths.

There was a common bedroom on the ground floor for the guests where everyone received a bed consisting of four piles driven into the earthen floor with ox-skins stretched taut between them and each traveler had his own blankets.

The next morning the prince had to pay one and a quarter dollars per man and horse and all Texan landlords were in collusion about the emptying of pockets with their high prices.

Captured by the abundance of things new and foreign, the expedition silently rode on to Industry where a larger number of Germans lived. Notice of his arrival had already preceded the prince and the troop was greeted festively and escorted to the inn.

The riders looked like a miracle from another world in their immaculate uniforms. Industry was a poor nest where industrious people were struggling to make progress and everything was still in its infancy but the climate was devouring people. Only the tough could see their way through and hardly any of the Germans in the city had been able to achieve that which they had dreamt of at home.

Everyone had to come to terms with just one bitter lesson that meant that inhuman diligence, the abandoning of all good habits and dogged tenacity were necessary if anything was going to be achieved. Anybody who was unable to manage that perished. The country was without mercy with some sitting half-heartedly upon the soil they had begun to work because they dreamed, worrying at night, that they might be able to make more progress elsewhere.

The black earth seemed inexhaustible in its ability to bring forth the best crops yet the climate was against the people. In the rainy season everything gave way to a bottomless porridge and the settlers had take cover on the few stable places amongst the shifting earth as the soil became drenched, leaving only swamps and marshes behind.

Abundant and excessive growth welled up from the damp ground but with it clouds of mosquitoes and obnoxious vermin too. Illnesses rose like ghosts from the mud and the swelter, devouring people and clearing the settlements of whites so those who could afford it bought Negroes and let them work for them. Neither the terrible thunderstorms and subsequent floods nor the unexpectedly threatening Norther, with its sudden fall in temperature, could breach the faith of the toughest amongst them.

The Germans were the most stubborn when it came to sticking it out. Some knew that they were on a lost cause for the rest of their lives but one day their children would reap the blessing of their commitment, which made them hang on. "Get on with it, dig or die!" They said.

Many Americans just could not understand this and they changed their settlements often, always searching anxiously and looking for new and better places. They went from one day to the next, never looking back at what they had done in months of hard work. The Germans, however, gritted their teeth and only gave up when there was no other choice. Mothers died with a quiet glow in their eyes, knowing that their sacrifice had not been in vain and that their children would be their heirs.

That was the thing that was different about the Germans — they thought in generations and it was not the benefits that they were able to impose on the country from one day to the next which determined their decisions but the belief that the final victory of their diligence would be transferred from the parents to the children. So they planted trees, planned roads, dug ditches and built dams and locks whilst they rooted themselves to the ground, wrestling with it, and did not throw it away as if it were a thing to be detested. Yet the country even made its selection amongst them but in the end, the best and the ones with the strongest resistance won through.

Thus were the Prince's thoughts on his ride across the flat, stoneless expanse.

In the scorching midday sun they camped under a group of live oaks as deers passed in packs, awakening the desire to hunt. They shot a hefty animal but only slowly did the guardsmen realize that hunting was nobody's prerogative here and the adventure began to entice them.

The best pieces were roasted and a butcher, by the name of Hermann Nahm from the land of Hessen, handled it with skill. It all seemed like an irresponsible waste when they had to leave the greater part of the deer and move on.

The prince laughed when he saw how hard his people found it parting with the beautiful meat and said, "You'll learn it yet — you're in Texas now — not back home where you have to buy a small piece of meat in a store for loads of money."

In the evening, the men sang the prince's anthem for the first time as the troop saw the weatherboard huts of Industry appearing before them.

In the brief dusk a swarm of people met them, waved and welcomed them in German.

The prince stayed in Industry for a few days drafting the memorandum to the Texas Congress, requesting the extension of the concession for the grant of Bourgeois d'Orvanne. He sent it with a courier to the capital city of Austin, which lay in the rolling countryside northwest of the Colorado.

Compatriots from all over the area came together to hold a festival in the prince's honor. He allowed himself to be celebrated as the great supporter of all Germans in Texas. In an address he invited them to make lively use of the offer of the Mainz Adelsverein and to resettle themselves in the Society's area.

"The Society will not rest," until it has collected all the Germans here into its care and a strong German state in Texas is our goal. The Germans on both sides of the Atlantic Ocean will soon see the benefit of our sacrifice. I drink to the future of a united Germany in Texas!"

Glasses filled with schnapps and wine were enthusiastically lifted and clashed together. Later, one of the oldest pioneers, Friedrich Ernst, made a toast. His eyes shone as he shouted, "Let us now drink to the good of the noble and generous German princes who also think of their subjects on the other side of the great sea!"

Many eyes filled with tears. Now all the men and women felt themselves back home for a few moments, which touched everybody's heart.

In Austin, the officers of the government and the congress were in no particular hurry to promote the Society's cause. The president was hard to reach as he traveled around the country a lot, preparing for a final, decisive confrontation with Mexico.

The Prince was received honorably in the capital and with all possible pomp. He rode with his people in front of the government building in a solemn procession and the representative of the president paid him homage. The prince, very receptive to such formalities, was gratefully moved.

This was followed by a festive meal accompanied by torrents of great speeches. Solms floated in exaltation, knowing how to praise the importance of the Mainz Society for Texas in always varying and more colorful phrases. In a report to the homeland he wrote:

"I have the best impression of the country and the people, and I am hoping for the renewal of the concession. Everywhere Germans and Texans greeted me honorably. One drank to the welfare of the German princes and the compatriots living in Texas who will once again feel happy to be safe and sheltered under the care of our Society."

However, the Texas government, following its own law of gravity, was not moved by such sublime words. The prince was burning with impatience so he made visits, gave presents and appeared as an ambassador when it came to making an impression, yet the renewal of the concession was delayed in spite of everything and he did not know what to do.

"People," he said one day to the guardsmen, "get ready! We're riding as fast as possible to the grant tomorrow so we can see what's going on there and I hope the government has decided by the time we get back."

They were on the road for many weeks. They rode boldly through the soft waves of the prairie. Traces of Indians appeared and they saw buffalo moving on the horizon. The distance, from which bushes and trees rose in clusters, was endless and rivers had to be laboriously crossed.

Rows of hills rose one behind the other to the southwest as new ones continued to emerge on the horizon. The troop of riders disappeared amongst oak forests free of undergrowth and with tree trunks standing like columns. Occasionally they passed by lonely settlements and in narrow river valleys they marveled at the fertile dark earth.

The mountains rose ever higher, whilst the valleys continually narrowed, growing more and more barren. The horses had to climb steep, bare slopes, dry, stone-strewn plateaus stretching prosaically and incalculably into the distance. The prince became more and more silent as he increasingly pulled out the map, shaking his head. There was no doubt that this stone desert was the Bourgeois d'Orvanne Grant.

The riders returned tired and dejected to Austin in the second half of August. The prince was almost glad when he was informed of the government's decision to definitively refuse the renewal of the concession. On August 20, Solms wrote to Germany, "We should be glad to get out of a bad situation in this way. It is unthinkable what would have happened to our people if we had brought them into this grant, as most of it is desolate limestone mountains on which no blade of grass thrives. The good land in the narrow valleys has been populated many times before so our colonists would have received only what was left. What should be done now? I hope that it will be possible to control preparations in the home country so that nothing definitive happens until I have a really useful area solidly at my disposal."

At the same time back home, the Society was putting together the first transport to the grant purchased from Fisher. The first ship was to transfer the advance party that had been put together with much thought. Only healthy and capable persons in the prime of life were selected out of hundreds. Families with many children were told by the leadership to wait for later crossings.

This advance party was to clear the way into the interior, the pioneers breaking through to explore and determine the march route into the unknown. Farmers, craftsmen, teachers, doctors, wagoners, millers and pharmacists were selected who were sent lists showing in detail the equipment required, asking them to arrive at the port of Bremen on September 15, 1844, three days before the departure of the first ship. Three more ships should follow by the end of the year.

Management on behalf of the Society for the first advance was given to the Darmstadt engineer Nikolaus Zink[17]. He was instructed, employing the help of American experts, to survey of the land and to begin the construction of the first settlements immediately upon arrival at the grant.

After prudent consideration by the Society management, a number of strapping peasant whores were mixed among the healthy men. That would give everyone enough zest for life and cohesion and would additionally create the possibility of soon seeing a tribe of genuine German-Texans emerge.

Women were recommended to protect themselves with suitable underwear for the voyage in the steerage. The Society management had thoughtfully suggested this because the planned sequence in building the intended structure should not be hampered by any randomness.

In many places in the German fatherland, the preparations for the move to Texas were now beginning. In the first days of September 1844 people traveled to Bremen on carriages, ships and by rail. There was a big, happy farewell in towns and villages, which the many who had been left behind could only watch with envy.

## III

The reddish late summer moon climbed contemplatively over the roofs of the houses in Bremen. As it freed itself from the highest ridges and chimneys, it swam peacefully in the soft blue sky looking sleepily down on the glittering harbor basin and the maze of alleys and streets. The harbor was silent without the hint of a breeze as the day's activities came to rest, leaving a slightly melancholy autumnal odor in the air.

The guard on the brig "Johann Detthart" pushed the gangplank over to the shore, hanging a lantern over it. "For goodness sake," said the helmsman to the sailor, "some men have got things to do here and the gangplank won't be drawn back until they return!"

Aboard the stately three-master all was quiet. Some of the emigrants had already moved into their quarters into the steerage whilst others were still staying in the guesthouses at the harbor.

Hermann Koechert sat with his young wife on a roll of rope, "Lie down now, Luise," he said to her, "lie down, it won't be long and I'll soon be back. Zink asked a few men to come over for a briefing today in the 'Letzte Traenel'. At ten o'clock someone is going to arrive from Berlin wishing to join the travel party. We've got to talk to him because he's been in Texas and even wrote a book about it. A discussion with him would be very valuable for the instructions he would give to everyone tomorrow, the day before we leave, Zink said." Koechert led Luise to the companionway to the decks and she descended the steep stairs.

A male voice called from the shore, "Herr von Wrede[18] has arrived!"

Many startled people in the steerage were occupied by the loneliness of the thoughts that they had spun for themselves after the fullness of the day. Footsteps trailed hollowly over the wooden deck but soon it became quiet. Hermann Koechert and a troop of men entered the back room of the Gasthaus "The Letzte Traene" opposite the anchorage of the Brig.

"Gentlemen, I'd like to introduce Captain von Wrede to you," began Zink. "He's just arrived and wants to take part in this debate despite the late hour. I'm very pleased, Captain, that you could at the last moment still decide to accept the Mainz Society's offer. I've selected a few of the men who'll form the advance party into the Society's territory and I'd like to make you familiar with everything that concerns our journey. From the experience you gain from local conditions you'll hopefully develop a broader sense of responsibility and a higher conscience as a commitment to the whole, which is greater than searching for any personal advantage. Captain, if I may ask, why did you hesitate with your decision right until the end?"

Captain von Wrede stood up, serious eyes burning in his gaunt, tanned face. "That's very easy. I've been following the work of the Mainz Adelsverein since its establishment and anyone familiar with the Society's thorough theoretical preparation can form the opinion that every effort is being made to ensure the success of the operation. Everything on paper, is correct and in this respect has had a tremendous influence on people. The preparation betrays a great sense of responsibility but it still remains in many respects just what it is, theory — paper and ink."

"Captain, please don't forget our money, our supplies, the weapons, the healthy, impeccable people and let's not forget the reputation of the members of the Society. These are tangible facts! These are not theories, they're realities!"

"Certainly, but thinking plans over can mature to the point where everything is so clear that in the end it becomes easy to confuse perceptions with reality and one forgets to take opposing forces into account. So because you don't know what they are going to be, you assume them not to be there. However, they finally determine the course of events and sometimes the most mature plans are thwarted. This is where my sense of responsibility finally seized me and so I want to risk my own skin once more because, as the way things are, the whole project can neither be called off nor reduced to the extent, which I from my experience would consider necessary."

Doctor Kuester, a young doctor from Frankfurt, jumped up, "Permit me, Captain, the Society stands behind everything with its tremendous moral weight. Very significant funds have been made available and we, correct gentlemen, will do our best to reach the goal!"

Everyone looked at him approvingly.

"You'll have to, too," the captain continued. Good. Money, you said? Nice but be careful. The Society has been equipped with a working capital of two hundred thousand guilders. That's a huge sum to the poor but suppose you sent only twenty-five hundred settlers to Texas in the coming year and supposing everyone took along the four hundred pounds of baggage allotted to each person, then that would give you a million pounds, or ten thousand hundredweight.

"A Texan covered wagon actually carries two thousand pounds at best. So if you wanted to bring the people to the Society's territory, then five hundred wagons would be needed and another hundred for women and children as well as another hundred for tents, provisions, utensils, tools and much more. Even the procurement of so many wagons is almost impossible and they would cost a fortune.

"If the enormous fleet of vehicles is to be kept in motion without any problems, then one needs seven hundred Texan wagoners because only they master the difficult business of driving oxen in every type of terrain. They must be fed and paid for, whilst one and a half to two yoke oxen are necessary as draft animals for each wagon. That makes twenty-one to twenty-eight hundred animals. So again, a very huge financial requirement becomes apparent and that's *my* reality!

"The Society is promising to build finished homes. It wants to procure the first pets, cows, horses and pigs and it wants to make sure that every fifteen acres of land can be secured by fencing but rather, because of cattle and game damage, regulated agriculture is quite unthinkable. Three to four pairs of oxen often have to be yoked to a plow in order to break up the matted sward. Three thousand oxen, three thousand cows, and fifteen hundred horses are necessary to commence agriculture to any degree.

"Since the Society has decided not to follow a cautious development of the settlement but rather to immediately throw masses of people at Texas, the great danger lies in trying to do everything at once. It will require millions. A good horse alone costs a hundred and fifty to two hundred dollars so what are their two hundred thousand guilders? Besides, I am only calculating here with twenty-five hundred immigrants at first."

The farmer Thomas Schwab from the Black Forest groaned because he had deposited his entire fortune with the Society before departure. Now he rested his head between his hands and stared at Wrede as if hoping to finally hear a liberating word from him.

"You see, Texas is like everywhere else in the world—only money seems to matter. Yet not only money, not even the sum of your wishes and hopes will make any difference to the success of the operation. There is something special to add to everything I said and that is the reason I came. You can't do it with money alone but only with the strength of the man who wants to achieve something!"

His gray eyes gleamed and his fists were firmly planted on the table. "I don't want to discourage you but you do have to face things honestly and look the facts straight in the eye. No beautiful apparition, no dream and no wish is going to help us! I travel with you because I know that things will be tough on man and beast. A ruthless natural selection is coming upon us and that what has to fall will fall. This is what attracted me because I wanted to work with men again. Is there anything greater than subjugating the earth?!"

He reached his hands across the table as the others reached for them. "He who wants to lead here should know that! Anyone who is weak can still go home. What I said is not fitting for everyone, yet the men of trust, and Herr Zink has chosen you as such, must be greater than any single speck they can see beyond just satisfying their own personal desires."

Zink and his trusted companions let these last words sink in for a long time. "Thank you, Captain. We understand you and feel the heavy responsibility that lies upon us—yet it's almost not a burden anymore."

Zink shook hands with everyone once more and many things were discussed late into the night. At last, they parted like conspirators, borne by a great, transpersonal sense of duty. On the following day, September 17, 1844, the traveling party was to be informed of the set of tasks that it had to perform whilst living together during the crossing.

Hermann Koechert crawled into the bunk next to his wife. In that hour he felt as if he had shed all of his previous life. He thought for a long time about one of the captain's sentences, "Was it right to send a prince to Texas to prepare things? One has to understand that Americans marvel at such a thing as if it were a legendary animal, yet remain the more suspicious and reserved."

Early in the morning, those arrived who had spent the last nights in the taverns at the harbor. Zink made his appearance to the one hundred and fifty people, married and unmarried from all over Germany and different in dress and dialect, as they gathered on deck—even before the multicolored luggage had all been stowed and the still empty berths had been allocated.

"The anchor will be lifted tomorrow morning," began Nikolaus Zink. "We are the vanguard that the Mainz Society is sending to Texas so that we can open the way for the thousands who'll come after us. We have to be conscious of this and aware of our obligations at every hour. We're now forced to live for seventy to ninety days in the confinement imposed by the narrowness of this ship. There'll be many hours when we are tired of closeness and weary of human company yet the peace of all must be more important than the petty quarrel of individuals at all times.

"This group of travelers is to be divided into cooperatives of ten people. Each such group forms a kitchen duty and each chooses a leader, the kitchen duty master. In the evening he receives the meat from the helmsman for the next day and attaches the kitchen duty number. I will hand out the corresponding metal tags to the duty master as required. Everyone picks up the meat and additional food items for preparation the next day, according to his number.

"The large utensils will be returned after the meal and the small ones kept for the travelers to clean themselves. Bread and toppings are assigned to the mess master for the whole week.

"Every kitchen duty has a common kettle for tea or coffee. A just person will have to be chosen in each group for apportioning and distribution. No one is allowed to crowd the kitchen to cook or fry something special for themselves. The kitchen duty chooses bunks side by side and above one another. Crates are to be used as tables.

"Speaking to the sailors during working hours and smoking are prohibited. Weapons are to be given in to the captain for the duration of the crossing. Nobody needs to lose heart in the first few days due to seasickness or storm as everything passes. In the evening music and dancing are permitted until ten o'clock if so desired.

"All the captain's instructions must be obeyed and any complaints about the ship or its crew should only be made through me. Below the intermediate deck lies the bilge where the provisions, drinking water and general luggage are stored. No one is allowed to descend there without permission. If rats show up no one needs to be frightened because they are to be found on every ship and we'll have to get used to the creaking of wood too.

"The upper bunks and likewise, the passage between the two rows of bunks, are to be cleaned at least once a week. Domestic appliances are to be hung on the tarred ropes that are strung to the intermediate deck. There mustn't be anything left lying around and the boxes in the corridor between the bunks have to be tied together with ropes so that they don't fall on top of one another when the sea gets rough.

"As long as the weather permits, the entrance to the steerage should remain open during the night because this is necessary for ventilation, there being no windows.

"Everyone should keep any valuable property in their bunks. Depending on the severity of the case, theft will be punished by food deprivation, attachment to one of the three poles or flogging. Jurisdiction is the sole responsibility of the captain.

"The decks are to be sprinkled with vinegar or fumigated with the smoldering end of a rope dipped in tar every other day.

For safety reasons, three night lanterns will remain alight. Nobody may leave their sleeping place without good reason after ten o'clock in the evening.

"Essential medicines for every voyage will be dispensed by me. We have sufficient quantities of castor oil, vinegar, Epsom Salts and lice ointment.

"In severe cases the captain is responsible.

"I see that some of you have brought duvets but they have to be sold sometime during the day. I advise you to turn everything unnecessary into cash because over there money's worth more than luggage.

"Make sure to use fresh water sparingly.

"That's just about everything essential for now and further instructions follow. So now comrades, get to work! In the west lies the land we are looking for so let us be worthy of our great commission because the better life can only be attained through sacrifice!"

The captain boarded the ship on the evening of September 17 1844. He asked Zink to share his cabin with him but he refused saying, "I belong in the steerage — with my people."

The ship sailed down the Weser with the tide on September 18. Captain von Wrede and Lieutenant Wilcke[19], the two soldiers of the advance party, leaned against the railing and Wilcke said, "I have the impression that we have a good number of able people on board. Zink is fit for the task and then there's Koechert, the schoolmaster from Thuringia, a firebrand in love but nevertheless reliable. The milliner and a tailor brothers, Hilpert, the farmer from the Black Forest, Schwab, and the merchant Birkel from Wiesbaden. Dr. Kuester, the doctor from Frankfurt, does not make the same good impression on me that Zink seems to have of him. Then there are a few able-bodied women and all sorts of adolescents so I think it's important to keep an eye on people so that, when it comes down to it, we can entrust everyone with the right tasks."

"Good, good," said the captain, somewhat concerned, "but what will our prince have been up to over there?"

They did not yet know about Bourgeois d'Orvanne's deception, the acquisition of the new grant also being unknown to them.

Fisher was so far ahead that he could make arrangements with the prince for the reception of the first ship.

He had already arrived in Galveston on September 15 and learned that the prince's main luggage was still with the German innkeeper, cobbler and preacher. He did not spend much time in Galveston but drove on to Houston where he was lucky enough to meet the prince at a festivity in the company of the German pastor Ervendberg[20]. There they were able to drink to the welfare of New Germany.

The prince was very depressed after the land acquisition negotiations with all sorts of people had not taken him one step further. He was already thinking of buying individual farms for the first immigrants and then traveling home to call off all further transportations. Pastor Ervendberg also considered this to be the only possible solution.

Fisher introduced himself, "Your Highness, my name is Fisher, I am a Bremen consul in Galveston and I have just come from Germany having signed a contract with the Mainz Adelsverein for the purchase of my grants at the upper Colorado. I am commissioned to negotiate with you as the second commissioner of the Society and here is my mandate." He pulled a bundle of papers out of his pocket and slid them onto the table. The prince was so startled that he forgot to take them as he stared at the stranger asking, "What did you say?"

Ervendberg rose up, stepping forward and saying, "Of course, it's you Herr Consul!" He turned to the prince. "As far as the personality of this gentleman goes, it's true what he says, your Highness, Consul Fisher is known to me."

He shook hands with the merchant and it was only now that the prince reached for the papers and hastily scanned them. "There, read, Pastor! Truly, the man sends us heaven! Rest assured, Herr Consul, I saw almost no way out—but now let's get to work!"

It was as if all the pressure of the last weeks had fallen from his soul. "Imagine, Herr Consul, Bourgeois d'Orvanne's grant has been bought from the Texan Government by the Frenchman

Castroville. I almost envied the man, but now I feel sorry for the people he settles in the stone desert and now we've been helped too. You are my savior!"

The pastor had tears in his eyes.

"This is a visible sign of the divine will that will bless your work," he said, his voice obviously moved.

Fisher now narrated the course of events, as far as he was involved. Finally, together they were able to see the new, common task, when he said, "On September 18, in three days' time, the first ship leaves Bremen. It may be here by the end of the year and by then we must have everything prepared!"

Fig. 8: Germans on the way to New Braunfels

The guardsmen, who had suffered greatly from many illnesses and from the prince's depression, pepped up. Fisher left to carry out the deliveries of goods corresponding to the Society's program having been provided with sufficient bills of exchange. He was to present his accounts to the prince for checking after the ship's arrival.

Solms recognized as his next task the necessity to find a harbor from which the Fisher grant could be reached by the shortest route. For weeks he rode with his people along the coast, through swamps and rivers and examined every bay. They came to Bolivar, crossed the Brazos, touched Colombia and Brazoria, arriving in Matagorda after a difficult ride. Often the horses were up to their stomachs in mud. At Matagorda the Colorado River ended in a wide, shallow bay, with its headwaters wrapping around the Fisher grant in a wide arc, which seemed to give the prince the direction of the march into the settlement area. Further explorations along the shallow coast, traveling around the Lavacca Bay, they finally found a suitable place for the construction of ships on its southeastern shore. The land belonged to an American by the name of White and he gave it to them cheap. The prince called the calm bay "Carlshafen[21]" and all those arriving should be brought into the grant via this place in the coming years.

"People," he said, as they went to sleep the first night on their own land, "this is the beginning of a new chapter of German emigration history!"

He loved making such sonorous impressions.

---

Difficult weeks began for the guardsmen with messenger services in all directions keeping the men on the move. The surroundings of the new port had to be carefully explored because the location and nature of the trek into the colony was of great importance.

It took a lot of money to procure the necessary wood for constructing the camp because neither tree nor shrub grew on the coast that rose gently from the sea, white and sandy, and there were no stones either. The prince rented all the vehicles that could be acquired from the farmers in the neighborhood and had to bring logs, boards, and ironware from long distances. Solms did not act frugally as he was able to spend well as long as he had sufficient cash. The farmers knew how to take advantage of the situation so they demanded prices for material and services that often far exceeded the local value. The money melted away like snow in the sun but Solms paid because it was necessary to make the most out of every hour. He enjoyed creating, commanding and forming.

Fisher sent the main luggage from Galveston and the cannon also arrived. Crates, bales and rolls were stored for the time being in a corner of the main hut a little way inland, the heap growing continually in height.

As the first paddle steamer from Galveston was looking for the entrance to the Matagorda Bay in front of Passo Cavallo, a shallow sandbank lay across its path as the breakers whispered deceptively and their roar could be heard from afar. Only with the utmost strength and genuine American daring was it possible to guide the light ship as it slithered over into the deeper, calmer waters upon a high wave. For all ships arriving later, the tall weatherboard hut became the point of orientation.

Meanwhile Fisher bought as much corn and bacon as he could get but usually he had no time to check the quality of the goods. "Come on, let's go," was the word, "into the Lavacca Bay to Carlshafen!"

Galveston became lively whilst the Consul cashed in commission for himself.

Wheelwrights and blacksmiths found work because about thirty covered wagons had to be assembled quickly with full equipment. Draft oxen, slaughter cattle and salt beef were traded and Fisher quickly earned the reputation of being an important person to earn by. The whole city knew, that in the past, despite many dubious dealings, he had always got nowhere. That was all over now and Herr Henry Fisher had returned from Germany with his pockets full, opened his locked up house again, aired it and was now going into very big business.

It was November and the air blew cold and rough from the north as the supplies soon began to grow up to the roof in the barn in Carlshafen. "Well, it will soon be time," said the prince to Ervendberg one morning as they had crawled shivering out of the tent and looking out to the white foaming sea, "I can hardly wait for the ship with our people aboard to appear on the horizon."

He became more and more impatient as the days went by and on November 28, he sailed to Galveston with three of his guardsmen on a returning steamer. "I want to be there beforehand to welcome them and they'll have to be transferred from the sailing ship to a coastal steamer which has a shallow draft. I am not completely satisfied with Fisher and want to see what's going on for myself. He has not provided a statement for any of his shipments to date. The man has been allocated considerable authority but at the end of the day, who is he and do we really know him? I have no peace of mind on this and believe that it will be an important task for the future to keep this kind of American away from our compatriots."

Unfortunately he came too late because his ship got caught before Galveston in one of the terrible Texas storms and the sea was boiling, meaning that landing was first possible on December 2. Galveston looked just like a huge puddle.

"Your Highness is just unlucky," Fisher said to the Prince, blinking slyly, whilst in his office. "The ship with the people from Germany sailed out to Carlshafen last night."

That was true because the storm had driven the small coastal steamer into the open sea after it left Galveston and for that reason had not been noticed by the prince's ship.

The call "land ahoy!" broke out among the exhausted and weary people on the German sailing ship at the deliverance from the long sea voyage as they thereupon pulled themselves together. Many attired themselves in their holiday clothes and something like happiness dared to start showing itself. Koechert's wife, Luise, took her best gown out of the suitcase and dressed herself in the narrow bunk, doing this with her last strength because the journey had taken its toll on her. It had become almost too hard for her to share everything personal and to see her own life and shame eroded away. She had become pale and thin and now she and the others looked longingly over to the land beyond where all their wishes were to come true.

Hermann Koechert and his trusted companions were sitting in front of the chart room. They discussed with Zink everything that was to happen upon arrival in Galveston. A faint glow of joy ventured its way to the surface—the goal was near! Hope flew from one to the other but actually a wearying disappointment was gnawing its way into each of them. Their trek into the garden of the world had initially ended very soberingly in front of a shantytown that lay strewn over a pile of sand. Some had eaten and drunk their secretly hidden supplies in the last hours before arriving at Galveston, lifting the mood somewhat, yet everything remained restrained and subdued.

The sailing ship docked but nobody was allowed to go on land. Sailors got hold of as much white bread as they could lay their hands on and the emigrants greedily devoured some fruit that they negotiated for excessive money from on board.

Now they were crammed together on the upper deck of the small paddle steamer and the lower one was clogged with luggage. Above the city lay a harsh, steel-blue sky as the last part of the journey began.

The night fell fast upon the sea, devouring the light, and it was so cramped that you could hardly see your hand in front of your face. Valves hissed and soot and smoke whirled over the travelers as it began to rain. A storm was brewing whilst hunger stirred but nobody could get to his luggage.

The Germans clung to each other soaked to the skin. The paddle wheels often whirred freely in the air when the ship lay on its side. As the lamps went out no one could see the other as somewhere on the vast ocean, forgotten and tiny as a feather, sailed a helpless boat packed with frozen, moaning people as the night covered and the storm juggled with it.

They finally arrived at the entrance to the Matagorda Bay on the afternoon of the next day. The pilot flag was hoisted as the pilot ventured across from land in his flimsy boat. Climbing aboard, he pushed himself through the motionless barrage of people into the wheelhouse. The storm was getting stronger and the surf was raging whilst house-high waves were driving them backwards. One wondered if the pilot would lose his way as the ship turned back and forth looking for the fairway. Sandbanks were lurking just a few feet below the ship's hull and it was hard to tell where the entrance was.

Water greedily pawed the ship as if the sea would grab the almost extinguished human cargo and drag it down with it. The surf was increasing and walls of water obscured the view as the fire under the boilers was intensified. The pilot yelled something into the captain's ears that made him turn pale and downcast. There was a crunch and a jolt that moaned like the lament of wood and iron and people fell over each other. The ship was now sitting on top of the bank, the wheels becoming suddenly stationary as all wondered if this was the end.

Ropes and tethers were passed up from the belly of the ship as frozen hands reached out for them. Everyone held on to each other. Entire groups girded themselves with ropes, wrapping them around railings and anything solid. Hell was cooking under the boilers and the engineers hung weights on the safety valves. Sails were set and the ship creaked and crashed in all of its joints under the blows of the surf. Planks bent and water began to penetrate into the interior as crying and whining could be heard between the surges of the storm whilst some dropped onto their knees and prayed.

Koechert had tied himself to the railing with his wife wondering if she was still alive, her eyes wide open staring past him with her silk dress sticking to her like a black skin.

The sailors started to prepare the lifeboats as the boilers were overheating with steam sharply issuing from all the cracks. The storm, the sea and the ship were all fighting together with their utmost. Suddenly the wheels began to turn again, cracking, erratically, irregularly, forwards and backwards then hitting the ground and lifting the ship whilst one wondered what would happen should the wheel shaft break.

The storm threw the watery desert against the ship as house-high waves broke in and buried the people under it. Then the ship broke free as the water ran off the boat and they strove into the quiet Lavacca Bay.

Koechert was holding his wife in his arms. She leant against him feebly, only the rope keeping her upright. Her head dropped onto his shoulder and once he loosened the rope, she collapsed beside him. Although he caught her, she hung like lead in his arms. Wondering what had happened, the crowd moved closer to the two as Koechert lowered the woman gently onto the deck. She was dead and in the storm he had not heard the fainting scream that passed his ear just as the wheels began to run.

The ride became calmer although outside, beyond the boat, the sea was raging. People were becoming humans again whilst the news of the death of the young woman was whispered from one to another. Pity grew out of the isolation and fear of all those bound together in this life and death community of fate. Luise Koechert was the first to land in Carlshafen in her silk festive dress, that lonely man sitting next to her in the boat. Ervendberg stood upright in his cassock like a black pillar on the white sand. He was surprised that there was barely a sound from the ship and that a boat, where he could see only one man besides the two oarsmen, was heading for land. The boat crunched on the sand, the man within it remaining seated, slumped, head tilted forward. Ervendberg stepped into the water and, going out a few steps, he could now see the dead person lying on a blanket. He folded his hands and he now would have to say something other than what he had previously prepared for greeting the advance party. In fact he said nothing but, pulling Hermann Koechert up towards him, he kissed his forehead only saying, "Brother."

It took several days for the Germans to come back to themselves again after this terrible journey but Ervendberg was able to give some consolation.

Now they stood again on solid ground, "on German soil," Zink said to them but that was hard to understand at that moment. They looked beyond and could see the sea stretching into the distance, peaceful and smooth and they wondered slowly whether they had ever really experienced the storm. It was not easy to organize and to come to terms with the wealth of impressions that were still suffocating all thought.

However, the grave, the first one, just beyond the storage hut, was real enough. A flat, white heap of sand lay with its dry substance slowly blowing away under the faintest breath of air.

Impatience soon began to stir and gossip flew whisperingly along the tent rows as people wondered when they would break out for the colony. The arrival of the prince from Galveston bringing a huge amount of material, cattle for slaughter, fruit, potatoes and vegetables provided plenty of material for conversation for a while. His Highness in his romantic uniform permitted himself to be marveled at and whilst retreating to his tent was somewhat disturbed by the confident—almost too confident—demeanor of some of the leading men.

"People can't stay here without anything to do," Zink told him one day. "We have to set up a veritable, permanent camp that will provide safe shelter for transports arriving later. I suggest that Koechert become the manager of the provisions whilst Wilcke develops the camp, builds defenses and takes command. We shall increase the guardsmen to twenty men to protect the undertaking and all other men able to bear arms are to make up the reserve. The patrol service in the foreland will be looked after by Herr von Wrede, whilst Dr. Kuester will be the camp doctor. The supreme command remains in the hands of your Highness."

The prince made a sour face during these brief sentences. He wondered if there was some force at work which was pushing itself up beside him and which was able to see clearer and work more consequentially than he himself could ever have.

Zink went on to say, "The women in their turn have to prepare a plan around the cooking of food and the related procurement and Koechert will supervise those responsible. It should be ordered that all garments that have suffered during the crossing are immediately checked and repaired and Thomas Schwab's wife can be in charge of that.

Fig. 9: The farmhouse of Nicolaus Zink near Comfort, in which he died in 1887.

"Water must not be taken from the freshwater ponds but we've got to dig a well immediately. I'll see to that," Nikolaus Zink insisted.

The prince felt himself being cornered more and more by each demanding sentence. The assuredness of the man, who as an engineer was not given to dreaming, seemed uncomfortable and annoying. The abundance of demands tired the high and mighty Lord. He questioned whether this was not just all petty common sense which reasonable people would arrive at by themselves. He would have liked to start off immediately into the colony with the whole troop with himself at the head, then his guardsmen and then the people of New Germany.

Zink's sobriety clouded his employer's joyful ambition and it seemed as though he was already a bit outside of the self-forming events. Zink, Wrede, Koester[22], Schwab, Wilcke, Koechert and, whatever they might be called, were putting their heads together too much.

Following Zink's instructions, the emigrants went to work and ramparts were constructed with nine canons soon sticking their round mouths over them. Inside the outer fortifications, around the storage hut, they built a strengthening wall of sand, stakes and boards. The men were trained in shooting and guard duty. Koechert overcame the helplessness of his grief with the will to work, pushing aside every whim and encroachment. Three forges were working from morning to night and blacksmiths and wheelwrights built fourteen two-wheeled carts. Everything was orderly and according to plan.

But also many scoundrels were seen to be drifting day and night around the camp. Failures from all over the world were being attracted to the undertaking's reputation like mosquitos are to the light. Captain von Wrede led the patrol service and prevented all precarious people from approaching Carlshafen.

Christmas was gradually approaching as Koechert and Captain von Wrede were sitting in the pastor's tent.

"Agreed," said the Thuringian, "I, with a few women, will prepare everything—but of course it doesn't really feel like Christmas, does it?."

After a pause Herr von Wrede said, "The prince is worried."

"In what way?" asked the pastor.

"He hoped that money would arrive with the first ship from Germany but Zink brought only as much as was necessary to secure the transport. What now? The bill of exchange business will have to carry on. Hopefully the people won't start pushing for their money they entrusted to the Society before they left to be paid out. Otherwise we'll really be in the soup."

Just at this moment the prince was saying to the engineer, "Herr Zink, I've asked you to speak to me because I need to talk to you about something that's worrying me very much."

Zink sat down on a field chair as Solms closed the door in front of the entrance to the tent and whispered, "I'm disappointed that no money was given to you in Mainz. What are their Lordships thinking about? There are already a large number of exchange bills circulating in Galveston and New Orleans. Fisher avoided my questions when I addressed him at my last meeting with him and he pretended to be overworked looking after the Society's affairs.

'That's not the most important thing,' he said, 'but that we equip and look after the handful of people who're now in Carlshafen. We have to think of the thousands who'll be coming afterwards. What you have spent so far on funds is only a beginning.' Not only that but he was still pressing for the payment of the sixth which is contractually assured him as commission. However, I can't make money out of sand—the only thing we have in abundance!" he sighed deeply. "When will we move on from here? I have to do something to help me over this stress. Riding, hunting, pushing forward! All this messing about is killing me! Above all, why doesn't Fisher send the wagons that I've long paid for? In Germany I'd know what I had to do. But here? I feel like I'm paralyzed."

Worries upon worries, yet the least were had by the Prussian Ensign Julius von Coll[23] who would drive cows and oxen into the pasture, singing and whistling all day and had a happy word for everyone. Everyone liked the herdsman Julius and women enjoyed it when he spoke kindly to them.

One day the prince presented the engineer with a plan. "You see," he said to Zink, "I've drawn the route of a railway as I imagine it onto this map. A large proportion of the men who migrate in the coming year could be employed in its construction. As rails we'd use oak wood and the locomotives would be imported from Germany. Think about it, you're an engineer, how could it be done? I think it would be great if we could reach the Society's territory from Carlshafen by the most direct way, then anyone arriving in three or four years would simply go onto the platform and travel with a ticket to the end station. Great, eh?"

Zink felt as if he had been kicked in the teeth as he glared at the prince, shaking his head and wondering that he had been given such a man as his superior. The lives of all the hopeful and faithful working outside in the camp were at his mercy and it was immediately clear to Zink in that moment that the only thing that would help now would be resistance.

On the night after this interview he stood for a long time behind the storage barn with Herr von Wrede. "I saw it all coming," said the captain. "Let's wait for the right moment to make the man harmless and I think that things are gradually moving to where this point in time will come. The next ships from Germany will be arriving soon and we'll be moving forward to the grant, taking the prince along with us and then we'll have him amongst us. I'd suggest leaving Koechert here as he's demonstrated an extraordinary skill in keeping boozing and grub in order. The schoolmaster can then receive and look after all incoming transports."

Worries spread around the camp as many of the people were asking why things were not moving forward, where the wagons were and what had happened to the horses and oxen the Society had promised. "After all, we paid-in our money in Mainz," they growled.

Christmas Eve came and Herr von Wrede brought two oak trees with him, one larger and one smaller, after a long ride with some of the guardsmen. Koechert unpacked lights from a box and the women had been baking a lot in the last two days whilst one or the other brought out some sweets, donating them from their personal supplies. The evening was mild, the sea was so calm it seemed as if it had fallen asleep and the stars were bright and clear in the soft blue of the sky. All work rested and families came together and they spoke quietly whilst they washed, combed and dressed in their Sunday clothes in readiness. The camp streets had been swept clean and it would normally have been the time for bells to be ringing somewhere. The cattle were complaining in the pen after Julius von Coll had driven it there earlier that day.

A light flickered up in front of the barn, then one more and then another, ever increasing. All eyes were looking up as the tiny flames hovered silently in the mild night. Then, yet more flared up out of the darkness quite a way from the others, burning upon the oak tree that the pastor had planted on Luise's burial mound.

People remained still as their eyes fixed upon the lights, taking their thoughts back home in so many ways. Christmas had arrived in their midst.

A voice arose reading the Christmas Gospel from the area where the candles were burning and every word fell upon open hearts until finally the voice said once again, "Peace on earth!"

During the night, Ervendberg shared Holy Communion amongst the members of the church and only then did Christmas carols start to be heard. Cakes were handed around, there was coffee and milk and it seemed as if home had come to them there. Gathered together with many, in a quiet corner on one's own or in loving devotion as a twosome, the German emigrants celebrated their first Christmas in Texas.

---

"Your Highness please try to understand what I'm saying! The Society has started an undertaking for which it would have needed not two hundred thousand but two million guilders. We've got to move on from here as soon as possible because everybody's getting impatient. They're fed up with listening over and over again to your well-meaning speeches and stagnation is doing more harm than good. The blood of the young is running hot and is about to boil over so that if there's any prospect of reaching the Society's area in the spring, we can no longer hesitate or the time for planting will be over."

"Herr von Wrede, you are speaking in a manner which does not become you."

"That may be, but it's essential because in a few days we have to make room for so many new people who'll be arriving from Germany. Your money worries are understandable but if you think that Fisher is a crook, then throw him out—should he cause trouble, we're still around. So let's pack the bull by the horns, the sacrifice will be enormous anyway—Texas just devours people—it's always been that way."

"All right, you go to New Orleans with the steamer that's leaving today, get credit and buy food and tools. We shouldn't strip the camp too much by what you take with you and also when you're there make sure the wagons finally arrive," Solms decided.

"I'll play havoc with Fisher if that doesn't work."

"Good, carry on! The emigrants arriving in Galveston must stay there until we get there. Fisher has to provide for accommodation and food whilst Wilcke tries to raise wagons and servants from neighboring farmers."

"It'll be difficult, because they need livestock and farmhands now for the spring planting and whatever you do, your highness, get hold of money, money and even more money!"

"I hope the next ships bring enough with them."

Wrede left.

Five ships were docking in Galveston in those days, new emigrants were unloading but nobody was prepared for them. Four hundred and thirty-nine Germans landed plus more than a hundred others who had left home on their own bat because things were not moving fast enough for them. Some thought they were too late and that the land had already been divided whilst others had plans of their own. Among them were the Jewish20 men Nußbicker, Reinfall and Kuhschmerz who were seeing trading opportunities and had provided themselves with all kinds of goods.

Herr von Wrede came out amongst a wild throng of people that filled the harbor when his steamer docked in Galveston. After a long search he found Fisher in his office, stretching his legs over two chairs and reading the notations on the New Orleans Stock Exchange, which had just arrived.

The captain startled him.

"Am I the Society?" cried the consul, "Am I Man Friday? If money is there, fine, then you could do a lots of things here." He pulled out his empty pockets and held them away with pointed fingers, laughing scornfully, "But that's the way it is with us!"

Galveston quayside was a colorful collection of people and luggage with all sorts of characters wandering around which did not amuse the captain as he surveyed their ranks. Poor, frightened people lay between others who had built mountains of luggage around themselves. Good-for-nothing women folk were drifting around and nobody knew where they belonged.

Some sat there dressed up for the city, a little crumpled but nevertheless with a little hat upon their head and a parasol under their arm. A long, skinny man was trying to hold it all together.

Some distance away from the travelers' bustle were mountains of boxes, bales, equipment and sacks over which men were standing guard. These were supplies that the Society had sent from home.

"A lot of unwieldy stuff," thought the captain, "they bought it according to their lists because they think we need it. If this could only be slowed down! Here other types of plow and axes are necessary and the Americans have better saws and mills, so much of the stuff is just worthless. Colonization from a desktop — one should have sent the pen pushers with it at the same time!"

"We've been looking for you," Fisher shouted as he spotted the captain behind a tower of boxes. The tall, lean man stood beside the consul as Fisher introduced him, "Lieutenant von Claren[24]."

The captain bowed slightly. "Von Wrede, from Carlshafen. Man, what fairground of people did you bring with you? The ships should immediately take the whole heap of scum back home — I don't like it at all!"

"I've been hanging around here with my people for a week as the first transport with the 'Johann Detthart'. The other ships will be coming in short intervals and with every one that comes, things will get more gaudy."

"Did you bring any money?"

"Yes certainly, I delivered it to Herr Fisher, according to the instructions."

"Peanuts!" he said with a sneering gesture. "Not even a drop in the bucket. I bought all available ship provisions in the city as there was not enough money for anything else and people can't be expected to starve."

"That's really upset everyone's mood now," Claren interrupted. "The people have had a very miserable crossing and long for fresh food. Now ship grub again."

"Who is the tall, blond woman over there — look there — she's leaning against that wall of boxes?"

"That is Countess Reitzenstein. Her husband died from smallpox during the crossing. Both came from Thuringia and she is still stunned by her pain so you'll have to leave her be."

"So you have received some money, Herr Consul?" Wrede asked insistently.

"Of course, as was already mentioned."

"I need a larger amount immediately."

"Impossible, sir." Fisher seemed turned to stone. "At last, I have been able to think of satisfying part of that to which I'm entitled."

"Sir, you have to live and will certainly know how to look after yourself!" Wrede flared up. "You have to realize that, whatever happens, I need to have money!"

The Consul displayed a superior grin and the captain's blood began to boil. He grabbed the huckster with his left hand on his buttoned jacket, lifted him a little, putting his right hand on the revolver and continuing, "I know Texas and know how to deal with you rabble. If we meet in private, then you'd do well to get ready for what's coming to you!"

Fisher re-adjusted his crumpled jacket.

"Lieutenant von Claren, you'll now escort me to the office of this gentleman and in my presence will receive from him the money for better provisions for our people."

The captain was able to obtain credit and goods in New Orleans and Fisher had fifteen ox-wagons loaded. He formed his own considerations about the course of the enterprise ensuring that the Society's loan should be increased to the utmost and the use of the incoming cash be concealed as much as possible. Deliveries in kind would have to be delayed. The outcome will be an illustrious crash in which anyone in the know would nevertheless be able to extract all sorts of personal advantage.

Three days later Herr von Wrede returned and the emigrants were still waiting at the harbor. Those who had money had crept into the line of shabby guesthouses that lurked in the harbor alleys looking for prey. Those who did not have anything had to starve and freeze in the open air. Sharp gusts of wind, interspersed with evil rain showers, pushed the last resistance out of the bones of the poor. Rogues cunningly plundered the luggage stashed under blankets and tarpaulins. All sorts of scavengers hung around and tried to persuade fickle people to part from the Society.

"Dear Sir," whispered someone into the ear of Christian Kauz from Volkstedt, one of the farmers, "what can you hope for from this bankrupt outfit? Pay me a hundred dollars and I'll get a farm the Society could never give you. Where is the grant? Nobody knows for sure. No one was there yet. The land belongs to the Comanches[25] and they will fight back. Remember, sir, the Comanches are one of the last wild Indian tribes! The whole area must first be conquered. Did you come here with your wife and children to be scalped? I'm sorry for you!" The guy first made a movement with his index finger across his throat and then around his flaxen mop of hair.

Every word burned itself into the farmer as his wife groaned and hugged her two small children tightly thinking, weren't they already in hell. The stranger knew how to tell more and more gruesome stories until he had achieved his goal.

This way whole families disappeared with their last money and belongings and nobody heard a thing about them again.

Individuals who had nothing to lose but a messed up life, set off on their own daring everything and mostly losing everything. Wages in Texas were high and labor was sought after. Farming families had often brought servant and maid from their homeland and cunning agents made it clear that contracts they had concluded with their masters in Germany did not need to be kept to in Texas. In the night, the inexperienced boys and girls stole away, enticed by the money and stunned by the hope that they would soon be released from servitude and be able to work on their own soil.

Shady women, troubled children who the local communities had coaxed to go, landed in the whore pubs at the harbor. Habitual thieves ran away fast when they realized that in Texas you do not get anything for nothing and that only work – hard work – was waiting for them. "Hein," said one of them to his sidekick, pointing with his hand over to the camp, "man, be sensible, we're staying there! Make sure to only march at the back of the group and not at the front where you have to face the music. If there's something to inherit then the rearguard have the best prospects. What may well be packed in all the boxes and crates? My fingers are already itching."

Nevertheless, the overwhelming majority held out and their confidence in the Society could not be shaken. They were respectable peasants, artisans and business people who believed firmly in the security of their contracts.

"What's lost is lost and it makes no difference now," said the captain to the lieutenant before returning to Carlshafen. "The more we get rid of the unreliable ones here, the less they are likely to become a burden on us later."

He allowed his eyes to wander over the camp. "Hey, hello, you over there, come here." he waved to the two Berliners.

"Hein, he just waved to us. What does mister General want?"

"How did you get here?"

"Yes, you see, mister General, it was like this: in Prussia there were too many — our number doesn't fit there anymore — so they begged us to go to Texas. You can become something there, they said and so we went."

"Profession?" asked Wrede.

"Casual laborers", answered Hein, "but usually without work."

"Well, there's no lack of that here. Get ready immediately and drive with me to Carlshafen. Our herdsman will be happy to get help from such hardworking people."

"What did you say, Hein, rear guard? Idiot, we're at the top of the list," growled the other. "Aha, maybe it will be something of a little Heischen and an Iriene and a few flower pots in front of the window!" They put their package under their arms and followed Herr von Wrede.

"Leave with the first transport from here in four days time. Fisher has been instructed and is liable down to his last shirt button for making sure everything goes well."

Herr von Claren smacked his heels together and slightly bowed. The captain sought the Countess from Thuringia and found her behind a mountain of boxes. She sat on a suitcase and rested her head in her hands. "Permit me, madam, to make you a simple suggestion."

Sunk in thought, she awoke and looked at him with wide eyes. "I'm going to Carlshafen in half an hour and I'd like to ask you to come with me. The head of the trek will be leaving for the grant in three days and if you want, you can be one of the first to reach the colony with us. You just have to get out of here and forget what's behind you."

"Thanks," she said dully. "OK, I'll come with you."

The camp in Carlshafen was buzzing like a swarm of bees. At last they would be on their way and they could leave the sand dunes. The resistance that had accumulated during the weeks of inactivity vanished like a shadow, as trek oxen came and then, later, the wagons from Galveston, but it was not possible to find wagoners. Zink chose the most reliable among the farmers and gave the teams over to them.

Koechert held in-depth discussions with the prince and Wrede and Zink were freed of the supplies and equipment from the shed that were to be packed up. In several musters, Wilcke examined the weapons, horses and equipment of the guardsmen and each driver received a rifle as well as a belt with cartridges. Zink sorted the women into riding groups so that they could always take it in turns to walk and then again ride, whilst nursing was organized and cooking allocated to a number of women. Everyone accepted the post they were assigned to without opposition as life had once more gained a purpose.

A bitter north wind[26] swept over the camp before they could make their start and both people and animals were shivering with the cold. When it was over, Zink put the wagon train together. The heavy yokes lay wide on the brows of the oxen and the horses danced with impatience. The men and women stood next to the wagons as Zink had allocated them.

Thomas Schwab with his family drove the first one. The guardsmen were arranged so as to cover the flanks, front and rear guards. The lead was taken by the prince, the captain, and the countess. Zink rode with the rearguard.

The herd was driven by Johann Julius von Coll behind the wagons and the two Berliners acted as assistants assigned to him, keeping the animals together by using long whips.

"Well, what d'you say now, Hein, we've managed to get into the rearguard — that's the thing!" said the other, letting the long strap of his whip sweep over the cows. "We two would never have thought in Berlin that one day we would be driving cattle together with a real live baron."

Four huge bloodhounds, as used by farmers in the south to trap escaped Negro slaves, jumped around the long train. Before it started to move, Pastor Ervendberg spoke words of encouragement to all.

Wilcke and Koechert, who had made the great sacrifice on behalf of everyone by staying behind, took leave of everyone as departure commenced.

The prince stood in the stirrups and turning backwards, he pointed westward and exclaimed: "Forward to New Germany!"

The wagons ground their wheels in the sand and happy voices were projected ahead of the train accompanied by the yapping of the dogs. The lead had to stop again and again so as not to lose the wagons. Koechert and Wilcke stood for a long time on the parapet in front of the barn and waved until the train disappeared into the distance. Before the day came to an end, a song flew across the string of wagons, one of the guardsmen having written it and composed a suiting melody:

> *Free around free German land*
> *Doth the Colorado River flow.*
> *On the green edges bravely stand*
> *Grave primal forest row on row.*
>
> *Southern sun greeteth cedars tall,*
> *As old as those in Lebanon;*
> *And birds, frail as feather do call*
> *Fluttering, chirping stock and crown.*
>
> *From forest night doth proudly peak*
> *The fragrance of magnolia.*
> *In evening breeze the treetops shriek*
> *The greeting for New Germania.*

## IV

The wagon train slowly crawled its way into the country like a multi-limbed worm. The lead group scouted the path ahead and was not infrequently hours ahead. Captain von Wrede led with the pertinacity of the experienced pioneer and they would often see him in the distance, sitting erect on his horse with his gun resting across the saddle.

To lead a cohesive train through the alluvial land of the coastal region was an extraordinarily difficult task. The ground was deceptive because nowhere were there any trodden and hardened roads. Rivers and streams ran into swamps and marshes or crept there way lazily to the sea, dried up clumps of yellow grass forming broad nests. The train crawled slowly between harvested cornfields, sugarcane plantations and cotton plantings, with here and there a tree ascending into the sky above the flat land.

Lonely farms with somewhat quick-tempered people lay scattered as far as the eye could see, howling dogs revealing the distance, whilst Negroes could be seen working in the fields. The wagons often sank up to their axles and it took the daring of men, willing to give their all, to repeatedly extricate the sinking cattle from the insidious ground.

Frequently, when mastering dangerous places, the wagons had to be unloaded and subsequently re-packed. The wagon train became increasingly dirty and began taking on the color of the earth. During each halt the women scrubbed and scrubbed, craftsmen repaired and tired men dropped down exhausted in order to briefly recuperate.

Added to this was the difficulty of steering because the Texas oxen were bulky and stubborn. Nobody had experience in dealing with them and it would often be that sufficient men would have to be harnessed in front in order to pull the oxen along. Suddenly they would break off to the right or the left whilst drawbars splintered, women shrieked and the wagons rattled against each other, yet it went forward in spite of everything as they were lured on by their final destination.

Packs of deer chased past them whilst wild ducks and geese sailed in droves upon the water surfaces and fish were everywhere in abundance. Spring was already gently stirring and between sharp winds from the north, a soft, enticing breeze swept across the earth that brought courage and confidence to the pioneers. The hunters' prey stewed on skewers and roasted in cauldrons. Corn patties were baked for each meal, which, after much aversion, the emigrants had learnt to accept.

Julius von Coll and the two Berliners had learnt to work well together by now and their jokes swept invigoratingly along the wagon train, conjuring bright laughter from strife-torn faces in many a desperate moment.

"The lads are more useful than I first thought," said the captain to Zink at the following night's camp. "Someone who slides down the slippery path in the tussle for survival in the city can become a person of substance if you put him at the right time in the right place."

The prince sat in the third place in the circle and after a while he asked, "Have you seen how the people of Victoria infiltrated the camp, trying to wheedle their way in with our people? I saw one coming to do business with a whole armful of liquor bottles. Immediately I closed the camp gates and strengthened the guards during the night. I don't like these Texans—hucksters and a pack of rogues—always out to trick the inexperienced."

"It's the same all over the world," laughed Zink, "only it's more or less cleverly hidden and labeled with different honorable words"

"That's why I always come back to my plan, which I have talked about so many times before," the prince went on, "the unified German nation state that we want to establish in Texas must be kept from getting too close to any local inhabitants and certainly not to mix with them. The way stations, which are to be built from the coast, a day's journey apart to the colony, must not be located near settlements. Each place shall be appropriately built for protection. The roads and railways, which are to connect the way stations later, are part of the long route between New Germany and Germany. Every day we get nearer to the realization of these things and will soon have to decide where the stations should be, because I will have to purchase the necessary land."

Zink and von Wrede knew enough about the Prince's plans and now looked at each other with a mutual skepticism. For weeks they fought in vain against the high-flying dreams of His Highness and often had to speak very determinedly to bring him back to earth. As soon as he felt any resistance, he would rise up, sometimes becoming insulting, as he had vainly fallen in love with his own thoughts. Now the other two felt that the time had come to act.

"I want to make my position finally clear to you once and for all," the captain began, wanting to force the outcome no matter what transpired. The prince looked up. "Please," he said curtly.

"The point now, is to be soberly clear about what we can achieve and not to assault our people with thoughts and plans which are to their detriment. We are marching with about one hundred and fifty people. The grant is somewhere in the distance and I estimate the trip to be at least fifty days, with just a few of them behind us. Anyone who coolly estimates what a human being is capable of can imagine what the trek to the west will be demanding from us. The way into the colony will be the hardest test for the advance party and we can be happy if we are able to bring everyone to the goal alive. The more we take our path closer to cities and settlements, the easier it'll be for us to face the unforeseen and unpredictable.

Thus I'll not only follow the straight line determined by the compass and entered into an inaccurate map, but I intend to make the best of every advantage of the terrain and all existing areas, as well as making use of all the paths and streams. I worry less about what could and should be but rather see what is. What use are stations on a way forward that we don't even know and can't know. The size and location of the respective way stations can first be determined when at the destination.

I'm only willing to allow myself to be guided by my own experience and I'll not go one step further if your Highness doesn't abandon his plans and submit to reality. Our people are too precious to us for anything else. If Highness takes it to the ultimate, then self-defense is the only answer—that is, I'll let the people decide themselves into whose hands they wish to entrust their leadership.

The prince rose from his folding chair, took a step toward the captain, measuring him from top to bottom, resting his hand on the butt of his bulky Colt pistol.

"Your highness doesn't need to get worked up," Zink commented. "Nothing'll happen if you submit and nobody'll notice that you allowed our views to determine things."

"Our views!" snapped the prince. "So you as well, Herr Zink?"

"Certainly, your Highness."

"So you're letting me down right here in the middle of this wasteland? If I didn't feel irreplaceable, gentlemen, I'd shoot it out with you here and now!"

Herr von Wrede let out a loud hearty laugh. "From your words I gather that you, Commissioner-General, clearly see the outcome of such a stupid shootout and you could just be right! However, we're in Texas and don't want to transplant European salon chivalry here."

The prince had turned pale. "The last word on this has not yet been spoken, gentlemen!" He turned hastily and slipped into his tent but for a long time he was not able to get to sleep. His unease fluctuated back and forth between annoyance and uncertainty and even as his anger faded, uncertainty still remained.

Half asleep, he heard Fisher's name. No one knew, until now, that the consul had not yet settled more than the sum of thirteen thousand three hundred and sixty dollars. They had been handed over to him by the Society in cash or bills of exchange and he avoided all requests to account for it. Did he understand the prince's way of consequentially avoiding objective firmness whilst remaining afloat in his dreams?

Solms sensed, almost physically, the captain's severity and Zink's rational directness. In Germany he would not have tolerated such people near him but here he was at their mercy now. Never before had he felt this as painfully as at this moment, yet if only he could have taken his guardsmen and storm the country at their head! In his mind, he saw sabers flashing in the bright sun, heard shots cracking, deer and buffalo falling and turkeys flying cackling to the ground.

Nevertheless, there were always these two men — serious, calculating and sober. He wondered if they were taking the leadership out of his hands and whether his authority was sufficient to ultimately prevail. There was no way he was going to ask the people. They had to march because the whole thing was about their well-being and he had herewith taken on a thousand dangers, venturing life and limb, only for the sake of the people. They therefore should be grateful to him and obey him, persevering for their own sakes — and that's the end of it!

The next morning the journey was delayed because during the night, some of the grazing oxen had wandered away from the camp. It took almost two hours before one of them could be caught again and the other had sunk in the mud and was already dead by the time the men found it. In its place, a strong cow was placed in the yoke in front of the first of the two cannons, which clunked heavily at the middle of the wagon train.

Slowly the land rose and became firmer, clear water flowing in the watercourses. Green new growth already shimmered under the previous year's dry grass as "The rolling country" opened up in front of the Germans — that's what the Indians called it — with one gentle wave of earth rolling behind the next in monotonous regularity, like a sea frozen in a storm. Up and down it went for days, monotonous and tiring. All eyes were full of yearning, set on the horizon thrusting itself mercilessly and unattainably before them, wondering what could be beyond. From time to time, the ragged wasteland was interrupted by a group of trees or shrubs as the woodland became denser at the rivers.

At night the wolves howled and now and then a buffalo herd would thunder past. Undoubtedly Indians would have been passing by in the distance and the loneliness caused anxiety, creating all sorts of visions. There were those with dysentery too, as the footsore arduously dragged themselves on.

The prince always rode far ahead and shot whatever came in front of his gun. The journey made few difficulties for him but Zink was on his feet from morning to night, struggling to hold the wagon train together. Every day there were involuntary stops caused by axle and wheel breaks that kept the craftsmen's hands full. Nevertheless they moved forward, knowing that they would have to reach their destination in the end, a thought that everyone was tenaciously clinging to.

One night they camped in a shallow depression through which ran a thin stream of water. The captain had ridden westward for a stretch but did not see a trail or notice anything else. Making frequent stops, inhaling the air in long drafts, it smelt of burning, with the smell continually growing stronger. At this point he tore his horse around and rushed back to the camp.

"Hello! Everybody listen! The prairie in front of us is on fire! The wagon corral needs to be opened in one place to drive all the cattle in! Then close the gap again and tie them together tightly! Buckets out! That's what the women have to do. The wagon tarpaulins and all wooden parts must have water poured over them immediately! The men take the spades and dig a shallow trench around the camp! The turf should be lifted off and thrown over with the earth side upwards! If we have time left, the forecourt must also be flooded. The cattle are to be packed together into the interior of the ring of wagons so closely that they can move as little as possible!"

He got off the horse, giving it to one of the guardsmen.

"Where is the prince?"

"Not yet back from the hunt," called a voice.

Everything in the camp stirred in a frenzy but it was difficult to drive the cattle, which were used to freedom, into the corral and Julius von Coll and the two Berliners had to make use of all their skills. The women formed a chain from the watercourse to the wagons passing along bucket after bucket and soon woodwork and tarpaulins began to drip.

The smell of burning in the air became sharper as the men shoveled what they could. The prince had still not returned as he was probably following a pack of deer. Zink had a deep pit excavated at the point opposite the advancing steppe fire and in it they sank tin boxes to take the powder and cartridges. After it had been filled, he poured a few buckets of water over the loose earth. The men worked like machines with nobody obviously feeling hungry or tired.

"The drenching of the wagons must continue as long as possible," ordered the captain, "place a number of full pails in front of the ring! When I give the signal the women should get into the wagons. You have to watch out for any sparks that fly under the tarpaulins and the men should take all available sticks, poles and shovels and line up around the camp. Pour a bucket of water over yourselves and keep your moistened hats on! Hang up damp blankets and towels!" He gave his orders curtly and calmly.

As night began to fall, a fiery streak could be seen glowing in the distance. Tongues of fire licked out and hit the blue darkness as stinging smoke blew past them.

All at once it was said, "Mrs. von Reitzenstein has ridden off with the prince and she had taken her rifle and a good supply of cartridges."

A spattering of sparks brought the hissing air from the fire long before it arrived. The captain poured two buckets of water over his head and the rest he passed to the others. His instructions were executed in a controlled manner, despite his fears to the contrary, thus avoiding confusion. The terrain had been submerged a long way towards the fire to act as a barrier in front of the camp.

Now the fire became clearly audible.

"The women onto the wagons!" exclaimed the captain.

The fire came in gurgling and howling at a tremendous speed spewing out its breath of glowing embers. Some men were still running to the water, carrying it in buckets and pouring it over the foremost carriages but soon the men were forced to duck under the wagons.

Outside they were hounded and trampled in fear of their lives and the smell of burning flesh was clearly noticeable as much was lost to the flames. Game from the rolling land rushed wheezing before the fire and birds fell to the ground, embers scorching their wings. The earth groaned.

The cattle inside the ring became restless. The glow ate more and more glaringly into the darkness, the night becoming as day. The form of things and people were traced hard against the light, everything alive hunching together as if under a glowing dome.

Somewhere, two fearful voices called out as a man and a woman climbed into the ring and grasping hands dragged them in and whilst their horses pressed fearfully against the wagons, rearing up precipitously.

The fire stopped for a moment at the watercourse, jumped over and ate the short distance up to the ditch. It could not go any further and hurried around the camp and on into the endless distance.

Everyone felt the searing bite of the force of nature right down to his bones. The animals within the coral tumbled over each other, crashing and thundering against the wagons.

Oxen and horses stomped everything down in fear of death as wood broke, people shrieking. Sooty arms swung heavy buckets, letting the water sizzle down onto the burning belongings. Squashed, scorched and weathered by fear, many of the emigrants had crept into the frame poles where at least they were safe from the raging animals.

Then followed that deep, heavy silence in which only hearts beating wildly, panting for breath is to be heard. A few minutes seemed like a fearful eternity as the fire continued to crackle beyond the camp.

The congestion of animals gradually freed itself and people began to speak softly and to check that they were all in one piece. The night seemed all the blacker around them after the gaudy burst of flame into which they had been immersed for several minutes.

Lanterns were lit, their light penetrating drearily into the darkness and wax candles could be seen wandering back and forth. Pain became apparent once the horror had passed, as burns evolved into blisters and broken bones and bruises caused people and animals to moan. Smoke-clogged lungs coughed freely and Dr. Koester was stretched to the limit.

Only the morning showed clearly what the fire had done. The Countess von Thuringia lay rigidly outstretched under a cart — dead. "Snake bite in the ball of the right hand," Dr. Koester diagnosed after careful investigation.

"We hopped from the horses in a hurry and I helped her into the ring between two wagons, climbing in behind, but then she was gone," the prince said wearily. "Whilst running away to escape the fire, a poisonous snake may have crawled under the wagon."

The faces and arms of the men were covered in soot, their beards and hair scorched. Black-rimmed holes sat like plague lumps in the wagons and covers. In the animals' turmoil, many valuable items had been trampled. "Lucky we tied the wagons

Fig. 10: Costume designs for Samiel and Caspar in the original production of "Der Freischütz" ("The Marksman") - Opera by Carl Maria von Weber

together as it's unthinkable how we would have felt if the animals had broken out," said the captain.

The cattle lay terrified within the ring of the wagons, their eyes wide open with fear. The horses were allowed to run free and with trembling nostrils they sensed the burning smell that still stood over the scorched earth.

People found there way back to the habit of daily work only slowly. The Sick and injured were laid under the quickly pitched tents and there was much for the craftsmen to repair.

The cattle had to content itself with a meager diet for a few days, for there were only just two narrow strips of grass running like green streaks into the distance along the banks of the gully.

"Today we've got it easy with the cow dung," said Willem, the Berliner, to his friend. "This time, they're putting it all in one heap and so we don't have far to go for it."

They had started gathering it with Julius von Coll because that was often the only fuel under the cooking pots for days.

Butcher Rahn had to slaughter two oxen and one cow that had broken their legs in the wheel spokes.

---

"Your Highness, the idea of a straight line with railways, stations and roads from Carlshafen to Kastell and on to Leiningen or whatever the places should all be called, which you drew and named after your calculations with a divider on the map, is now surely all wrapped up! Now reality has ruthlessly caught up with us and it could truly get even worse!" he said, glancing past the prince.

He eyed the old officer sharply and suspiciously, not sure that these words should shame him, because he lacked the power to flare up in the old way, the fire having devoured something within him.

"We've been stuck in this burnt-out wasteland for two days already."

The prince was silent and rubbed over his crumpled uniform. The big hat sat limp on his head since the fire had chewed away at the front edge.

Nicholas Zink approached him. "We cannot stay a day longer if the animals are to be rescued — and our lives depend on them. Corn stocks are shrinking because we've had to use a lot of them as animal feed. The sick and injured still needed some rest for a few days and our pastor was badly hit by dysentery and is terribly weak. Despite everything, I intend to break camp tomorrow morning, whatever happens! We have to look for areas that the fire has spared and from now on everything depends on finding cattle feed."

The captain took out his compass: "If we turn half right, we'll get safely to the Guadalupe. Perhaps we'll reach one of the watercourses leading into the great river and can then march along it. If the fire has reached that point it'll have spared the damp valley floor and we'll find food. River upwards lies Seguin and there our supplies can be supplemented and several yoke oxen bought. Only one grave has been left behind — that's luck, we got off lightly."

The wagons were reloaded according to Zink's instructions. Room had to be made for the injured and the sick. When they had finished cooking, the women plucked every accessible blade of grass along the watercourse and a tiny reserve of green food was piled up on one of the two-wheeled carts.

They now moved on, the wagon train crawling forward wave upon wave. The hooves of the animals threw up ashes and soot, irritating lungs and smudging faces. Every now and then, the fire had eaten around a damp area leaving a green spot that resembled an island in the endless brown. The animals were put out to graze but they did not get enough to eat and started to lose weight appreciably.

"They look as if they would've eaten barrel hoops, with their flatulent bellies. One can feel sorry for them but it can't be changed," said the drovers. The oxen's strength weakened and often the wagon train stopped suddenly, as if everything had fallen asleep.

On the third day after the prairie fire, the captain stopped late in the afternoon and pushed the wagons together, wondering what was going on.

The sky hung hard and cold, shedding a strange light over the earth. The prince looked angrily around for the cause of the layover.

"Tents close together! Lash down the wagon tarpaulins! Stake down the cattle! The sick must remain on the wagons!" One command rapidly followed the next. Peasants and artisans immediately got stuck in and hammers swung, lunging onto the heads of the piles.

No sooner had the wagon coral been assembled than the sky suddenly opened. A hurricane swept across the land, ice-cold streams rushing down and flooding the camp, which almost vanished under thrashing torrents. The storm tore off the tarpaulins so that they pounded like flags. The wagon covers, already scorched by the fire, were shredded to pieces, allowing water masses to pour into the wagons' interiors.

The farmer, Christian Schilling from Kleingoelitz and the clarinetist, Weinreich from Rudolstadt, squatted huddled together under a wagon. "Dammit again," growled the farmer. "We're certainly used to many things and I've already had many a cloudburst back home whilst working in the fields but something like this! That there's such a thing as thunderbolts and such icy cold it goes right down to the bone!"

"I'll soon be tired of it all at this rate, neighbor. This is not what I imagined. 'It's standing on the green shores of Texas, waiting for you,' 'twas said back home. If only I'd known that when I helped out in the court orchestra one evening for the last time and received twenty silver groschen. It's good that my colleagues can't see me now. How they envied me when I left — yes, yes, he's standing on the green shores of Texas and waiting."

The musician growled grimly to himself and his voice was weak and hoarse. "Will I ever be able to blow an instrument again?" His scrawny, torn fingers pulled the blanket he'd been struggling with tighter around him.

The sick were groaning in the wagon above them.

"Anyone who survives all of this has been tested by fire and water," said the captain to Zink. "We've won once it gets to the point where our people can watch such weather from the door of their log cabins — but a lot needs to happen before we get that far. Each of them must first undergo a complete character change and whoever still has the strength after that is over the worst. It all starts with dysentery and I'm afraid we'll still have to bury more than a few before we get there."

The water seeped into the maize sacks and nothing was safe from its rush as sugar dissolved and salt washed away with the rain. The women were shivering in their wet clothes. The storm mercilessly destroyed the last traces of painstaking care with which they had tried to fight conditions until the last. First the fire and now the water! In the face of this destructive frenzy, none of the little vanities that were otherwise always important to women, regardless of the severity of the situation, could be kept up, robbing them of a good piece of their self-confidence.

Only after many hours did the weather abate and the water could be watched seeping into the parched earth. Zink and the captain went from wagon to wagon checking the damage. Then the sun came out and soon the whole camp was like a laundry room. Crates and boxes were cleared and the contents spread out in the sun in whose softening warmth the will to life stirred anew.

After a long search, clarinetist Weinreich found the case with his instrument. Secretly, he crawled under a wagon and opened the lid. A few glistening drops of water stood upon the blue velvet as he gently lifted it out and put it to his cracked lips. A sound arose, at first hoarse and pointed, whilst everyone listened, wondering what it was and whether it could be music or whether such a thing could even be possible.

Weinreich was lost within himself as his fingers jumped over the flaps sounding the great solo from the "Freischuetz". Tears were in his eyes thinking that perhaps they were still human after all.

The sounds flew alien across the prairie and for a few moments all hands stopped, every conversation coming to a standstill as Weinreich continued. Then a few voices timidly joined in:

> "I went through a grassy green forest,
> As I heard the little birds singing:
> They sang so young
> They sang so old,
> The little birds living in the forest,
> I do like hearing them sing so well.

The sun went down as the Germans were still singing, forgetting all the torment because their homeland had now joined them as cooking fires glowed under cauldrons and the sick felt hope once again. As long as there was enough power to sing, then they could take whatever came their way.

A few lads took a girl as partner in a folk dance as Weinreich played, skirts fluttering, joyous exaltation arising from the dusk.

"That's good," said the captain, "as long as they can do that, we've won."

The prince shook his head. "I find something like this quite out of place, it should be forbidden. The seriousness of the situation really demands a different kind of behavior."

"Under no circumstances, your Highness! Anyone who understands people must rejoice that they're finding a way out of the misery of the last few days."

The prince shook his head. "Incomprehensible to me." he mumbled, taking long steps and striding off around the coral.

Then he heard the two Berliners talking to one another.

"Willem, what's such a prince anyway? He hasn't a clue, scrambling around all day like a dog with a bone! If we didn't have the old'n and if Zink weren't around, I wouldn't bet a penny on His Highness. He's not even as much use as the stopple on a bottle."

"Let it be, Hein. If this goes on, I'll be taking the first, best opportunity homewards — via the dirt road — that's shorter."

Solms moved on. He had heard something that he often felt in the last few days — that he remained a stranger among these people. They were drawing and fusing ever more closely together whilst he stood way apart from them. Every day the laws forming the coexistence of all were forming themselves ever more resolutely and clearer and yet nothing drew him into the circle of forces that were welding the community of fate together.

During the night he had a decisive confrontation with the captain, Zink, Koester and Schwab. There were many things said that filled their hearts to the brim with a sense of responsibility for days.

"The toughest demand on us will be the march from here to Seguin," said Herr von Wrede seriously. "I'm sure we'll soon find green fodder. If things don't work out, only very radical measures can save us."

Zink suggested: "In Seguin we'll have to give people and animals peace and quiet until they have sufficiently fortified themselves for the onward march. Supplementing the draft animals, the supplies and repairs to the wagons will all hold us up for some time."

"The sick also need to rest," said Dr. Koester thoughtfully. "Some of them are in very bad shape and symptoms of fever are appearing that I don't recognize."

"So we'll again need to dig deep into our pockets, gentlemen," said the prince. "But do not give yourselves any false hopes—our cash has run out. I can't say how far we'll be able to get credit, so let's hope for the best!"

"Just as much a scoundrel as Bourgeois d'Orvanne," the captain summed up the prince's report "but not so coarse and brutal—he sucks the blood out of his victims more slowly."

"As soon as we find the first suitable place, it will particularly be the Society in Mainz that has to be informed about the actual situation", suggested Zink. "In Germany people are still being put aboard ships and the masses are gathering in Carlshafen whilst confusion continues to grow. When I try to imagine what might come out of it all, it makes my hair stand on end." He paused.

"I venture to speak, whatever may come out of it: Your Highness, I do not have the impression that you are as capable of things as the gravity and responsibility of our tasks demand. In my opinion, the advance into the grant can now only be carried forward as far as our strength permits and I estimate the journey to the colony to be forty to fifty days."

The prince's eyes ran hot. The engineer had said something plain and open that had pierced and ravaged him increasingly since the fire and nobody was saying anything about it. So that was the verdict that the men of his confidence were passing on him—yet he did not reach for the pistol and neither did he challenge Zink.

The moon shone high above the camp as the Germans lay sleeping with exhaustion, whilst the earth was awake and everything growing, stirring secretly and alive—faster than back home.

The men in the tent made a number of important decisions. Five of the guardsmen were awakened and told to keep their horses, as well as those of the prince and Herr von Wrede ready for sunrise. A troop of riders riding northwest left the camp in the time between night and day.

On this morning, Zink had the wake-up call blown early. Thomas Schwab announced that Herr von Wrede and the prince had ridden ahead to carry out important business in Seguin and would go on to San Antonia de Bexar.

They set off early in the cool of the morning, Zink leading and riding at the head with some of the guardsmen, whilst Herr von Coll, with the two Berliners and the herd, took to the rear. It became more and more difficult to drive the hungry animals onwards and the marching capacity of the wagon train shrank from hour to hour.

The earth burst open as the rain worked wonders and after a few days, the bare brown was covered with a green veil, but still the grass was not long enough to satisfy the hunger of the cattle. Zink had the corn rations cut in order to better feed the animals, yet people put up with it in silence. Taciturn but unbroken, the wagon train pushed forward in a world which seemed to be without end.

Zink had ridden ahead equipped with a piece of paper in his hands which could have been taken for some sort of map. Rivers without names, points that should be cities and something in the west that looked like a centipedes' nest which could have meant mountains and there was a lot of white space, terra incognita, between everything. "Buffalo herds," could be read in one place and at another it stated, "extensive woodlands, Indians, salt-desert."

On March 12, 1845 they finally saw a broad water expanse glistening to their right—the Guadalupe. The Germans' eyes lit up as they shouted, "fodder, fodder, fodder!!" Now there would be milk and butter again and the agony of the animals would come to an end.

They entered Seguin in the evening, the city consisting of six wooden houses and there were trees, real trees—cypresses, oaks and peaches. There were bushes and fields too and it seemed like a miracle but once again, shadows, other than those of animals, wagons, and humans, could be seen creeping forwards in the sun.

As Spring made way for early summer in the valley of the Guadalupe, Zink started to relax and the Germans collapsed exhausted into the grass, caressing the stalks. The week before, the prince had ridden to Seguin with Herr von Wrede and had been able to raise credit. The three storekeepers of the place, who were also hosts, had time to prepare everything and were able to take advantage of a good deal, hoping to dump some of their old stock onto the Germans.

---

The Prince, Wrede and the five guardsmen flew across the prairie at a gallop along the old Spanish Trail that led down to the Rio Grande, Mexico. The two men had now reached an understanding.

"The danger of the Indians has never been considered important enough in the Society's calculations," the captain said by the fire in the evening. "From what I can envision about the colony so far, the land still seems to be owned by the Comanches. They are one of the few tribes who've kept clear of alcohol and likewise, they consciously avoided any widespread contact with the whites, tolerating no Christian missionaries in their territory. They renounced the blessings of European civilization and therefore remained healthy and strong. While our goal will be to settle peacefully with them, we need to be clear that they see us as inconvenient intruders and there could be difficult and bloody Indian-style conflicts. Our people, neither in number nor in their physical condition, are capable of defending themselves effectively or of attacking the redskins.

Therefore, the conditions that the Society has allowed to happen, need to be completely eliminated. You should go back to Germany and settle everything based on the experiences you've made here because if someone practical doesn't support their Lordships in Mainz, they can cause the greatest harm, despite all their good intentions. I hope it's not already too late.

"I wrote all this to Mainz in my last report from Seguin. In addition to able soldiers, experienced merchants must be in the vanguard to Texas and I agreed that the requirements arising from the Texas realities exceed my capabilities. The Society needs to immediately appoint a new Commissioner-General. I agree with your proposal to set up a main gathering point, where the arrivals should get their breath back before setting out on the last part of the journey, before the trek into our territory.

Hopefully things in Germany can be reorganized according to the current situation, otherwise I see the day coming when the Society will be facing an economic and moral collapse that it won't be able to justify to posterity. That's the bitter realization to which this undertaking has brought me. Nevertheless, the priority lays here, Captain, yes, unfortunately first here, the prince replied.

They arrived in San Antonia de Bexar[27] on March 10 and soon heard of an opportunity to buy land. Messrs. Gaza and Veramendi offered them a large area on the Comal Creek. It lay on the wooded mountainous bottom that gradually flowed into prairie land. San Antonio was an ancient Spanish foundation that was once the capital of Texas when it still belonged to Mexico. Veramendi[28] had been the last governor.

Both buyers and sellers had set out to visit the country by March 11. The hills became closer to the river the further they rode up the Guadalupe and oak forests filled the valley bottom with meadows on fertile, black soil lying between.

Then they turned into the Comal Creek Valley where the mountains became higher, bare peaks rising above the oak forests and game passing through in herds. The water was cool and crystal clear and there were so many fish in it that the Germans could not cease to be amazed. The right bank of the creek extended level and flat out into the prairie whilst the left bank rose steeply, the earth promising fertility. The mountains lay like a protective wall in front of it all.

The purchase agreement was signed on March 15 in San Antonio de Bexar. "If not everything, then at least something has been achieved," the prince said with relief as he placed his name under the document. "I am reassured. Here our people can recuperate and the area is big enough to offer all development opportunities for a middle-sized city. It will become the entrance gate to the colony. Captain, this March 15 1845, shall be a day of remembrance for the Germans in Texas."

Messrs Gaza and Veramendi entertained their German guests and joined them in a toast to the future settlement. "The target is still far off," said the captain, "but his Highness can claim the merit of having helped achieve this end, so please allow me to give your name to the first German city in Texas," he stated, raising his glass. "It shall be called 'New Braunfels'."

The prince gave thanks and was overjoyed. They clinked glasses and drank to the good of the new community. Two of the guardsmen had already left for Seguin on March 12 and the prince's messengers were able to tell some marvelous things about Comal Creek country. The sick crawled out of the wagons and nobody wanted to display their weakness as they were coming nearer to meeting their goal.

By March 17, Zink and his vanguard had come across the prince. With the setting sun on Good Friday, March 21, 1845, the wagon train arrived at the land that had been bought from the two Spaniards. Thomas Schwab's wagon was the first to drive through the Guadalupe, opposite the mouth of Comal Creek, where the new city was to be built.

---

Ship after ship left Galveston, on Herr von Claren's instructions, as it was getting hot and everything had to be done to get the emigrants out of the unhealthy city as fast as possible, so he rented every accessible boat. Fear and death were lurking whenever crossing the sand bank at the entrance to Matagorda Bay and the Americans who ran the ships made bets on whether they would make it across.

Claren had pushed the prices down and only by moving fast was it possible to earn anything worthwhile. More and more new ships arrived in Galveston from Bremen, Hamburg or Rotterdam, whilst luggage piled up in mountains and the city did splendid business.

Fisher paid with bills of exchange on the Society, the debt continually rising. He held back cash remittances and, whilst passing from one hand to the next, the bills lost value and became a measure of the level of trust that the Society had with American businessmen. That trust climbed and fell whereas, over time, falling prevailed.

The ship owners got out their oldest barges, which were no great loss when they went down. For good pay there was always some sort of captain to be had and some foolhardy lads who dared to go with them. Later, the ship insurers refused any cover for vessels going to Carlshafen so people and goods entrusted to the ship owners were left to their mercy.

Things got worse and worse in the course of the year 1845 and until the autumn of 1846 and the privateers got plenty of chance for practice. They cast off in Galveston so that the way across the dangerous depths of Matagorda Bay had to be negotiated during the night. If one of the ships capsized, then they just let the people drown, when their screaming would first be silenced once they had run out of strength to stay afloat. The crew always managed to get to safety, since they reserved the lifeboats for themselves. The Americans began working hand in hand with all sorts of criminal folk that contracted along the coast. Under US Maritime Law, all cargo and beach goods pulled out of the sea became the property of those who took it, if none of the lost owners could legitimately lay claim to it — and those sailors made sure that did not happen.

The reserve of retired ships in Galveston continued to get smaller, at which point New Orleans had to help out. Disused coastal schooners were thrown back together and placed back into service.

The influx of emigrants from Europe remained just as strong. Besides those in the care of the Society, there were countless others who wanted to make their fortune without the help of the Society. Many, who could not stand it in Galveston out of impatience, went off alone. Men got together and left their families behind in order to find somewhere in the enticing distance as a place to settle. If they found it, they intended to come back and pick up those left waiting. For weeks and months, women and children hoped for the father's return, yet he never returned, as the prairie had devoured him and only a very few found what they were looking for.

Anyone who had entrusted himself to the Society had to stay in Galveston until their turn came for the crossing and when they disembarked the boat in Carlshafen or Indianola, as the Americans called the landing place, to wade the last stretch of land through the shallow water, they all they ever saw was sand swarming with people.

"What will come of all this?" Hermann Koechert often wondered. With the help of a few men, he had weighed out the cooking rations for the day ahead. Driven there by worry, Wilcke joined him in the storage barn.

By now, almost a thousand people were lying on the sand. "Where is the prince? Is the advance party already in the Society's territory? What will become of us?" When they were alone, the two men would often ask themselves these questions. They were crushed by the impatience and complaints of the people in the camp. Finally, even the most timid man was no longer able to remain silent: "Where is New Germany? When do we leave? Where are the wagons and the oxen which are going to take us there?"

Wilcke, feeling the need to do something, stacked some maize sacks with Koechert. "Something has to happen," he said dully. "The beach is filling with rubbish and rubble. Filled with suspicion, families are beginning to set themselves apart and their disappointment and undirected rage is making them sensitive and irritable. Laziness causes friction as gossip and meanness run along the camp streets so we need to provide employment. Tomorrow I want to put together a work party to build earthen huts. I will gather together the young, single men to form a security force. They will be trained strictly and thoroughly, so that they know they have a special task to carry out. If I could, I would put some of the dubious ladies they sent over to us in sacks and drown them like cats.

"The children have to be put together in play groups and I also want to look for work for the women. Most of the lazy lumps cause filth and create strife. Claren has to come over from Galveston and help us here!" he sighed.

"Wilcke, if I could scream about it now, I would say, 'give it up! Your good intentions will become a crime! Send money and some decent people!' They have thought of many things at home but, that the people and all that is human can get out of joint here, that has not even occurred to those pen-pushers. Create a reliable defense guard! How many rifles do you have? Is enough ammunition available?"

"I can fully arm one hundred and sixty people," answered Wilcke, "plus two hundred cartridges for each man."

"An appeal to common sense, insight and good will promises little success in our situation. The storage barn is to be guarded more strictly than before. Maybe I'll have to cut the daily ration soon, which means hungry people who can only be met with suspicion. Fisher wanted to send slaughter cattle but all that has become of it is two hundred barrels of stinking salted meat."

Hermann Koechert sat down on a cannon and looked down into the camp.

"Best of all I like the people from Baden with their prayer circle because they have left home to avoid religious intolerance. With a true voluptuousness in their endurance, they put up with everything, because they recognize in this torment the will of heaven and thereafter want to begin a purified new life. One must defend them from the ridicule of corrupt city dwellers."

The responsibility and gravity of the task that Koechert had to shoulder had been growing continually since the prince's departure. His own desires and goals melted away under the force of the duties imposed upon him by the camp leadership.

It was different with Wilcke. Despite everything, he always felt in himself the will for adventure. For many a sleepless night, he found himself uneasily tossed back and forth between duty and longing. Back home, love had thrown the young officer off track and he had now ended up in Texas with all the others. He had found himself in taciturn friendship with Koechert, every day the two growing closer together.

Koechert felt that the Prussian was a complement to his unconditional nature and he had become even tougher after the death of Luise. "Anyone who wants to speak of philanthropy in our situation cannot allow themselves to be shaken by anything." he mused, placing his arm on Wilcke's shoulder. "The good of all is our highest duty and every troublemaker must be rendered harmless—even fools can be dangerous. If today the Hessian schoolmaster down there, the one with the long hair and rolling eyes, speaks of a Christian community having to endure everything, then that man is wrong. That's just the goal now but the actual way goes through purgatory. A belt of cartridges is worth more in our situation than a barrage of beautiful words."

They looked out upon the sea, Wilcke pointing over the parapet: "Down there, left to the water, there lies the Mayor of Anklam in that circle of people, that's Klappenbach. He very much imagines building a friendship with Ervendberg, whom he knows from university. His mayoral past is still poking out from each and every buttonhole. He attacked me today because of our strict camp rules and spoke strong words about building a community with a democratic constitution. The man, it seems, is infected with ambition and wants to become something special here, so we need to be careful. But he has a beautiful daughter, you have to give him that."

As they looked across, the girl was standing right in front of the water. The wind was pulling back her dress, clearly exposing her tall, slim figure.

The two were silent and after a while, Wilcke said, "The day before yesterday, a merchant came along, his name being Wessel, and I got into conversation with him. He pleased me and he could certainly be of use to you, if you were to involve him. He understands both goods and people."

The two went to the camp, passing Luise's tomb, looking for the merchant Wessel.

The days passed in grueling monotony, getting hotter and hotter. The hospital tent filled up and children died, as a fragile blanket of fear and faintness resembling order lay over the camp. Deep down, however, dissatisfaction raged as hunger ate into the people but many could not face the hardtack gnawed by worms and the over-salted, greenish salted meats. The wealthy had eaten the last of their own supplies and rioters and adventurers found willing listeners in clandestine meetings.

Koechert sensed that all sorts of things were going on and Wilcke was also wary. The camp guard became firmer and more soldierly with each passing day. One evening a meeting was rallied in front of the storage barn. Koechert stood on the parapet as people flocked together from the tents, huts and alleys.

"Compatriots!" began Koechert. "I do not need to say anything about our situation as everyone is experiencing it firsthand. Senseless rabble-rousers and agitators are spreading their poison, which is irresponsible and we have to render them harmless.

"At the moment, things are like this: there are still ships coming from Germany and the Society is obliged to get the people to Texas whose passage it had assured by the summer of this year. The necessary funds for us have been delayed for reasons that are unknown to me. The available food corresponds to this situation, so Herr Wessel is traveling with some carts to raise fresh meat, flour and other food in the area. Hunting is to be undertaken in the near future under Herr Wilcke's leadership.

"To what extent there has been misconduct in Herr Fisher's business dealings in Galveston, will be examined by the Society's management and is the Prince's job as Commissioner-General. In my estimation, the advance party should have reached the colony and every day a message could arrive that calls us away from here.

"So therefore patience! Only stupidity can believe that it'll all be manna from heaven. We are not on a trip to Cockaigne. As difficult as it may have been for many to leave their homeland, it will be just as difficult and perhaps even harder to create a new one.

"The people of the advance party who ventured beyond all misgivings into the unknown do not expect us to become faithless. If anyone should be among us who thinks they would have done better under the circumstances in what was done here in Carlshafen, they should please step forward and are obliged to help us. We will know what consequences to take based on a fair judgment of our guilt.

Hermann Koechert allowed his eyes to wander over the crowd. Nobody stirred whilst many a head was lowered. Yet, in some, resistance had hardened and stiffened.

Koechert raised his arm and pointed east. "In the next few days a load of oxen will be arriving from Galveston. It is extremely difficult to muster draft animals at the moment as the farmers are in the middle of fieldwork. Carts will arrive with cattle for slaughter. However, there will not be enough vehicles available immediately to make it possible for everyone to set off into the Society's territory with the next wagon train.

Only a regular shuttle service between the colony and Carlshafen will relieve us from the overcrowding. Those who are left behind should not despair. Hastiness and all individual enterprise are meaningless, it being easier to make demands than to make sacrifices. The American public is watching our undertaking, so let us not forget that we are Germans!

They drifted back to their berths individually and in groups. The night was mild, the wind fanning over the camp, and much humanity was released out of its cramped rigidity. Some were brought together who had been separated during the day — living was more powerful than necessity!

Wilcke was looking for his girl, the mayor's daughter. Koechert was sitting on a sack of beans in the storage barn and calculating, a candle pouring its yellow light over the serious man.

It was March 27, 1845. The guard at the camp's western exit stopped, holding his hand to shield his eyes and looking inland into the distance.

"Two riders? No, one. A single horse is running after him!" Like living shadow puppets, humans and horses were moving in front of the sun.

The watchman cried out and Wilcke jumped onto the parapet. "A man with two horses for sure — he has stopped and is turning around and shooting!"

It was not until quite a while that a soft, dampened bang was heard. The rider kept on chasing, getting bigger and bigger. His floppy hat hung on the storm strap on his back. Sand was thrown up, the horses flying in a racing gallop across the plain. The guards quickly pulled back the gate and the rider stormed in, heaving the reins back with a jerk that made the horses stand, and falling into the sand.

"The dogs!" he gasped, his eyes wide open. He lay there for a few minutes before straightening up. "First Indians, then these devils of bandits. They shot my comrade Schach and I had to leave him lying there if I was going to get the letters through."

He breathed heavily and slowly and getting up, he took a bundle of tight-laced papers from the saddlebag of his horse. "I should give this to Herr Koechert."

Wilcke sent a man off to look for Koechert and the camp began to stir. Leaving cooking fire and dinner where it was, people ran up to the parapet. Soon the rider was inundated by the many questions rained upon him.

Finally Hermann Koechert came and an alley was cleared for him. The rider reported: "Balthasar Waldbaer from Lengsfeld in the Rhoen and Wilhelm Schach from Leutnitz in Thuringia. On March 15 ridden from San Antonio. Should deliver letters to Herr Koechert. On this day purchase of the site of New Braunfels. Indians in the area of Seguin. Bandits back beyond Victoria. Schach was shot down. I came through. They were on my heels close to the camp. Smell booty. Are eager for horses, rifles, cartridges and money."

Everyone hung on every word the messenger spoke. Meanwhile, Koechert had undone the complicatedly bound letter parcel and looked up. "New Braunfels you said? What is that?" he asked in astonishment.

"The new city between Comal Creek and Guadalupe. So it has been named by Herr von Wrede."

Now the guardsman Balthasar Waldbaer told of the wagon train of the advance party to the west, then of the prince's ride with Herr von Wrede and the two Mexicans to Comal Creek. The emigrants were sitting silently in the sand, taking in every word.

"We haven't got to the colony yet, but it shouldn't be far away. The advance party will stop in New Braunfels, because people and animals have to rest. I saw the country of the new city myself and there's good farmland with plenty of water. My comrade and I rode from San Antonio on the day of the purchase. When the advance party has arrived, Herr Zink should immediately survey the city map and stake out for the landless. For the time being, every family shall receive ten acres in the urban area, and a single person half as much."

The audience were now no longer able to keep silent, questions bursting upon Waldbaer like wildfire. At last everyone knew that the advance party was at the end of its strength and before the march into New Germany, a city had been founded as place from which to sally forth. Later, it was intended that everyone coming from Carlshafen was to gather there to go on into the grant. New Braunfels would be like a fortress at the fore of the new state, pedantically checking anyone who wanted to go in.

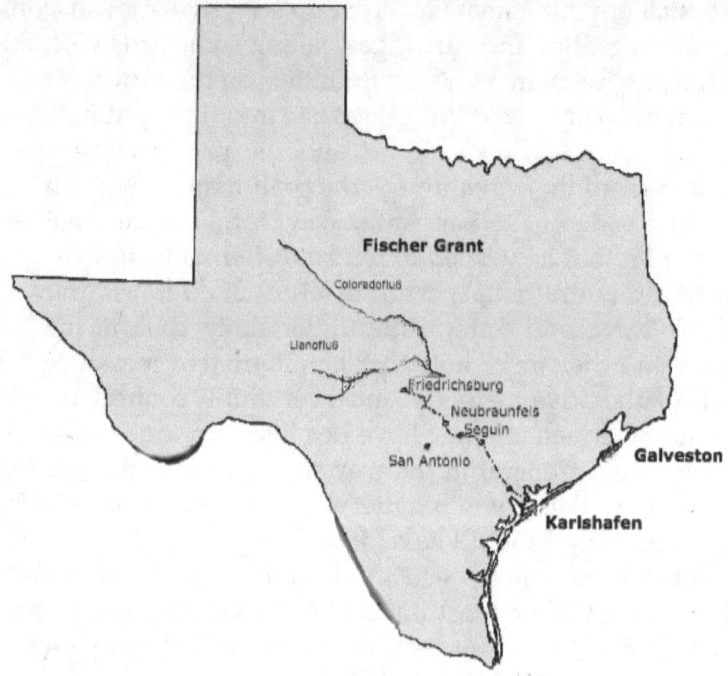

*Fig. 11: March Route*

Only when the horn player had blown the call for sleep three times did the excited crowd get up and look for their berths.

Most of them did not sleep that night, their thoughts unable to find peace. They asked themselves about land that was going to be handed out and whether enough had been bought. They wondered if there was better and worse soil and according to which criteria the lots were awarded. They questioned whether the Society would now have the houses built as promised. The people of the advance party would then have first choice so perhaps one should set out immediately to secure land, house and farm.

Such questions stirred people up, as mistrust and greed burned in their hearts. They huddled together, whispering, and wondering what to do. "Could the leadership be wrong? After all, have not I alone to answer for the fate of my family? Do I have to take what is assigned to me? Can I buy something else if I scrape my pennies together?"

A bunch of young men had crept up secretly, seriously considering getting rifles and cartridges, taking some girls with them, and starting the march to New Braunfels on their own.

Koechert, Wilcke, and Wessel sat late into the night in the storage barn reading Zink's report and the prince's instructions. Zink described the way through the prairie up to the hour when the prince rode out to San Antonio with the captain. Solms informed him that he wished to return to Germany as soon as circumstances permitted. Apart from letters and reports, they need to know the actual state of the undertaking back in the home country in order to be able to take alternative measures. "The march of the advance party and everything connected with it has made me realize that I have not lived up to the duties of a Commissioner-General in the way demanded by the burden of responsibility. Herr von Wrede and Herr Zink actually have done everything I should have done."

"That may not have been too easy for him," said Koechert and continued: "The most important thing is the next transport to New Braunfels, so get two hundred people together as soon as possible. They are to be provided with wagons, livestock, and equipment exactly as the advance party. Herr von Claren will take the leadership and, if he's still in Galveston, he should be notified immediately. The two guards Schach and Waldbaer will support him, since they certainly know the way, whilst Mr Wilcke will remain at your disposal in Carlshafen. The second wagon train will be made up of the innocuous as well as precarious individuals and every weapon holder needs to be checked for reliability. Sick people may not be taken along.

"New Braunfels is established as the exit gate to the colony. Increasingly closer Indian voices suggest many dangers. We have advanced as far as our strength permits and on the first night after arrival, two people from the High Rhoen died of exhaustion brought about by dysentery.

"Convince Herr von Claren to extend the march breaks at the hottest hours of the day as long as necessary and then to march into the evening. The risk of fever goes up with the increasing heat and care must be taken to ensure that no one sets off on the journey without a hat. Bright headscarves are the best for women."

Koechert looked up and asked, "Is that still our prince? Think about what would've happened to everyone if he'd not had the captain with him!"

The candle flickered as Wessel raised his head. "I'm ready and, if you can spare me, I'm available for the administration in New Braunfels. I feel as if I can hear a buzzing and whispering coming up from the camp. It seems that everybody first rises up and fights for their rights, each one of them out there putting themselves first with nobody wanting to back down. I'd suggest choosing the Baden folk as the core of the expedition company because they have reliable women and well-bred daughters — also the two Hilperts from the Black Forest, the tailor and the milliner — I know another man, Gustav Schleicher is his name, he knows what he's about."

So they went through the camp streets until late, deep in thought, taking measure of things long after midnight.

Fig. 12: Georg Jochim Jacob Friedrich A. Klappenbach, 1860's

Once Koechert said: "The Mayor Klappenbach from Anklam[29] may also come along. In New Braunfels he'll be better able to prove himself than here."

Wilcke was startled. "Why? Leave him here — I mean, you could…"

Koechert looked at him blankly. "You made me aware of the man first, some time ago, and I just thought we should just get rid of his banter."

"Yes-but-I did not really mean…" Wilcke said nothing. Here he was in a position and time as a man when personal issues had to take second place but he made another attempt before they parted.

"Perhaps I could substitute for Herr von Claren…" Again, he did not finish this sentence because, confronted with Koechert's severe glance, everything that was trivial and all too human paled into insignificance.

They first stepped out of the barn at dawn. Wilcke went to his tent feeling crushed and falling onto his coat, groaning and contemplating whether Barbara would be able to endure their separation.

Koechert thought about Wilcke's last words before he fell asleep, wondering if the man was unsure and what was going on inside him because he was not able to understand him.

---

The camp was already stirring before the wake-up call on the early morning of March 26. People rushed up and down the camp streets asking themselves whether what Waldbaer had said was true, the prince had already distributed land in the new city to the people of the advance party and yet they were still sitting at Lavacca Bay.

People wondered why the camp administration was silent, whilst even the mistrustful already saw completed accomplishments, hardly visible in the early days. The terms "city" and "Braunfels" in the meantime sounded familiar to many, as if one were talking about an old established community.

At last the assembly signal came from the parapet. Everyone ran as fast as he could up to the empty space in front of the storage barn, driven by an enormous tension. There was a silence as Koechert climbed onto the parapet and made his report.

"The city to be built will be the last stop before the colony. Because the first and heaviest jobs can only be done by the healthy and strong, at first two hundred should be selected and made ready for departure as soon as possible."

Everyone was listening feverishly to the words being spoken.

"Last night, after careful consideration, a list was drawn up that I'll now read out to you. It contains the names of those who have been selected for the second migration and only in exceptional cases can something be changed. Those designated have to prepare for departure within the current week."

Some felt like screaming with impatience, wondering if they were included. They hung onto Koechert's every word, as if it was a matter of life and death. The names were read one after another, precisely and clearly, and those who heard themselves called, awoke from their anxiety only after some time had elapsed, whilst others stood standing in crippling fear. It now seemed that each of them was just on their own, considering themselves to be either favored or disadvantaged.

Two hundred names were a lot but the list finally came to an end and Koechert was silent. Suddenly a storm broke out and men jumped out of the crowd and pressed against the parapet. Curses came up savagely to Koechert as women screamed and howled. "Fraud! Rigged! Rogue! Criminals!" was the threateningly sound across the square. Clenched fists, tent pegs, piles and knives were held up above the heads, as the anger became infectious. Those chosen withdrew and went to their camps but the indignant crowd however, crowded ever closer to the parapet. "Fetch him down!" screamed furious voices from behind. "Who gave him the right to tell us if we should go to Braunfels or not? — Heh, you benefactors at our expense, aren't we not all equal?"

Koechert stood quietly on the parapet and let his eyes swoop across the rebels, having no weapon with him. Wilcke let the guard step forward and load their rifles and gradually it was becoming clear to people that the list would tear families apart —here a father would be taken away, there a son, brother, or groom, daughter, bride or maid.

Koechert's firm voice sought to be heard again, having to make a fresh start several times. "He who doesn't yet understand that his welfare for better or worse is bound up with everyone's fate and who sees only himself and not the whole, is unworthy of standing in our ranks!"

His words were lost.

"Only allocation according to the plan made by the leadership can guarantee the success of our work. In comparison, the individual is worth only as much as he fits into the whole. I'm not stopping anyone and so everyone can decide for themselves— but then they needn't expect any help from the Society if they thus disassociate themselves. Only those who have the interest of all over and above individual advantage have the right to protection, upkeep and leadership."

It took hours before the camp came to rest again. Rigidity, stubbornness, and obstinacy dissolved into powerlessness and dullness.

The preparations for departure soon smothered the annoyance of those who remained behind. Only a few trouble spots continued to smolder. Under the direction of the Hilpert brothers, women tailored suits for the men from heavy linen sheets. The laundry supplies were checked and it was amazing what some peasant woman had brought with them, despite of all their complaints.

At the end of the week, Herr von Claren came from Galveston. "I hope the last two hundred people left in Galveston will be here in a few days. Then there'll be a break for some time because, during the hot months, it'd be murder if the Society would continue to send ships over. I don't know what they're doing back in Germany because things seem to have grown over their heads and they are bringing us mouths to feed for which I'm not able to provide."

Koechert took the list of names from a barrel full of sauerkraut, gave it to the lieutenant, adding a number of explanations as he looked through it with him.

"Waldbaer knows the way, as I discussed everything with him. Conserve supplies, take care of the cattle and watch out for the oxen, so that they don't stray too far from the wagon corral during pasture! They are the most precious possession I'm giving you and it seems doubtful to me if I can find any more for the next transport. Fisher's hours of management are numbered —I'm just waiting for the return of the prince and then the guy'll be thrown out. That may be the easiest bit, but is there a successor for him in this nest of robbers and pirates?"

"I've already told you," answered Claren, "in what criminal manner the man sought his advantage. On average, three to four people died of dysentery and scurvy daily in the last week. The heat is increasing and Galveston is getting empty with only the profiteers staying behind. I met a German merchant— Klaener is his name—who accepted our bills of exchange despite their questionable value. I owe a part of the equipment and food to him alone and he's also taking care of the ships and will guide the passage of the last ones. He wants to help us and without him I'd not have been able to bring a single wagon here."

Claren received the horse from the guardsman Schach who had been shot. He put together an armed escort from tried and tested men.

"Because your equipment is not nearly as complete and good as the advance party's, you'll have a harder time than Zink. I've allowed you to unload some more barrels of vinegar so that it can be mixed abundantly with the drinking water. Here are the marching orders of Herr von Wrede, signed by the prince," said Koechert, "plus some money and" — he squeezed Claren's hand — "as much luck as you are going to need!"

The intention was to break camp in the morning yet the camp seemed to be still sleeping but in fact, unrest had kept most of them awake. Many a couple that would have to part at dawn lay closely entwined together.

"No, I couldn't tell him, dearest — it was just impossible. You can't talk to him about such things because he misinterprets what you say. It's as if whole areas of human feelings don't exist for him."

Barbara Klappenbach sobbed quietly as Wilcke said that to her. "Then I'll go to him right away, even if he's sleeping," she said.

"If he's sleeping, you say?" Wilcke gently stroked the girl's thinning hair with his hand. "In fact, does he sleep at all? I don't know. He lives only for all our sakes. Don't cry. When all is ready, I too will come to New Braunfels."

She snuggled closer to him. "Ludwig, go with me, or let me stay. You, you, are you listening? Because this Koechert has said I have to go away with my father, no one dares to do anything about it. Who is this man to whom you also submit? Are you more committed to him than to me? Ludwig, do you hear? Should I go and kill him? The camp would be able to breathe again!"

Her tears came in gasps and Wilcke remained silent. He could feel her breathing as he lowered her head to his chest.

She continued, her body shaking, "I don't think anything good will come of all of this and I don't know why. Ludwig, if this will have been our last night together! And you say that you love me and yet keep silent?"

Her hot breath whispered these words into his ear as the man held the exhausted girl in his arms and thought anxiously of the morning that was going to take her from him. He had to use all his strength to resist her plea.

Morning came and a fresh wind blew from the sea driving away everything sultry and clearing every bleary eye. Yokes were lowered upon the brows of the oxen as they were stretched into new, white traces and the carters tried out the whips with their long leather straps. The ten cows trotted mooing down to the rear as they drove them out of the pen — much earlier than they were used to — and the dogs were let loose.

Joy, sadness, austerity and pain lay in the hearts of the emigrants. At six o'clock in the morning the trumpet signaled for departure and the train started moving. Hermann Koechert stood at the camp exit as the long line of people, wagons and animals, passed him. He shook hands with everyone and he had an encouraging word for each person as he said goodbye. Relatives and friends accompanied the departing ones for hours.

"Make sure you get a building site on the market place," a woman impressed upon her husband. "Then our bakery will have a top location. Take care of the money I've sewn under your waistcoat."

"I'll shoot you a bear — you can count on it. The fur will make you a good winter coat." one of the guardsmen assured the farmer's maid accompanying him. A young couple walked together closely embraced in wordless silence for hours, sharing glances of hope and promise.

Then came the parting moment. Those who remained behind went tired and silent, individually and in groups, back to the camp, going to their sleeping places and letting their thoughts follow the departed.

Some young men went missing from the watch the next morning, taking their rifles and a larger supply of cartridges with them. Only an intensive interrogation, which Koechert held with four young girls, showed that the flight had been prepared several days before. The girls had assisted their lovers, entrusting them with the remainder of their cash, to then be notified if the runaway had found a place to settle.

Koechert had a hard time dampening passion and bitterness and having to make tortuous explanations that sometimes depressed him. "It's no longer about arguing about what should be but we have to cope with what is. Anyone who runs off to his own destruction cannot count on help and I hope for your sakes that the lads get through."

On the third day after the exodus, two families had disappeared overnight, their tracks being lost in the cornfields of the nearby farms. They could not be brought back and Koechert had to delete some from his lists who, by their own decision, sought their own way out of the camp. Some who stayed were just too cowardly to lay everything on just one card but they fanned the flames of their secret resistance, which exacerbated what they already had to endure.

It was four days after the departure of the second migration had passed when Koechert found a note in the morning in front of his tent. "I had to leave, for reasons that concern me alone. Either I'll be back in a week — or…"

What was that? He read the note repeatedly. Wilcke had absconded — Lieutenant Ludwig Wilcke — the soldier Wilcke! The thought made Koechert shiver. He would have done anything for him so was there anyone who could be trusted?

The camp had not come to rest at all and everything was on a knife's edge. People shouted for better food, demanded a doctor and cursed the Society.

During the night the Society's program posted on the barn was struck a blow with the word 'Swindle!' written in chalk underneath.

The escape of Wilcke, the leader of the guard escape, was not allowed to be known. "So I have to lie," whispered Koechert desperately. He let the guard stand to attention and said firmly and harshly, "I'll take command until Lieutenant Wilcke returns. He was sent on the second wagon train last night with important orders and should be back in a week. Mahr, you're the oldest man of the guard, you stand in for me! I really have to be able to rely on you." putting his hand on the man's shoulder and looking at him astutely. Emotion welled up in

Koechert's heart, as tears welled in his eyes. "The watch remains as it was ordered by Herr Wilcke." The crew looked at him anxiously. "Nobody who helps me get the camp through the present emergency will be forgotten." Koechert dismissed them.

"Something's wrong," the men said as they crept back into their huts. Soon the camp also learned that Wilcke was no longer there, whilst thousands of reasons were sought and found to explain his absence.

During the next few days two ships came from Galveston bringing the last Germans. They had been packed on three disused coastal schooners. One had been smashed to pieces on the barque.

A large amount of money from the Society as well as lists with the names of the travelers had been found on the sunken ship, so that it was now possible to precisely check who was missing and the names of the dead.

People climbed passively ashore, allowing themselves to do just what they were told. The number of sick unloaded was greater than from any ship so far and the hospital tent soon became overcrowded.

Koechert was startled when he learned that there was no doctor amongst the new arrivals. The merchant Klaener decided on his own initiative to send a load of corn. Fisher was reportedly out of town on the day of departure and it was said that he was dealing for oxen in New Orleans. A letter from him to Koechert had gone down with the third schooner.

It continued to get hotter and everyone was looking for shade and cool. Since there were no longer enough tents to go round, earthen huts had to be built, the supply of wood having become exhausted. The heat paralyzed people's mood and there were complaints of theft whilst order and cleanliness diminished as people became idle and filthy. Nevertheless, some families fought bitterly for cleanliness and health, refusing to give up. Koechert had to threaten harsh punishments in order to succeed.

Every day, a number of wagons were on their way bringing fresh food from the hinterland. Koechert transferred the business of purchasing to a man from Darmstadt. "Herr Altstaedter, see that you first of all get fresh vegetables because the number of scurvy patients is increasing alarmingly. I'm relying on you and we should not let Texas get the better of us."

Altstaedter drove from farm to farm but every day cash was getting tighter. Some of those who accompanied him had already disappeared, having hired themselves out as servants or daring to seek their way into the unknown.

"Mister Altstaedter," a farmer said to him one day, "keep your bills. I already have so many that I can wallpaper a room with them. Here, have two sacks of corn—I'll give them to you—I feel sorry for the people."

Koechert was sitting alone during the midday heat in the shade of the storage barn with the door standing open. In the morning he had been informed that two unmarried women had disappeared. He knew a few things about their past from the documents and was glad that they had left. They were among the shady characters that were not willing to abide by camp rules, having been shoved over by the state.

"In the end, it'll probably be the case that only the able-bodied will remain whilst above all for the others, the unknown holds a terrible judgment in store," he considered, wondering how it was that this thought did not disturb him. "Would it perhaps have been better to accept Klappenbach's proposals and to democratically expand the camp rules, burdening all with the responsibility?"

There was not even the slightest of hint of breath outside. Not even children's voices could be heard. "Nonsense!" He looked across the camp. "How few there are left who can be relied upon now—most have become heaps and mush thinking only of themselves, seeking their own way out of the suffering for self and kin. Each person can only see only their own need and that's driving them apart. One thing they all agree on is in their condemnation of the Society."

A woman rushed in through the gate of the parapet, her wrinkled skirt flapping around. "Herr Koechert, come quickly into the hospital tent, my husband is dying!" Her voice sounded dry and hoarse and the pale face beneath the tightly parted hair was rigid and furrowed with horror.

Koechert stood up. "Who is your husband?"

"The linen weaver Balthasar Teichmueller."

With heavy strides he stepped out into the burning sun, walking behind the woman into the hospital tent.

"Nobody can help! What is this disease at all?" she asked, crying.

A group of people from the Rhoen had arrived with the last ships, poor that the club wanted to settle at its own expense. Some of them had to be immediately transferred to the hospital tent and isolated. Worst of all was weaver Teichmueller who had already been complaining of headaches and shivering in Galveston and then he had begun to shake in fever. His skin turned white, his pulse began to race and it was in this condition that he allowed himself be taken onto the ship. As the weakness increased, he was forced to lie down and thus they carried him ashore in Carlshafen in a linen sheet. The woman knelt beside him in the corn straw, at a loss as to what to do.

Everyone passed by his bed filled with fear, for no one recognized the disease. As his condition rapidly worsened, his tongue swelled, becoming crusty, his eyes murky and yellow, sunken deep in their sockets. In her fear, the woman was speaking all the sweet words she knew into the man's ear, yet he lay with indifference and absently upon the straw. His face rescinded into a rigid wood-like mask, he neither ate nor drank, and one wondered if he were still alive.

Koechert pulled back the curtain at the entrance to the tent and walked between the two rows of patients where men and women lay side by side, just as they had been brought in. Relatives who cared for them stepped to one side. The air in the long room was thick and heavy.

Teichmueller was in a corner and fear had ensured that a wide area had been kept clear around him. Everyone sensed, with the linen weaver from the Rhoen, that something new and terrible had come amongst them. Koechert knelt down, parted the patient's shirt, and saw the brown-yellow, leathery skin, whilst the sufferer with the fever remained indifferent. His pulse was very weak.

"Is that yellow fever?" passed through Koechert's mind. Rather early—usually it first climbs out of the marshes at the end of May or at the beginning of June. But maybe it found a victim for its greed ahead of time in this emaciated man."

"Frau Teichmueller, I will have a smaller tent made available at once where your husband can be isolated. We can do nothing but wait and see and trust God will help us." he thought to himself standing up and giving her his hand. "Hopefully he'll survive the crisis. If my guess about the nature of the disease is right, and it's true what I've read about it in a book today, then this night will be decisive."

A tent was set up outside the camp with a ditch dug around it. Koechert had announced that no one was allowed to cross the ditch and enter the tent. Those who did not follow this order would be immediately locked up with the patient. No one could associate with his wife but she had to look after her husband and address all requests to the sentry, who would be placed in front of the gangway over the ditch. Food for the wife would have to be deposited with the guard.

The news of the unknown illness paralyzed life in the camp for a while as families anxiously moved apart from each other, each in dread of the other. They could see the lonely tent down at the waterside in front of which the guard strode back and forth, his rifle glistening in the sun.

In the evening, Koechert, filled with foreboding, again went down to see how the sick man was doing. Touching him, his skin felt damp and cold, the face becoming more and more drawn, with the bones protruding to such an extent that one could think they had been sculpted and profiled by a knife. In front of the tent he had a barrel of water set up which was heavily saturated with vinegar. His unrest drove him along the seashore, thinking whatever would come of them if this were just the beginning of a widespread plague.

His attention was drawn to bright, laughing voices a little way away. Children were floating paper boats and rejoicing as the light waves threw their white toys with a gentle sweep back and forth on the sand. Hermann Koechert bent down and poked the small vessels out into the water again, only to return time and time again, until they became soaked and disintegrated. He then took the children by the hand and brought them to their parents.

That night, Teichmueller's wife lay down next to her husband as she felt the illness creeping up inside her too and his lips whimpered quietly as she snuggled against him.

It was well past midnight when Koechert left the guards again.

"It's very quiet in there," said the guard outside the tent. "I haven't heard anything from the woman for a long time."

A white disk of a moon hung shining in the sky. Koechert listened as a weak child-like groaning became clearly noticeable. "Mrs. Teichmueller, can you hear me?" Koechert called several times, yet there was no reply. He crossed the ditch and pulled back the curtain as the moon shone brightly into the tent. Black bile had oozed of the man's mouth and the woman was throwing herself back and forth in fever. Koechert leaned down and pulled the blanket over the dead man.

"I'll get some people and have lime made up so that we can bury the man before dawn," he said to the guard, dipping his hands into the vinegar water. Thus the yellow fever had come over as a stowaway with the last ships from Galveston!

Everything was bristling with activity as Koechert came up to the parapet. A horse was stomping and snorting, the guards were chaotically running around as a voice called Koechert's name.

"Is that Wilcke?" Koechert pushed back the gate. Wilcke's horse was led past him, sand dusting up like snow in the moonlight.

Wilcke stepped in front of him, with disheveled hair and without a hat, leading Barbara Klappenbach, the daughter of the Mayor of Anklam, by the hand.

"So that was it!" said Koechert, disappointed. "Yet again, Wilcke goes off for the sake of a woman! I thought I could rely on you right now when I need every level-headed person. You were an officer!" He did not want to go on talking in front of the guardsmen.

The girl stepped between the two men. "Herr Koechert," she said firmly, looking him straight in the eye, "if we are guilty, then do with us what you think is right. I came back because I sensed that it would be more necessary to make use of me here than on the wagon train that Herr von Claren is leading to New

Braunfels. Ludwig Wilcke did not ask me to return—I asked him to take me back—that we are in love with each other is our business alone. Now I want to make good for that which he was guilty of in the fulfillment of his duty."

Koechert shook hands with both of them and they went into the hut together, talking amongst themselves for a long time. When Barbara Klappenbach emerged again at dawn, she stepped resolutely down to the hospital tent and began to look after the wife of the linen weaver.

# V

Whips lashed across the backs of the draft animals and, as if they knew that the journey was nearly over, they braced themselves in the traces to take the last climb.

Thomas Schwab led the first team by the head straps as cheering calls flew along the wagon train, clinking and rattling as it went, the animals sweating and men and women grabbing the wheels by the spokes and pushing with all their might.

The prince was riding ahead with the captain through a grove of slender live oaks, cedars and elms, the horses struggling to climb higher and higher. Like huge paws, the washed out slopes of the next mountains reached out towards the riders. The forest, gray and yellow, fell behind them, the layered limestone, growing more and more arid as the horses gingerly placed their hooves upon the brittle rock. A plateau, bathed in warmth by the last light of the sun, spread westwards into infinity in front of the horsemen. Looking eastward, back the way they had come, they were reminded that in some places on the slopes they had encountered traces of Indian camps. On the other side, the Guadalupe lost itself between softly bulging slopes and craggy rocks, below them Comal Creek burst out of the forest.

"Captain Wrede, we've reached our destination," cried the prince, patting his horse's neck. Herr von Wrede, holding his hand over his eyes said, "On the left bank of the creek forest, rocks, ravines and crests, on the right fertile prairie ground—not bad! It should be possible to do something here. How wonderful this view is!"

From afar they faintly heard the sound of the approaching wagon train, almost lost in the wind. "We'll have to go back, Your Excellency, so that the wagons don't drive beyond the place we chose for the settlement."

They carefully led the horses back down the slope, rode past the source of Comal Creek, waiting in the woods for the arrival of the wagon train.

"Is it not a wonderful feeling to have arrived at our goal, Herr von Wrede? New Braunfels, the German city in Texas, will be built here." The Prince glanced east, eyes shining brightly.

"At the provisional goal, your Highness! The grant lies somewhere behind us. If it isn't worth more than the lime plateau that extends into the sunset, then God have mercy on us. I'm suspicious of everything connected with the machinations of Herr Fisher. The last ones always carry the can, so hope to God that it won't be our fate."

Down below, the wagon train moved into the forest, one wagon after the other penetrating into the green-gold twilight under the treetops.

Zink stopped. The words "We've arrived!" flew from mouth to mouth. Wood was being gathered, and soon the fires were burning, cracking and spitting under the cauldrons. Night was coming on quickly, the fires brightening the world around them against a backdrop of impenetrable darkness beyond the narrow circle of light, standing like an alien and heavy wall weaving a net of secrets around those tired people.

"The two deaths we had today I've put under blankets outside the camp," Zink told the prince. "We still want to bury them before dawn. They died of exhaustion, dysentery having taken away all their resistance."

The night air rustled amongst the high branches of the oak trees as coolness crept up from their roots. People were squatting around the fires speaking softly amongst themselves, their faces illuminated by the fire. In the cauldrons, the abundant fruits of the hunt were stewing and boiling but nobody was in the mood to eat.

"We're here—in New Braunfels," they kept saying, looking around everywhere. Only very few had grasped that the journey would not be continuing tomorrow. This was where they would stay and build houses, plough fields, cultivate, sow and harvest. Here, one day, families would be founded and children would be jumping around and eventually, one would die and be buried here.

Gradually the light from the fire dimmed, the night covering everyone, and soon only the steps of the now reinforced guard could be heard. Now and then it crackled and rustled in the distance, the silence amplifying every sound. The cattle had gone off to graze and people slumbered restlessly in a light, brittle sleep. The fact that they had now reached their destination after so much torment and so many terrible experiences ensured that many remained devoid of sleep.

"Man, Willem, you fool, can't you grasp that we're now in our Society town?" Hein Klarvutke huffed at his friend and Willem Piesicke groaned, "No, no, no! Beautiful city, nothing but trees. What've they promised us? Everybody has a comfortable home. Have you seen one? I don't think so; Trees, trees, nothing but trees. Are we supposed to be the ones to build the city after all? No, I don't get it—and such a thing is called New Braunfels!"

In Zink's tent, the trusted companions were still sitting together, discussing the work plan for the foundation of the settlement that they had gone through many times during the march, for the last time.

"So, to sum up," said Zink, "ruthless care must be taken to avoid confusion and disorder in all the work which has been scheduled. Basically, everyone should stick to their own job and only tackle other jobs at the beginning, until they can go back to the work for which they have been trained. We must convince people that they have to be subordinated to the whole, despite many special wishes, until the first major works have been carried out through working together. Before we allocate the land lots, the city must have been surveyed in its entirety and we have to clear the trees in the urban area and drag them to collecting stations. The organization of the community, as we'd like to have it, has to be structured in such a way that everyone finally ends up with a certain degree of self-evidence of where they belong.

"This will be difficult in some cases because the march didn't make angels of our people. The fact that we've made our halt here is contrary to the Society's original promises—like so many other things—and there's no point arguing about it. Our tasks now arise from this piece of earth that we want to colonize. If stubbornness and pigheadedness of certain individuals become too dominant, then you'll have to come down on them like a ton of bricks.

"As an expression of our firm will, both internally and externally, we'll first build a castle-like fort on the same level where the leadership is residing and within which the Society's property is securely housed.

"Planting this spring is out of the question and as a result, the Society will have to feed the people at its own expense.

"In order to obtain fresh meat, the prince will be in charge of the hunt until his departure. Herr von Wrede will set up a patrol beat. We are in the hunting grounds of Comanches, which must not be forgotten for a moment because, the more we expand, the more we restrict the redskins' feeding grounds and I don't think they'll accept that without putting up a fight.

"Here we've stepped out beyond the usual bonds and traditional order—but what do we know about Texan law? So we have to find and shape justice ourselves. Our Germanism, as it transpired from all the shires of the fatherland, should show us the way as our most precious possession. We've got to start all over again with everything. Gritted teeth, axes, and shotguns are now worth more than beautiful and eloquent speeches." He shook hands with each of the men and looked them straight in the eye. "God bless us!" said a miner from the Westerwald when they left the tent.

The camp was on its feet early the next morning, extreme curiosity driving them all out of bed wondering where they were. Zink then allocated the working groups and had the Society's property unloaded, set out and sorted, a few pilferers having to be tied to trees.

The two merchants, Wessel and Birkel, took stock of the tools, equipment and supplies. The first tree fell under splinters and crashes as a few experienced men from the Vogelsberg led the lumberjacks, the tops of the trees crashing dully upon the ground and the clearing spreading out from the center to all the sides. Women chopped up the tops and branches making firewood, whilst oxen dragged the smooth trunks onto ever-growing stacks. An oval area was thus created, on which several of the most beautiful trees were left standing.

Around ten o'clock, when the heat was most oppressive, they took a break until the afternoon. Some who had taken off their hats had collapsed due to sunstroke.

Things went well and in the evening the singing of songs from home could be heard once again. With every passing hour, people became more at home on that earth which was soaking up their sweat.

The prince was able to find plenty of game, riding daily and hunting with three others. Deers and turkeys made up the main food and the skins were carefully stretched and dried, pulled as roofs over hurried huts, or stretched between piles as beds across the forest floor.

Still feeling worn out by the devouring dysentery, Pastor Ervendberg was sitting on a tree stump watching the hustle and bustle. He had been entrusted with the pastoral care for the community and the care of the graves since the dead were no longer being left randomly along the wayside. With trembling fingers he had begun to create a church register and Zink had entrusted him with the administration of the seeds, later employing him as a mediator because, in his quiet way, he was well able to balance and mitigate things.

A troop of young people under Zink's guidance, equipped with chains, laths, and stakes, busily set about surveying the terrain. It had to be done quickly, because one was permanently mindful of the pressure of the people who finally wanted to have their own ground under their feet.

During the last days of April, at the highest point above the camp, the foundation stone was laid for the "Sophienburg". That was how it had been decided to name the fortified administration building but the celebration actually caused the prince lots of occasion to worry.

"What sort of flag should be hoisted?" He asked Herr von Wrede.

He replied bitterly, "Yes, your Highness, if I think of New Germany as you conceive it, then you would have to have a German flag."

"A German flag? Captain, if only there were such a thing! What should we do? In fact, for every group of our people you would have to draw the colors of their home state."

"It'd just demonstrate the same in Texas as at home—an emphasis of our German disunity which, your Highness, would not correspond with your intentions. Our destiny here is German destiny and this is how it is in Texas. Every day something crumbles away from that which separates people and soon they will no longer be Hessians, Thuringians, Prussians, Saxons, Badensers and Wuerttembergers, but only Germans. Yet we don't actually have a common symbol so your Highness will recognize once again that Texas reality asks us questions no one at home ever thought of."

Zink then found a solution, "It's just a way out," he said as he spoke to the captain. From the items left by the countess, who had died that past night from the bite of a copperhead snake, he took a heavy, yellow-silk shawl, and Thomas Schwab's wife sacrificed her black silk one, whereupon, away from the hustle and bustle of work, four women sewed a large black and yellow flag together.

Zink laughed when it was brought to him the evening before the ceremony. "Sad! We are going to raise the Austrian colors, which have brought so much mischief over us, with the Habsburg Empire always being Germany's misfortune. That'll not be clear to most, but that's how it is."

The captain shook his head asking Zink, "And what about a common German song that everyone knows and that should be the expression of our unity?"

"We've got nothing, nothing at all." Zink answered thoughtfully. "I want to suggest to the prince that we sing the Texas song that was written in the first few days after leaving Carlshafen."

Thus it was that the Austrian flag was raised on the day of laying the foundation stone for the "Sophienburg". It was a solemn moment when the first cannon-shot crashed and the wind unfurled the flag. Weinreich, the musician from Rudolstadt, played the Texas song on his clarinet, whilst the prince found sublime words praising the importance of the hour.

Zink's map gradually became clearer out of all the jumbled up confusion. The "Sophienburg" dominated the city with the streets radiating out from it. A generously dimensioned market should be at the heart, carrying and moving the life of the young community. The city lots, which were to be awarded after being surveyed, lay open and spaciously alongside the streets.

Tension among people mounted as work progressed and some were building their dream-houses on a favorite spot they were hoping to get. Mistrust was driving people apart because many had the same wishes and were now busy searching for reasons to deny the claims of their competitors. The pastor had many suspicions and much slander to unravel. Knives were at the ready and the women often used mockery, hounding people until their blood boiled.

All kinds of rumors were going around as the weeks went by. One of them claimed to have stood behind the prince's tent and heard Solms say to Zink, "We didn't see any Indians during the hunt but, the more one becomes familiar with the peculiarities of the land, the more evident is their omnipresence. We're certainly being watched all the time and we often hear strange birdcalls making us stop in our tracks. I have to spend a lot of good words to get my people to go riding long distances as they see and hear Indians everywhere and have already chased after a few bullets in their imagination. I, myself actually believe that nothing happens here that the savages don't know about and I'm worried about the moment when they decide to take action. The game stocks near the settlement have now been culled, the animals have moved on, the meat supply is becoming increasingly difficult. I believe that the redskins initially only taking stock of our strength in order to organize their strategy and it'd be nice if the second transport would arrive and we'd get reinforcements."

Zink said: "It's clear that we've got to deal with the redskins but as long as we have enough armed men, a bloodbath can be avoided. I want to set some riders in the direction of Seguin the day after tomorrow, where they should try to find Herr von Claren and get him to hurry. However, something else is bearing on me and that's that our supplies are coming to an end, some of which was ruined because it wasn't put under cover early enough. Once Claren is here, a command of buyers under the captain's leadership must try to raise corn and wheat and I'm hoping that Claren will be bringing money with him."

These words spread around in many variations and everyone exaggerated, fear piercing many a heart.

Concern and worry drove the prince and his hunters eastward towards the second wagon train and one day they finally came across the vanguard. They saw two riders stopped upon a mound. The prince rode towards them, his four companions accompanying him, but they did not let him approach, the two men shooting off their rifles and hurriedly turning around. Solms rode after them until he saw the wagon train coming from out of a depression in the ground. They came to a halt so suddenly that the wagons were shoved against each other, guns going off. The prince and his men shouted as loud as they could, "What's going on? What are the people so excited about?"

However, it was only when he finally gave his rifle to one of his men and, holding up his arms and beckoning to the wagon train, that the gunfire ceased coming from there and a horseman came up to meet him.

They introduced themselves.

"We almost killed each other," the prince said as he shook hands with Herr von Claren.

Claren reported briefly, "We're just a remnant of those who moved out. In Victoria, Gonzales and Seguin, each and everywhere some of the people disappeared, mostly taking rifles with them. The less we became, the closer the prowling bandits dared to approach us and often there were shootings where we suffered significant losses. On a stormy night, as we were waiting under the tents for one of the devastating rains to pass, the oxen broke out. We had to search over a week before we could round up enough of them that we could move on and some teams went missing. We had to burn the surplus wagons and with them all the load for which there was no longer room."

"Where are the two messengers that I sent to Carlshafen?" questioned Solms.

"Schach was shot on the way to us, and Waldbaer is lying on one of the wagons with a shot in his thigh. His horse is dead. He has behaved nobly. Eighteen of our patients have died, some still lingering between life and death."

"How have people coped with all of this?" Solms asked.

"Excellent, really excellent, even during the desperate days when we sat in the prairie without any draft animals—although everyone is bitter about the Society's failure. Forgive, Your Highness, but it's a fact that they put a plan into the hands of the people in Mainz, which seemed to be excellently construed —whilst everyone is sleeping it out over there, assuming that nothing can now go wrong. In fact, the more we are confronted by the reality of Texas, the clearer the contradiction between what the Society promised and what it has kept or could keep becomes clearer."

"Are you bringing any money?" he replied. "No, We needed everything to get us here as there were a lot of unforeseen issues which affected us on the way. Koechert did what he could but all blame and every failure should be laid at the Society's door. I want to emphasize this most markedly because we have had a terrible time, and it'll take time before the people can be put to work in New Braunfels. See for yourself, your Highness! We look like a band of robbers. The peasant farmers were the most reliable in every situation—both men and women—because they are physically the most resilient. What would've happened if I'd not had them I don't know!"

They arrived at the wagon in the midst of their conversation. People's eyes lit up when the prince told them they would be at their destination before sunset.

"I'm even bringing along a live mayor for you," said Claren, "Mr Klappenbach from Anklam. The man has horribly obscured our brains with his ideas of democratic leadership and, to be sure, despite the best intentions, has managed to make some difficult situations even more difficult. He suffered from dysentery for a while, which silenced him, but now he's got over that."

They visited some of the sick. Waldbaer was delighted to hear the prince's voice. "Only the good die young," he said, "and an old Rhoen thief, like me can take quite a bashing. I think some of those fellows who were after us ran out of breath when they got my bullets in their ribs and, if I could've sometimes poured a good Nordhaeuser schnapps behind the ears, then the bandits wouldn't have come even as close as they did. 'Target water' that's what was missing, Herr Prince—it helps you see more clearly, hear brighter and keep your calm!"

The people looked tired and exhausted and their clothes were hanging much too roomily on their bodies. They took a break until late in the afternoon before the last stretch of the trail was to be covered.

The prince rode ahead and reported the arrival of the wagon train in New Braunfels. The sun hung like a glowing disk over the mountains in the west as the train of wagons snaked its way across the ford through the Guadalupe. The people in the camp left everything standing, running towards the train as a piece of the home country rolled up to the founders of the city who had been worriedly waiting for them so long.

Compatriots, acquaintances and relatives came together looking apprehensively under the tarpaulins at the sick, the exhausted newcomers being almost startled by the noisy, gruff greeting of the people of New Braunfels.

"Willem, hurry," said Hein Klawutke to his friend Piesicke, "there are more boarders than workers. They've taken a bashing and are so worn out that they look more like baked fruit. And then all those sick—hell man—sending such people to us. Four cows they've managed to bring along—have you seen? As skinny as ballet dancers—they'll have to get something behind their ribs again." Since Julius von Coll had been appointed as manager, they were proud and confident in tending the farming of livestock self sufficiently.

---

"I demand that the man be shot or hanged on the spot," cried the captain. "The evidence of arson is clearly proven and our pastor's conciliatory reasoning may influence legal decisions once the city is established. The population growth that the second move has brought is a heavy burden and includes certain elements that are putting our forbearance to the test. We have to make an example so that those who are always up to something won't even want to think about doing mischief. Zimmermann tried to set the 'Sophienburg' on fire as revenge for being tied up!"

"Captain, I must interrupt you," the prince intervened, "it's your way of doing everything by hook or by crook but I think that in the circle of the leaders, amongst other things, we have educational responsibilities. I don't want to lower the severity of the offense with my statement but what opportunities do we have for increasing punishments if we already pronounce the death penalty because of a simple arson attack? I see Zimmermann as an inveterate weakling, whom we should bring to better ways."

"Nonsense!" Snapped the captain. "We're standing at outposts in the unknown west. The justice of the primeval forest and the prairie makes short work of it and it can let neither religious nor educational objections apply."

The captain stood up and put his fists on the rough table, looking at the men in the round, "Your highness, not only with this, but already through many other of your comments on questions of law and order, you've clouded and blurred the view of things. Had I have grabbed the guy myself, I'd have judged him on the spot." He put his hand on the handle of the revolver in his belt, "Only going the whole way can help us and I always feel the scent of the salon and over-refinement that emanates from you and which you are yet unable to rid yourself of. Behind the walls of the log cabin are our supplies, our powder is buried in the earth, our lives depending on it and anybody who threatens us can't expect any mercy."

"Captain, you go too far," said the prince.

"I want to finish this discussion. Frankly, something in me speaks against the demand of Herr von Wrede and I propose that Zimmermann be provided with food for three days, take his luggage, and leave the camp tomorrow. He's then outlawed and anyone has the right to shoot him if he lets himself be seen here again. I think that's enough and will make an impression," said Zink, with a compensating gesture.

Zink's proposal was approved but Wrede's infuriation did not cease immediately. As Ervendberg was writing down the resolution, he began again, "Too much precious time is lost when we talk and only ever talk. Highness should leave as soon as possible. We'll finish things here on our own."

"Captain, that's going too far!" said the prince.

"I know what you want to say, Your Excellency, but that doesn't change our situation. I only know one concern and that's how to get the people through who were sent here. There are still several hundred in Carlshafen and maybe the third wagon train is already on its way. So leave now and clear up any ambiguities with Fisher and hold your fist under the nose of the men in Mainz, making sure things get organized!"

"I am still Commissioner-General," cried the prince, his voice cracking. "Yes, I'm yet still that! I see it now, I've given way too much and too often."

"Well," the captain flashed at him, "you give up and take back as you please, you throw the money into the wind as you please, you dream of New Germany as you please and in the end you travel home, if you feel like it. Enough, sir! It's now all about the lives of a few hundred good Germans and no longer about your plans. Rustle up some money and get the heads of the people in Mainz sorted out before it's too late. Otherwise you have no further duties to perform at the moment."

"And my responsibilities here?" he replied.

"Have been our business for a long time, sir. Make it impossible for more people like Zimmermann to be sent over to us. I talked to some of his compatriots and the man only had a choice between the penitentiary and Texas back home and Texas made more sense than long-time imprisonment. Tell that to the Society.

"By the way, since 1840, the Cunard line has been maintaining a steamship connection to America[30]. The ships dock in New York or New Orleans. The journey from New Orleans to Liverpool takes twenty-four days. Get going, the sooner, the better, I beg you, and get some money together! Have you ever considered what it means to throw healthy, industrious people onto the sand of Carlshafen and on top of that, to endanger them with all the rejects that are being dumped from over there? I'd be a monster if I would stay silent for any longer!"

The prince looked around the circle of men sitting at the table who remained silent, looking past him.

"Herr von Wrede, I must express my disapproval…"

"Highest disapproval," grunted the captain mockingly.

"... pronounce my disapproval very emphatically. I gave you the leadership of this meeting and one attacks me now in the most uncalled for manner. In Germany I'd know how to put men of your kind in their place, Captain, I assure you!"

Zink looked up, his calm unshakeable. "Highness has no cause to be so agitated. Herr von Wrede spoke in his way only that which every decent person in the camp feels. I have to join Herr von Wrede's demands and cannot protect you."

The prince fell back into his chair, feeling as if he had been thrown out. The will of others stood against him like a wall, evaluating according to principles rather than inherited privileges. At last, pulling himself together, he said "I've already reported my resignation to Mainz from Seguin and I sent the report with the courier via Austin to Galveston and from there to New Orleans. I informed the management in Mainz that I only wanted to continue my job as Commissioner-General until a successor had been sent. He's not here yet, so what do you still want from me? Have I not already met your request?"

"Highness was influenced at that time by the impression which the prairie fire had made—for sure—but we have not been able to resist the thought that you regretted this step in the meantime, because you made no move to follow through your resolution with further action. I ask you, please leave! We have to cope here alone, no matter who the Society sends as your successor."

The end of the debate resulted in a list of demands to be presented to the Mainz Society.

A few days later, an American, coming from Austin and planning to settle in New Braunfels, brought a letter to the prince, which accelerated the course of events:

A Herr von Meusebach wrote that he had come by the quickest route from Germany and was destined to succeed the prince. He was already in New Orleans and wanted to start work for German emigration there right away. He was initially shocked by the poor reputation of the Adelsverein amongst the business people of the city. Since the hot season was approaching and fever was to be expected, he only wanted to stay there as long as absolutely necessary and then ride immediately to reach the advance party. After all, from what he had seen so far, the leadership did not seem to be in the best hands for there was much speaking for a great deal of confusion in the enterprise, which he would most emphatically bring to order.

The prince held the letter back a few hours before presenting it to Zink. Whilst the brief sentences of Herr von Meusebach, who was unknown to him, outraged Solms, they also touched his conscience. "Who is this Herr von Meusebach? According to the letter, he seems to fit all the way to Zink and his followers so why first wait for him? If he's here and his nose is in everything, there'll be more and more disputes. One is so rubbed between these sober stubborn heads that any enthusiasm is blown away wherever they establish themselves. They call their hardness responsibility and they're not capable of higher feelings. They're rebellious and without any nobler emotion! What will *I* get out of all of this?"

Downcast, the prince walked along the high palisade wall in front of the log cabin, which was growing higher and higher. The last question had left a bitter taste that he was not able to shake off for a long time. In the depths, a wide, deforested plain spread before him and thousands of stumps of the felled trees were to be seen. Flames licked through thick smoke where the tops and branches were being burnt in high piles, whilst ax blows pounded up to him from afar. He wondered how long that had been going on. The people worked doggedly, as if there were no tomorrow. Corn and meat, meat and corn, that was their food in hopeless monotony but they nevertheless carried on working.

The prince's thoughts were completely different. For him, such a bold piece of work as the founding of a German state in Texas should have inspired much enthusiasm amongst the people. Stopping for a moment, he heard behind him, in the courtyard of the "Sophienburg", the rasping of saws and broad axes splitting the trunks for the main building. The words of the craftsmen were bleak and sober as they went about their work and he heard a man's voice say, "I'm not going to do this much longer. I still have eight hundred Rhenish Gulden owing to me from the Society and haven't yet been able to find out about it. One must make it clear to the masters from Mainz that they promised us that they would construct log cabins. They would at least have to pay us for the work that we are doing here in the interest of the Society."

"Materialists," growled the prince. "Nothing of sacrifice and greatness, no vision of higher goals. Therefore, get away! Let's see how they get on alone!"

Zink approached him, having read Herr von Meusebach's letter.

"Then everything's fine, Herr Engineer," said Solms acutely and sublime. "I want to leave the day after tomorrow and ask you to give me a cart and two people as escort. I will ride taking the shortest route to Galveston and from there on to New Orleans. The men and equipment can return from Galveston via Carlshafen to New Braunfels."

"As you wish, your highness. Everything shall be arranged according to your wishes but will a cart be enough for your extensive luggage?"

"I will restrict myself accordingly," said Solms, wiping a fleck of dust from his coat.

At the end of the day, after they had washed and eaten, Zink summoned the camp community with a trumpet call. They gathered in the marketplace around a broad-trunked elm tree. He read out the most important passages from the letter of Herr von Meusebach and then spoke of the demands that the prince was to hand over to the management of the Society in Mainz.

"It'll get better now," most of them hoped. "Now everything is going to get sorted out and the Society will have to fulfill its obligations." Joy and confidence passed amongst them.

The patients learned of Ervendberg, the pastor, Solm's departure, and the arrival of the new Commissioner-General. "The return of the prince is a turning point. The letter from the new Commissioner-General reveals a firm intention and demonstrates strength and straightness in the style it is written. In a few days, the city lots are to be distributed and then the building of log cabin can begin for each and every one. The 'Sophienburg' will soon be ready. The five Americans who've been admitted to the community are to obtain glass for windowpanes, corn and especially medicines in Austin. Herr von Meusebach will bring money, whence we'll be able to cook better food. He should also clarify the question of remuneration for work that the association has commissioned. No one should allow himself to lose faith neither in himself nor in the goal. God's hands are cradling Texas and Germany."

The candlelight in his hand flickered quietly back and forth, the patients following the yellow flame with tired eyes. Before him lay a young girl on cornstalks and dry grass. She had folded her hands and was seeking his eyes.

"Have I not paid enough?" She whispered. "Write to my parents when I die, please, I beg you." She stroked her disheveled dress nervously. "At home, they wanted to get rid of me because I dishonored them. Mrs. Schwab showed me the dead child that did not want to live. I loved his father, Hermann, where are you? Hermann!"

The voice faded away, the light shaking and separating. Ervendberg put it on a wooden block and knelt down next to the girl, closing his eyes. Beyond time and space, he looked into a respectable German bourgeois room in which everything gleamed and shined with self-righteousness and decency. Of the four children, the assessor Harterich had brought shame upon the house and now the rumor about the daughter of the officer floated through kitchens and rooms, becoming exaggerated, beating every sense in the father dead, and building the idol of the honor of the house out of all proportion in his mind. Texas became a way out for the family to restore its reputation.

Ervendberg knelt for a long time beside the corpse.

That night, the prince looked through all the correspondence he had received from the management, disposing of anything superfluous. In the morning he brought Zink the books and papers: "Pass this to my successor. He can see if he can handle everything better than me." He bowed briefly and spent the rest of the day packing his belongings, giving anything he did not need to the bodyguard.

The nearer the hour of his departure, the warmer the prince's heart became. The joy of returning home seemed to take away the cloudiness and bitterness they had been through abundantly and ruthlessly in the last few days "They didn't understand me, and couldn't because they're shopkeepers and lack drive. While that is the case, they also have to bear all the responsibility" This thought made him happy as a burden fell from his conscience. He deceived himself over the heap of ambiguity he had left behind, projecting his thinking forward into the journey.

He had set off on the morning of May 15. Waldbaer had volunteered to accompany him with another man. The Captain, Zink, Ervendberg, Dr. med. Koester, Claren, Wessel and all those who belonged to the management took leave of each other at the gate of the "Sophienburg".

The prince had put on new gauntlets and climbed onto his horse, his weapons glistening. He did not shake hands with any of the men but leaning down slightly towards Zink said disdainfully, "Herr Zink, you didn't want to have it any other way."

"And *you* couldn't help it," he replied briskly.

The prince glared at him, spurred his horse and rode down the hill, beyond the camp at the Comal River, out into the prairie.

They watched him for a long time. "That's where German Romanticism rides home," the captain said, interrupting the silence. "Good posture, noble feelings, big plans, powerful words, nothing else. For us it means keep going and clench your teeth!"

"Take care, man! Pull and don't bump. You down and me up. That's the whole art. Remember at last! Ironically, they've put you on the pit saw, you unlucky devil! So you were a student of theology eh? I can see that! Leinduder is your name? Enough. Come on!"

The carpenter Christian Bader spat in his hands and pulled the big pit saw up to his chin. He was standing legs apart on two walkways above the round trunk of a live oak tree lying upon two saw horses that had been placed across a long pit.

Two arms poked out of it with the saw raised, and a bespectacled head looked out at the carpenter. "Herr Bader, yesterday we only cut six planks…"

"Man, I am no master and you need to get used to that. If you parsons preach, then you can also use first names with all mankind and know only one Lord. I am the carpenter Christian Bader from Hesse, employed by Theodor Leinduder, sawing planks for the official residence of the Commissioner-General."

"If I could only take a day off—my hands are burning as if I'd held them in the fire. Here, look at the blisters, like pigeon eggs —up, down, up, down. Not only that, but in a hole in which you can't move, smeared and filthy and my head feels as if it has been drained."

"Never mind," said Bader, "you don't need it either. Only tight arms, hard palms and a lots of puff." He turned around: "Hey, you, Carl, come here!"

Under a leafy canopy that was pressed into the corner formed by two wings of the "Sophienburg", appeared the roofer Goebel. For fourteen days he had been hammering shingles made from cedar logs. The roofs of the "Sophienburg" were to be covered with them as well as the floors of some of the rooms. The pieces sprang from the log evenly after each well-aimed blow with a bright tearing sound. Goebel worked fast and certain as high stacks stood to dry against a wall.

"What is it?" He asked.

"Come on, let the word of God rise for a bit out of the hole, otherwise it'll start slacking." Goebel jumped into the saw pit, pushed the student forward with a careful gesture and said: "So, comrade, climb out and sit down on my spot and if someone comes along, carry on as if you were splitting shingles."

He spat in his hands, grabbed the saw handles polished through use and pulled the flashing blade downwards. A trickle of fine sawdust followed every movement, the saw eating into the wood and moving forwards.

Leinduder sat under the leafy roof and looked at his hands. During a break from work, when the tree trunk was being moved one board width to the right, Bader shouted to him: "When we have lunch, you make sure to let our doctor pull a thread through the blisters and smear bear fat on it. This helps. He recently anointed my sunburnt back with it. Great, I tell you! The two bears the captain shot last week had pounds of it under their coats."

It was also busy at the front of the large log cabin complex. The beam walls were already almost stacked up to roof level, and they were just about to saw out the door and window holes. "As with the Gothamist simpletons," said one. "First the town hall is finished, then the holes to see through and to come and go are put in."

Carpenters were hacking the tree trunks with broad hatchets in the open space in front of the main house, each on two sides whilst others were sawing notches into the ends. The beams were stacked with the smooth surfaces on top of each other and the notches interlocked and held the growing walls in place.

Off to the side, two men were kneading mud and short-cropped hay in a pit, standing in the brown dough up to their knees. Women were carrying moss in baskets and cloths and were filling the joints between the layers of beams, after which they smeared clay mush over it all.

They worked hastily and with zeal for the fortress, with its storerooms and writing-rooms, the apartments, stables and guard-rooms, was to be finished before the arrival of Herr von Meusebach.

The men at the sawpit took a break whilst Leberecht Goebel smeared the saw with a dried pork fat stick and said, wiping his brow, "What a little job! If the third wagon train was to arrive right now, we'd know who to give the saw to."

"We're squeezing the very souls out of our bodies with this work!"

"How right you are," grunted the carpenter, "Zink said to me this morning when I grumbled, 'Bader,' he said to me, 'I know how hard your job is but it doesn't help. First when we are out of the woods, can anyone be allowed to think of himself. One of the first applications submitted to the new chief will be the one about paying any work done for the society. I want to work as hard as I can to fulfill the Statute,' he said!"

"Well, and?" Goebel asked.

"'We go along with that, Herr Engineer,' I answered him. Has there ever been such a folk-fraud anywhere? If we at least got back the money we paid in Mainz. Now that the Americans are here, there will soon be something to buy. With such boring fare, even the strongest man goes to the dogs in the end. Some are wearing their very last clothes and where should they get a replacement? Listen to people." They spat in their hands and carried on.

Zink had to stand and talk in many places during these days, "It'll be better when the new leader comes, I assure you. If we put our hands in our laps and moan then it's over with us. The harder we work, the stronger we can argue with the Society."

Each of them was occupied by two questions: "When will the third wagon train arrive? What do we expect from the new Commissioner-General?"

Zink had sent three riders towards Seguin to the third party. Finally, at the end of May, the first wagon drove through the Guadalupe ford and everyone went to meet the wagon train. Despite the heat, they continued without a break because they did not want to take a rest again just before the finishing line. A Herr Beneh was in charge.

The people sank under the trees in the Guadalupe bottom and were dead tired, letting the wagons be lead away by the New Braunfels people. At first the arrivals were shocked because the new city had been flying before them like a dream image for weeks. Everyone conjured it in their minds according to their liking, forming an image in their hearts. It strengthened them when the strain of the march threatened to put them down or when lying in the shadow of a wagon during a break in the marching, gasping the boiling air and blinking through the eyes closed against the glowing brightness. They mused whether that there was a town of peace and prosperity waiting for them in the distance with golden towers, bells pealing and colored flags flying. Hot blood then rushed through their limp bodies, causing miracles of yearning to blossom in half-conscious minds.

Now they were there, between huts and tents. The wagons drove up to the ring in a wide circle, forming on a hard-packed piece of ground. Pathways which were under construction, mountains of tree trunks and stakes and everywhere the uncut branches of felled trees, all under a blazing sun from which there was no escape—it was hard to see this as the golden city.

On the city hill above them, behind high, pointed stakes, the "Sophienburg" lay broad and massive. The wagon train had brought another cannon and soon it would be sticking its round mouth through one of the embrasures. It took days before people got themselves into the working fabric of the camp and came to terms with the sober reality.

The first children had arrived with the third wagon train as well as a number of families whose fathers had been sent on the second train. Only slowly did the shadows of mourning dissipate after it had become known who had died in Carlshafen and New Braunfels. Ervendberg had to give consolation to those who had lost relatives and were told about graves in Carlshafen or burial mounds in New Braunfels. Koester's hospital tent filled again but the rough life at the Indian border did not leave much space for reflection or allow one to become soft.

Zink's map was soon to become presumptuous. Everywhere were the stakes with their white heads that demarcated the city lots, the main tracks running between.

"I'd like to allocate the lots in the presence of the Commissioner-General," Zink told the captain.

"If only he were already here! We have to throw people their bits and pieces so they stick it out. Herr Beneh's report and the stories about the Indian attack on the third wagon train did not improve sentiment. If people could dig in their own gardens, then surely some of what is stirring up the unrest would evaporate."

"We currently have over a hundred and fifty rifles. Herr von Claren's drills with the security force have got to be continued. I think the redskins know everything about what's going on here as the traces of their scouts often lead close to the camp," said the captain.

"The mastiff hit by arrows a few days ago is proof of how far they are daring to go. I hope that we're already too strong for a major attack because the more we shoot game, the more they are forced to retreat to areas we haven't touched yet. Of course, they won't do that without resentment. My feeling is that rather than extensive raids, individual people are more likely to come under attack. Each group of lumberjacks outside must be accompanied by a few gunmen and, if possible, a dog. Children may only be employed and play inside the camp. Women should not venture too far to the border in the west. The savages have good cover in the mountains' gorges. Tomorrow I want to ride with some men over the Guadalupe to the east into the prairie where we found buffalo tracks. For the sake of the children, the cows must be spared, we need milk and a load of buffalo meat would help us a lot. Besides, Herr Zink, tongue and marrow bones are excellent I tell you, and something for connoisseurs! We'll take two bullock carts to load the loot, assuming we're lucky."

The next morning, just before dawn, the hunters rode out through the ford and into the rolling countryside. The captain stopped at every elevation and looked around.

The land lay before them in boundless silence as they crossed the extended track that came from Seguin and trotted into the tall grass of the virgin prairie. Only after hours did the dogs take scent with the wind coming towards them. The riders noticed a wide track before them on which the grass seemed to have been trodden down.

"This is the buffaloes route as they've rushed by. It must've been a big herd trampling all in its path," said the captain.

The buffalo track continued over many undulations into the distance and they rode along it. The captain dismounted several times, putting his ear to the ground. The two mastiffs ran with their noses glued to the tracks, sniffing and taking the scent.

Suddenly Herr von Wrede stopped. "Rahn, come here!" He put his hand over his eyes. "Do you see the little dots moving over the horizon? Those are buffaloes. The herd is feeding and has loosened up. We've got to try and get at them from the side. The wagons should be kept away so that they won't be trampled when the animals break loose. We'd better stand in that depression over there because if they flee, we'll most conveniently pack 'em in the flank."

Rahn and the other hunters looked east. "It seems to be a big herd, Captain. You can clearly see how the animals are coming individually over the elevation and then disappear behind the one before. The wind is coming towards us so that puts the weather against them."

They rode slowly beside the buffalo path. The dogs were put on a leash and led by the wagon drivers. The five gunmen put their rifles across the saddle in front of them, all hearts thumping. The captain rode ahead, Rahn staying beside him, "I reckon it's a few hundred head!"

Now the wagons had to stay behind and slowly the hunters stalked forward. The captain stood up in the saddle and stopped, "Did you hear that, Rahn? A shot!"

"No, Captain."

"There, now again! Look, the buffaloes are lifting their heads. There is actual shooting going on."

"I heard it too now, Captain. If that's Indians!"

"Doesn't matter right now, keep your eyes open! The buffaloes are starting to move towards us, walking back along their old track. Into the grass, go, spread yourselves out! Everyone take out one or two animals!"

The buffaloes began to run, the ground shaking. Behind them the dogs were howling and tearing at their lines. Again there were clear shots to be heard and in a thunderous rush the herd, a solid, black-brown mass, chased past the hunters. Several scattered animals ran behind them. There was shooting from the wagons as three or four buffaloes fell. The mass tightened even more, got confused at one point, and then carried on.

The shots found their mark, yet the captain remained as calm as can be. They swept over them like a raging tempest, blind and stupid, running for their lives with their heads bent and fearful — black, goggling eyes — shaggy tufts of hair swaying on their high hunches.

Nobody counted the massive, brown bodies anymore that fell from the herd, twitching and crashing to the earth and no one afterwards could say how long the whole thing had taken. When the last animals had passed, a few isolated shots crashed and the hunters turned their rifles eastward.

At the last elevation to the right of them were five riders and a row of packhorses.

"Indians?" they thought to themselves.

A moment of eyeing the strangers was filled with the utmost tension. "No, whites," said the captain. The foremost waved his hat and they now rode towards each other from both sides as the captain and the leader of the party met.

The stranger bowed in the saddle, declaring, "Von Meusebach, Commissioner-General of the Society for the Protection of

German Immigrants, on the way from Carlshafen to New Braunfels."

"I'm Captain von Wrede, leader of the hunting and raiding party, on the way to somewhat supplement the food in New Braunfels. Thanks, you chased the buffalo straight into our shotguns making the job much easier."

Once again, they both shook hands

At this point the wagons came alongside and Rahn had already jumped off his horse and got the men ready. The buffaloes that had been killed were dragged together, gutted and loaded onto the carts. Ten could be accommodated but four had to be left lying, their skins pulled off and their tongues cut out. Then they cut out the best pieces of roasting meat and wrapped them in the raw hides which work took several hours.

Meanwhile, Herr von Meusebach told the captain of his impressions in Carlshafen. "The Society management was greatly surprised by the report from the prince announcing his resignation. It was believed in Germany that, according to the estimates made, they had employed sufficient funds to secure the venture. My first task will be to ask the prince for bills and receipts and to send both to Germany by the quickest means, so that one can check the state of the enterprise as only then should new funds be allocated."

The captain laughed. "I can tell you already, the whole venture has gone off the rails from the very start. I've never understood that such an inexperienced man as the prince was endowed with such extensive powers. We weren't given the right to contradict his actions and could only mitigate and change a few things. Our life is always hanging on just one thread—money, money and money, Herr Commissioner-General! I suppose your packhorses are loaded to the brim with it."

"There you're wrong, Herr von Wrede. I've brought something with me but not enough to put all the damage to rights. However", he was searching for words, "what I saw in Carlshafen is so terrible that only a very big use of cash can really help. No one suspects such conditions in Germany. Koechert, Wilcke and a girl, Klappenbach, it is said, are defending themselves heroically against fever, laziness, hunger and dirt. I have advised against sending the fourth wagon train to New Braunfels now because I'm afraid that the epidemic that has been poisoning the camp for a week will be transferred to New Braunfels."

"Well, OK, then you should provide the bureaucrats in Mainz with fuel for the flames and then we'll see what happens. Nice prospects but you shouldn't be letting much of that reach the people because they're hoping for more from you. And how you want to hold the prince to account I can't imagine, since he left on May 15 and his two companions are not back yet."

Herr von Meusebach grabbed the captain's arm. "Gone, you say, leaving the post on his own bat? Is that possible?"

"The matter is thus: The course of events proved to us that the prince was not up to his task—I don't need to enumerate the tragic episode of this loser—Koechert will have provided that. The rest you'll experience in New Braunfels. To put it bluntly: We have deported His Highness with some vigor. The prince is taking the Society a number of demands from the emigrants and will report in detail. Whilst all future measures of the Society can then be taken on the basis of his experiences to our benefit, urgency is called for. No ifs and buts, no parades of the holy bureaucracy! Highness left behind a bundle of papers and something like a commenced accounting. Two of our merchants, who the Prince never consulted, in spite of the instruction to hand over this legacy sealed to his successor, have tried to examine anything that can be checked. From the records they calculated a shortfall of nineteen thousand four hundred and sixty dollars and two pence. What else is going on, we can only guess. Thank God that the creditors in Galveston, Houston and New Orleans are not so quick to find us and our reputation in the outback is better than on the coast. That is our reality, Herr Commissioner-General."

The two men stood silently side-by-side. Herr von Meusebach excitedly pulled his hand through his red-blond beard, biting into his lower lip. "And I'm supposed to now muck out this Augean stable? Wouldn't it be better if I turned around on the spot and tried to reach the prince before he leaves? I've got to know everything from scratch in order to get a grip on the matter. If that's the case, then there's not a penny left of the money I have brought."

"For a variety of reasons, I'd advise you, Commissioner-General, to come with us to New Braunfels first before making any further decisions."

Herr von Meusebach considered. "Fine," he said, then, "I'll ride with you."

"I don't want to be a prophet, Herr von Wrede, but I think we can only save the Society with very tough measures, no matter who they are. Do you want to help me with this?"

The captain shook his hand. "As far as men can do that," he said, "you can count on me. But Herr Zink, the leader of the raiding party, carries the biggest burden. Everything rested on his shoulders from the beginning, including that which the prince thought he was taking responsibility for. There is a circle of magnificent men standing by him who grew to their tasks and who the Society has to thank for the fact that the wagon train to 'New Germany' didn't go under."

They left in the late afternoon. A horseman chased ahead to announce the arrival of the Commissioner-General in New Braunfels. Some of the hunters harnessed their horses to the loaded wagons in preparation and shortly before sunset the raiding party passed through the ford in the Guadalupe and climbed up the steep track to New Braunfels.

The people had dressed up for the occasion, bringing out their best clothes from boxes and crates and stood now in two rows full of expectation and joyful hope along the way. It looked strange when the Thuringians, the Hessians and the Baden peasants in their wrinkled frock coats, the so-called "Wadenklopfer", prepared themselves for the reception. Tradition of the mother country in Texas!

Weinreich had installed himself with his clarinet at the front and when Herr von Meusebach and the captain rode up the path, he began to blow the Texas song, everyone singing along. Zink stepped forward and greeted the Commissioner-General. He dismounted and began a never-ending handshake.

Rahn had chopped into the haunches of the quarry left behind in the buffalo skin and was giving everyone a fair share of the harvest. The fires blazed again as the smell of roasting and cooking filled the air. After the meal, the youngsters danced under the elm whilst the elders told stories from home.

The Commissioner-General liked it all. "Isn't that a hunk of a man?" he said, "If he has as much guts in his brain as muscles on his arms, then it's going to get better."

"They've now sent us another Barbarossan," Klawutke said into his girl's ear as he danced. "Now nothing can go wrong anymore."

At the same time, Herr von Meusebach was sitting with the leading men at the table in the courtyard of the "Sophienburg". He held back his excitement only with difficulty, "You are right, Herr von Claren, the whole Society suffers from the wrong viewpoint held in Mainz. Their Lordships look at things like this: departure in Bremen, arrival in Carlshafen, onward journey to New Germany, arrival. Settle, start work, farming, sowing, harvesting and above all God's blessing and a real prince at the top, full of enthusiasm and daring. What I have just been shown by you, Herr Wessel, as accounts and a collection of documents from the prince, is so embarrassing and so depressing that I would like to call Highness to account even before his departure."

Everything was clear and concise which the new Commissioner-General said.

The first night behind the wooden walls of his room on the "Sophienburg" he found no sleep, knowing that the circumstances with which he had been met necessitated an immediate and fundamental change to all his plans. "The whole thing will at first be more of a rescue operation," he thought.

In the morning he was soon on his feet. Zink took the lead. "The most urgent issue is the procurement of food supplies and medicines as we're pretty much at the end because the third wagon train didn't bring much. A decisive blow to the funds of the Society was the purchase of the area of New Braunfels and as we advised the prince to do this, we're also therefore to blame for this expenditure."

"Well then, perhaps Messrs. Wessel, Birkel and Klappenbach would like to ride straight to Austin, taking their carts and go shopping. I'll give them some money. It'll have to be decided what is sufficient to cover costs and maybe one of the American merchants will ride along to speed up the purchase."

With a keen eye for all that was essential, Herr von Meusebach quickly overlooked the state of affairs and tried to purposefully intervene. Everyone he shook hands with and said a few words of confidence to was left with a new feeling of strength within their hearts.

On the third day after his arrival, Waldbaer rode past the guard on the way to the Guadalupe, "Man, don't ask me, that was quite a thing, alone from Carlshafen to New Braunfels."

He trotted up through the camp to the "Sophienburg". Herr von Meusebach was sitting over the map with Zink as Waldbaer stopped in front of the palisades. Zink sprang up. "Alone?"

"Yes, my comrade is lying in Carlshafen with fever. The cart is also there. Here's a letter from His Highness." The engineer read:

New Orleans, June 15 1845.

„Herr Zink!

"My journey from New Braunfels to Galveston went smoothly apart from a few shootouts. I have booted out Fisher. Now he is taking his revenge on me. Wherever I went and stood, creditors appeared with demands. I have no picture at the moment about what is really genuine.

"Herr Klaener's mediation made it possible for me to continue to New Orleans. Here Fisher hounded a whole pack of people on me.

"I am being held at the hotel and my luggage has been confiscated. The funds that I still have are enough to pay for the crossing, but by no means enough to free me from the hands of these bloodsuckers.

"I am sending the letter via Galveston to Carlshafen because I hope that my two companions are still there. I asked Herr Koechert to have it brought quickly to New Braunfels.

"Immediately initiate my release, as I gave you representation until the arrival of my successor and also all the money that you can spare. I expect quick help as I am burning to get to Germany.

"I have now got over the aftereffects of our last upset and despite everything, I believe in New Germany in the garden of the world! And what I can do for it in Germany will be done according to the old basic principles."

Zink read the letter aloud and then said, "The captain doesn't need to know the end of the story, otherwise he'll get into a terrible rage. Watch his fingers rather than his mouth," he said repeatedly.

"So, Herr Zink, this is how we're going to do this: I'll go immediately to New Orleans, find the prince in the Grand Hotel, and clean up what needs to be cleaned up." He sighed. "This will cost a pretty penny, and what gets lost there will be missing here. Yet it's still better to clear matters and then we'll have a better view of things. In the meantime I can't help but say some things to His Highness that he'll certainly not want to hear. In addition, I can give him a report of my impressions in Texas for Mainz, verbally and in writing. What do you think?"

Zink agreed. In the evening, the departure of the Commissioner-General was quietly prepared. Waldbaer volunteered immediately to accompany him and couldn't be talked out of it.

"So what?" he said, "that's a life just made for an old poacher. If it were up to me, I'd take some tough chaps, purging with them all the way up from Carlshafen so that the rabble would finally run out of the breath to disturb us at our work."

The next day, before the camp was on its feet, having selected a compatriot from the Rhoen, the three horsemen hurried out into the rolling country upon well-rested horses.

From morning to night the black hearses rumbled through the streets of New Orleans, collecting the harvest of death, in front of each a drummer, stalking wooden and stiff. Often they had to stop when they were given a sign from a house on the way. But many houses also stood empty, abandoned by or where the inhabitants had died off. In the summer of 1845 the fever was particularly severe and only those who for business reasons could not do otherwise remained behind, because the trade of the southern states and the path of the immigrants from North America and Europe to Texas went via New Orleans.

The merchants, who sent their families to healthier areas during the hot season but had to remain in the city themselves, never knew if they would see their relatives again. The dollar was stronger than the fear of death and the rush for success dulled the concern for life. Those who managed to accumulate a fortune in a few years could rest comfortably in quieter and healthier areas or engage in less dangerous business ventures.

---

During the summer, life in the big city on the Mississippi River tried to ignore the fear and worry. Theatre, opera and shows, schnapps, churches of all denominations, prayer houses of many sects, dubious establishments, whores, elegance and waste numbed the senses of the foolhardy robber barons.

When the Commissioner-General stopped in front of the Grand Hotel in New Orleans, he could already hear the ranting, screaming and threatening of the assembled creditors of the Society from within as he got out of the carriage that had brought him and Waldbaer from the harbor, the second companion and the horses having stayed behind in Galveston. Waldbaer forced an alley with his elbows through the wall of the waiting men in front of the prince's room. The policeman who was supervising entry and exit checked the papers of the Commissioner-General and let him enter.

The men outside the door fell silent as the guard told them who had come. They folded their invoices and bills of exchange that they had just been waving like flags through the air, putting them into their pockets, waiting like oxen that already have the imaginary smell of heap of hay in their noses before it is even there. The prince entered from an adjoining room when he heard the footsteps of Herr von Meusebach.

"I have the honor, Your Excellency." Herr von Meusebach bowed slightly. "Von Meusebach, Commissioner-General of the Mainz Society for Immigration in Texas."

"I am very pleased to greet you, sir," said the prince, "and think I am not mistaken in assuming that you've come to liberate me from this unworthy situation and it's about time! Get rid of this bunch and make sure that I can go in and out freely here—these people don't seem to understand who they're dealing with."

"One thing at a time, your Highness! The imprisonment imposed on you is very mild and you could have just as well been thrown into the jail. I don't intend to do anything about American law and if you had an orderly record of your management duties, I'd have dealt with the people in front of the door in no time. In this you have failed and we'll come to that yet but nevertheless, I'll still try to free you from your uncomfortable situation.

"But, sir, we haven't missed a minute. You personally are the least of my worries at the moment, Your Highness and other things are on my mind—I only came here because I wanted to make a difference."

The prince, dressed in his linen suit, fell silent, sensing the force that had amassed itself in the man standing before him, so he only made an embarrassed defensive movement with his right hand.

The Commissioner-General went to the door and saw that the number of creditors had meanwhile grown.

"Gentlemen!" He began. "I have the honor to examine the obligations of His Highness Prince Solms-Braunfels for the Mainz Society and to settle them if possible. At the same time, I am aware that a good number of honorable gentlemen have taken advantage of the versatility of paper and ink by considerably increasing the number of circulating bills of exchange and invoices presented and wherever possible, embellishing these— and that through the persistent use of numbers.

"That the benefits were more to your advantage seems to be more of a consequence rather than being the cause of your unselfish action. I will therefore allow myself in each case to examine carefully the claims you have submitted. A handwriting expert should also be consulted. It will be an honor for me to confront you, in accordance with the statements made and the appropriate legal provisions, as you did when you obtained legal culpability over His Highness. I can appreciate your precautions and would be pleased if you understood mine.

"Have the goodness to return here at five o'clock this afternoon by which time everything will be ready. I have the honor, gentlemen!"

He bowed and stepped back into the room. The swarm of people in front of the door retreated, grumbling and moaning, until finally only the policeman and Waldbaer remained. At the lunch stock exchange, Herr von Meusebach's address was passed from one dealer to the next and barely half of those who had disturbed the prince's life in the last few days appeared in the afternoon at the appointed time.

The Commissioner-General was able to deduct considerable sums from the abundance of demands because he knew how the men had preemptively fixed their amounts. Lastly, they had to decide not to get anything or to accept the quota he offered them as a compromise.

The funds of the Society were relieved of a good six thousand dollars and its credit thus received a blow from which it could never recover.

During the next few days, purchases were only possible with cash but Herr von Meusebach purchased large quantities of ship provisions, peas, beans, corn, rusks, sauerkraut, and salted meats plus a herd of beef cattle. He immediately had these supplies shipped to Galveston and ordered Klaener to send them immediately to the Lavacca Bay.

"Your Highness, I'm coming to an end!" The Commissioner-General went up and down the room in big steps. The prince slumped in an armchair, propped his head in his hands, and looked down at the carpet.

"I implore you, make sure that the Society keeps the number of shipments low this fall and only accepts impeccable people and seek to dampen the Texas fever in Germany. Be glad that you've not seen the conditions in Carlshafen lately." He stopped in front of the prince. "Your Highness, there is only one thing, either you send us two hundred thousand dollars or a thousand people will slowly die. Tell them that we should be spared this writing back and forth. I brought twenty thousand dollars with me and when the debts are paid in Galveston and Austin, nothing will be left. We've only come to New Braunfels this year and will only be able to prepare the fields, so this means people will have to be fed until next year, and that costs money.

"If the club can't accommodate my demands, I'll turn to the German press so that the public then may pronounce its judgment on their Lordships and the enterprise. It's just not enough to start a colony from a desk and from there to calculate the minimum expenditure possible. Texas eats people and money! And yet we're still not at the final destination. Our life is war, and that's why we need warriors and not skivers or dreamers."

He paused, stepped in front of the prince and put his hand on his shoulder. "I know your Highness wanted the best. Texas put you back in your place, so at least be our ally in the homeland!"

The prince's imprisonment was lifted the same day and he sailed to Liverpool with a Cunard Line steamer and from there to Bremen.

The Commissioner-General traveled to Galveston and Carlshafen. Hermann Koechert was standing on the beach when the boat came in with Herr von Meusebach and his two companions.

"Well, how's it going?" He asked, shaking Koechert's hand.

"Everything's taking its course! But where have you come from, Herr Commissioner-General? I thought you'd have been in New Braunfels."

Meusebach told of the recent events on the way to the camp. "This ends the 'Solms' era," he concluded. Then he pointed out to the paddle steamer that was setting boats out in the bay.

"They've started unloading. In the next few days there'll be two ships with full loads. Get Herr Wilcke to provide the people to help."

Koechert interrupted the Commissioner-General. "I have to take that over. Wilcke has been ill for six days with Yellow fever. There are currently thirty-two people in the hospital tent. That's why a few suspects had to be separated. From the day you left until today, we had twenty-seven deaths. Some families are extinct. Before the next wagon train can leave for New Braunfels, we have to deal with the plague here and you mustn't allow it be carried to the city under any circumstances. We've become passive and that's good because otherwise it would be unbearable. Since the cemetery has been expanding, the wolves have started to venture closer and closer to the camp. They open the shallow graves in the night and we're having a lot of trouble keeping the beasts off of us. Although I'm telling you this it is not because I want to complain. 'Who knows what's going on in these Germans' minds?' said an American to me who came to the shops a few days ago. 'There where Americans would diverge one by one to save themselves, saving any property which could be saved, their people melt into a single community — something unknown to us. That keeps them going and lets them overcome every necessity.' You see, Commissioner-General, that's what makes me believe in the success of our venture."

The two walked through the camp streets as all human life had crept into the huts and tents to escape the scorching sun. The air above the sand was shimmering.

"Keep your mind clear and strengthen the brave!" Said the Commissioner-General. "As soon as circumstances permit, I'll send an expedition to the grant — maybe I'll lead it myself. It's about time we saw what Herr Fisher actually sold us because everything was prepared in Germany and continues to happen that way, leading to the assumption that the Society's area corresponds to that which we expect of it. If we should be mistaken, Herr Koechert…"

The Commissioner-General was silent and looked down towards the sea. "Who's the woman standing down there in front of the biggest tent by the water and holding her hand over her eyes?"

"That's Barbara Klappenbach. She cares for the sick and is restricted from any contact with the camp residents. From her emanates a power that inspires even the lost with confidence and hope. Since she recovered after a fever attack, she seems to be immune to all illness. 'I simply didn't believe that I could and should die,' she once called to me over the ditch that encloses the sickbay. Now she's worried about the life of Ludwig Wilcke, her bridegroom — he's doing very badly."

They looked down as the girl stepped back into the tent. Meusebach and Koechert went into the oppressive dusk of the barn and fell exhausted onto maize sacks. Koechert had now learned all the essentials about the state of affairs. "You didn't say much which was good, Herr Commissioner-General."

"It'd be wrong to rouse the hopefuls out there from those dreams which they still dream, despite everything, but we have to stay focused, Herr Koechert, and keep our cool like chess players. Texas dictates the moves, and we've to defend ourselves so we'll not be check-mated."

While the sun was sinking and the evening settling softly over the sea, the fever in the sickbay was rising because between day and night the sick had their hardest time. Some lives were extinguished whilst others wrestled agonizingly through the crisis, holding on to the rest of a life that was trying to escape the glowing body.

Barbara Klappenbach went from camp to camp cooling the hot foreheads with vinegar water. She dripped cool water into the swollen oral cavities. Whilst having no medicines, she herself was the best remedy with her gentle hands. Confidence and faith flowed from them and even dying was easier when her hand lay on a dull heart.

In the corner where the linen weaver Teichmüller and his wife had died weeks before, Ludwig Wilcke was wrestling with death as Barbara knelt beside the sick man feeling his pulse. She counted only seventy weak beats and his skin was moist and cool. She tore his shirt open and began to rub the pit of the heart, knowing his blood should be flowing faster. The patient had his eyes closed and was groaning as she rubbed and squeezed and the traces of her fingers appeared bright on the tawny skin. This was all about his life, she thought as his thin upper lip quivered. The girl rubbed and rubbed, knowing that if his heart held he would be saved.

With strong fingers, she kneaded the weak body and whispered in her lover's ear that what he had liked to hear best back in the good days. The sum of her life compelled her into imploring incantations, as if she could let her healthy power flow over him. She sank down to him, her ear listening for a few moments to the passing beat of his heart. "Ludwig, Ludwig! Can you hear me?" she cried beginning to stroke more violently. "When our trees first bloom, when your future children are playing, when your son is hunting across the meadows on a nimble horse—Ludwig, it will be, come, stay there—you must not..."

As she rubbed and stroked faster, her head became empty and all her strength and the whole will to live gathered in her hands, feeling as if her heart was beating in the patient's body. How long this went on she did not know. Above them hung an oil lamp on a wire, the smoldering wick carrying a flickering flame gasping for air, as if it were about to go out.

Barbara Klappenbach was pouring all the fervor of her love over the passive body of the man who lay before her in the corn-straw. Putting her hands under his back, she pulled him up, rhythmically rocking back and forth with him to some covert measure of time. She clung to him, holding his head with her right hand as he tried to fall backwards, kissing the parting lips time and time again.

The little flame above her drowned in the oil. In the darkness she held her beloved tight, wondering if she would die with him. It seemed an eternity and she had no sense of hours, months or years.

When she awoke and opened her eyes, she had difficulty understanding where she was because of all the lovely dreamed images that had wiped out her memory of what had been before. Straightening up, she saw Ludwig Wilcke lying and quickly put her hand upon his heart. It was weak but regular and his skin was dry and warm.

"He's alive!" She looked into his now sharply contoured face for a long time, a refreshing sleep having erased all its distortions.

"He's alive!" She slipped a cloth under his head, opened the louvers in the ceiling and then stepped out of the tent. The first glimmer of the new day was speeding ahead of the sun across the sea, its purple fingers groping their way across the edge of the world and reflecting a sea, a thousand times broken, reflecting the golden glow. Barbara Klappenbach threw off her clothes and slowly walked out into the water, towards the new light.

The girl closed her eyes, the sea nestling around her body, soft and refreshing. Raising her arms, she threw herself into the cool tide. "Now, come what may, it can't get any worse," she said to herself on the way back to the tent.

The patient was still sleeping as Barbara took a sip of vinegar water and started taking care of the others. She would have to report two dead to the post.

The next day, the Commissioner-General set off once again for New Braunfels, as there was business to be done. Waldbaer always keeping his distance, Herr von Meusebach rode in the middle and Schmitz, the other companion, kept behind. On the second day of the journey they had strayed from the route, the track from Victoria to Gonzales having been lost in the grass thicket. They mistakenly followed a north turn and found a spot in front of them where the prairie was trampled, as hard as a threshing floor and smelled burnt. They tracked further and immediately saw a pile of junk and the corpses of a married couple and child who had been robbed of their clothes.

Waldbaer dismounted. "That didn't go off without a fight," he said as he searched the immediate area. "They were attacked there, on the trampled grass. The man had resisted with all his might and his left hand has been shot. The woman was cut down with a stroke of the butt whilst the child seems to have starved to death. They finally dragged them here and birds and wolves have already feasted on them."

Waldbaer picked up a note lying under the man's right hand. "From Galveston on our own with the last of our money. Attacked. Lost oxen and wagons. Wife, Antonie Berthold, killed. Dragged here. I, Heinrich Berthold, stabbed in the back and shot in the left hand. Wanted to burn us but could extinguish fire. Blood can't be stopped. Dortchen crying. Hunger. Letter to Brother Hermann in He-"

The Commissioner-General read the note a few times. "So this is the tribute we have to pay before we can count this country our own! The raid may have happened two days ago. Waldbaer, let's see if we manage to get those dogs in front of our guns!"

They buried the dead as best they could using Waldbaer's small spade.

"How many Germans across the world may have fallen victim to the urge to go abroad? They remained the seed, but the others often reaped the harvest. They remained isolated and weak when others became united and strong. They were tools, and others carried the work away. This Berthold should have waited, as the leadership had prescribed but he ran away and that's the sad ending."

Silently, the men got back on horseback and looked for the right way. It was two days later, shortly before Seguin, when they saw a wagon in the distance swaying across the prairie.

Herr von Meusebach took his binoculars out of his saddlebag exclaiming, "An ox cart—it's disappearing into a depression—wait—prepare rifles. At the peak in front of a group of trees and bushes the path is quite well worn so probably there's a settlement nearby." They waited, keeping close together so that from the front you might have thought it was just one rider. Over and beyond, the cart and tackle was emerging from the valley. "One is leading and another seems to be sitting up front. I can see the whip strap flying over the animals and they've tied their horses to the back of the wagon. I bet they're the rascals we are looking for. We'll ride around them in a wide arc and turn to face them."

The Americans were singing and feeling secure as the wagon drove on. When it disappeared behind the next hump, the three Germans spurred their horses, soon stopping at the height of the team, their rifles at the ready.

Meusebach called out to the bandits, "Stop! Hands up!" The song abruptly stopped and the robbers, terrified, stiffened like stakes. Their guns hung on the saddles of the horses behind the wagon. One of them wanted to jump to the back but Waldbaer chased a bullet into his thigh and he fell and the other stretched his arms straight up. The oxen were appreciative of the rest stop and were beginning to graze as the three men carefully rode up. The uninjured American had guns in his belt and in a flash he dropped an arm, trying to draw his gun. Schmitz shot his hand right through whilst the bandit was forced through the air by the impact, howling. The three Germans jumped down and in a few moments the two robbers were bound.

Waldbaer glanced into the wagon "A lot of stuff, sir," he said. "Household goods, clothes and supplies; certainly more than the Berthold family took with them. Therefore, the villains must still have a number of other things on their conscience." The prisoners wanted to talk.

"We're not going to waste any time beating about the bush with you" the Commissioner-General stated categorically. "There, behind the oak trees," he pointed with his thumb over his shoulder.

Schmitz subsequently nailed a carton lid to the trunk with the inscription: "This is how anyone will learn to swing who lays hands on Germans and their property!!!"

In the saddlebags of the bandits there was a considerable amount of German money. The rifles of the two men were of German origin and bore the same make as those of the guards in Carlshafen and New Braunfels.

"Thus things return to their owners," said the Commissioner-General as they moved on.

Three days later they arrived in New Braunfels. They were met with excited voices coming from the market. Under the elm the people stood crushed together as something very important was making everyone hold their breath—Zink was distributing the land lots.

The Commissioner-General was forcing his way through the crowd as Zink greeted him and briefly filled him in on the situation, "Look at all the shops around the marketplace as well as the most important crafts. Now everyone seems to want to open a junk shop and start selling. 'If you know nothing better to do,' I said to them, 'then you'll make it worse than it was back home. The distribution of goods must be in a healthy relationship to production and consumption and you can't all become shopkeepers. Above all, we need farmers because if nobody sows, there won't be a harvest!' But people have lost themselves in their plans. If I wanted to allow all the inns to be opened which are being proposed, there would soon be no such thing as a sober person in New Braunfels."

Despite the strains that he had behind him, the Commissioner-General immediately intervened, exclaiming angrily, "We've no use for lazybones here. That might suit you, crouching behind the counter, until the bell over the door tingles and then weighing up bags with your thumb on the scale. I know all about that. First something has to be produced and then we'll find a way to bring the goods to market. Grow corn, create vegetables, fruits and meat! Everything else has time. We'll have all this one day but we can only do one thing after another. It doesn't change the fact that everyone must build his house, tend a few acres of land, plant a garden and keep livestock. No one may misuse the other by trade and cutthroat dealing and if you want that, I'll smuggle a handful of devious sharks in here—then you'll soon see if you've any hairs left!"

"Did you hear that?" Shouted a voice from the rear, "we've got to build the houses ourselves now but the Society promised to build them. There you have it again!"

"Lie down and wait 'til they send some cardboard boxes full from Mainz," the Commissioner-General answered sharply. "You get the lumber for free, as well as the fence stakes. I didn't make up the Society's program and won't stand for uselessly harping on it. The first straw stalk and the first stake of the garden fence are more important to me than any futile hair-splitting. I call on all those who want to get on with the job. If it doesn't suit anyone he can go! Step forward one at a time and draw your lot."

The Commissioner-General stood tall and let his steely blue eyes glide clearly and calmly over the crowd.

Now, cracked brown hands reached into the box on the table, into which Zink had placed the folded numbered sheets. Eagerly, the notes were torn out, numbers leaping into brains. Those who received their lot forced their way out of the ring and ran out to look for the stake carrying the number of the lot.

With sparkling eyes, Heinrich Klawutke went to stand next to his friend Piesicke. "Man, what did you say? From today on, we'll be farmers. Can you understand that? I'm feeling quite serious—now only the pastor needs to preach and I'll start weeping—now I'll soon be getting married," he said pensively, trying to encompass his land with his eyes.

This day the earth to feed them was given to all. Apart from some who believed that they were disadvantaged by their lot, everyone consciously felt a new sense of home in their secure ownership.

## VI

The summer was hot and dry. The Germans in New Braunfels were almost dying in the burning heat yet they worked tirelessly as over each of them floated a dream-like image of the household they wanted to create. They spoke of nothing but their house, their business, their agriculture and many who were threatened by weakness, clenched their teeth and worked with their last strength, because their neighbors were enthusing next to them and they did not want to be the ones to stay behind.

No one knew what had become of all the enthusiastic young men, the students, officers and teachers, the scheming artisans and peasants! In tattered clothes, tanned, bearded and tough, secretly often quarreling with their fate, they stood up with the sun and first lay down their reins, saws, hatchets and hammers from their calloused hands when the evening sun sank over the horizon.

The women and children stood in front of the "Sophienburg" every morning in a long line to receive the daily cooking rations. There were not enough oxen, cows and horses to perform the necessary hauling services and it was a dangerous business bringing the heavy oak logs, the elms and cedars to the construction sites. Fathers, mothers and children stretched themselves before the trees, breathlessly dragging them over the hard-rolled paths. How many tree trunks belonged to even the smallest log cabin, what amounts of wood were needed to fence ten acres of land! One or two even were beginning to wonder if the whole effort made any sense at all, New Braunfels was only a station before the actual goal! So why break off here, if only to continue further? So people wavered between hope and despair, cursing their fate and beginning to believe again, becoming strong and weak in face of themselves. "Am I still there?" Many asked, feeling they had become completely remolded.

According to Zink's instructions, the log cabins had to be placed so far back into the urban plots that enough space remained on the roads for later stone buildings. He saw in his thoughts a true German city emerging with a proud town hall, wide squares, beautiful churches, schools and stately mansions one day replacing the construction of the temporary log cabins. Even the Texan reality could not drive away the otherwise sober engineer from such dreams.

Autumn was approaching slowly as the city was increasingly taking shape and properties were now visibly separated from one another and roads ran dusty and worn between the fences. However, the worries of the Commissioner-General were increasing from week to week. The monotonous food no longer pleased the people and they were beginning to demand a change. Now there were once again scurvy patients and the rapidly falling climate changes after icy Northers brought intermittent fever. Any improvement in the situation was ultimately dependent on money and that was not going to happen—bills of exchange were already passing through the hands of the American businessmen, as payment deadlines could not be met.

"Herr von Wrede," said the Commissioner-General, "what'll happen when the cold season comes and the houses aren't yet finished? On the coast, the weather was mild and friendly but here in the west there are many things to do, because we should be replacing tools and stocking up on food for the winter."

He was leaning forward in his chair, his head in his hands. "You've got to get hold of some money! Here is a letter from the Society management in Mainz promising a large sum, so ride to Austin and make sure that you get a loan based on the letter. In the long run, I can't answer for withholding that money from our people to which they have a claim. They're increasingly pushing for disbursement of their funds and they've started threatening. There's a lack of salt and spices and we didn't even have enough flour for a few cakes when Dr. Koester married the baker's daughter on the market fourteen days ago!"

"We mustn't lose our nerve," the captain replied. "You mentioned Koester—a less reliable man! I expected better of him. You should've heard him in Hamburg before leaving. I was told that he wanted to learn bakery with his father-in-law and that they both planned to start a restaurant. Koester is probably a good businessman but a bad doctor as well as a person to whom the word 'victim' is alien. Our situation urges everyone to own up and no one can hide behind puffed up words. The necessity calls for honesty, one way or the other."

"You've got to turn a blind eye to lots of things," said the Commissioner-General. "What can he actually do as a doctor? Damned little. More and more new diseases emerge that nobody knows for which we've got no cure. There's this peculiar rash again that quickly spreads and paralyzes the work. What is it? If you get water on it, it makes it worse. Koester is at a loss but oil and fat seem to help if you rub them on the itchy areas."

"I remember having experienced something similar in Italy," said the captain. "There they call the disease pellagra, rough skin. It develops after one-sided corn nutrition and therefore attacks only the poor. We've got to improve our people's diet."

"But that's just a matter of money again, Captain von Wrede," interrupted the Commissioner-General. "So you're riding to Austin!"

At the beginning of October 1845 Herr von Wrede rode to Austin with Lieutenant von Claren and Kaufmann Wessel. He carried the letter, indicating the transfer of a larger sum of money from the Society management in Mainz, in the pocket of his deerskin chaps. The three men raced across the prairie following the ancient Spaniard path that came from Presidio on the Rio Grande in Mexico and leading straight across Texas to Luisiana, reaching their destination in good spirits.

The captain managed to get two thirds of the sum promised in the letter from Austin businessmen. Part of the money was invested in goods, the linen bag with the remainder being stored by the captain in his right saddlebag. The three men then set out confidently upon their way back to New Braunfels, planning that the oxen wagons with the purchased goods were to follow. They now had to cover some fifty-five miles that did not lead past any settlement, making it necessary to spend the night outdoors.

In the early morning of October 24 after they had ridden away from Austin, encamping on the first evening under a group of slender live oaks. A spring emerged from the ground a hundred yards away with shrubbery and grass growing luxuriantly along the narrow stream. The men looked forward to a juicy piece of the deer they had shot and their rifles, powder and purse lay between the gnarled roots of the largest oak tree. Wessel stoked the fire, a white plume of smoke rising straight up, gilded high by the sinking sun.

The captain and Claren were lying in the grass, their saddles under their heads. They squinted up into a sky with a white cloud swimming over it and Wessel was leaning over to turn a leg of venison whilst heart, liver and kidneys were roasting in the copper kettle.

Suddenly the captain raised his head and listened. Then he bent down and put his ear to the ground.

"What is it?" Asked Claren.

"Shush—be still!" The captain waved. "Hooves."

Wessel had gone to the spring to collect water as Claren too put his ear to the ground, listening intently.

"I can hear something," he said, "but it could also be my heart—Maybe it's buffalo?"

"It's riders and they're getting closer. Take your rifle—better be on the safe side!"

They warned Wessel who laughed, "You don't want to spoil our meal, do you? Perhaps it's white men on the road just like us and then I'll have to put another chunk of meat on the spit!"

The captain's buff face tightened. Squinting, he peered into the distance as far as the tall grass permitted, reaching for his gun and putting his pistols beside him.

"Everyone to one side of the tree trunk," he snapped, then, "Lie down! Seek cover behind the roots—don't rush a shot—keep cool—they're coming from up front."

Claren could see nothing as yet but the hoofbeats were clearly audible and soon the screeching voices of Indians could be heard. They came from the front, then from the side and then from behind and the Germans were surrounded. The captain put the moneybag under his rifle to get better support. "They're circling us—take out each one individually—load calmly and aim well and don't tremble while shooting!"

Wessel saw the brown figures scurrying past as he crawled into the bushes, laying and holding his breath. The Indians were closing the ring more tightly now as they furiously rode around the campsite. Some carried rifles over their heads whilst others only carried bows, arrows, and small round shields.

"They've nothing good in mind," said the captain. "I've been waiting for a long time for such a thing to happen but I can't say that I feel particularly comfortable in this situation."

"It could be thirty redskins," said Claren, struggling to stay calm.

At this point the Indians must have clearly recognized the two. They rode even faster as the first shots crashed and Claren squeezed the trigger, shaking. "Keep calm," the captain warned.

"Aim lower!"

At first it seemed as if the redskins were only enjoying the cracking of their rifles as their shots missed their aim. They began to sing a shrill battle song, shooting at the oak without aiming at it. The trunk was riddled with bullets but they were all high above the heads of the two Germans.

"First let them get a bit closer," the captain advised. His eye was over front and rear sights.

Their superiority was making the Indians feel secure so they played with their victims.

"What do think they are singing?" asked Claren, controlling himself with difficulty.

"It's Comanches," the captain whispered. "I know their language."

The bullets that were digging into the oak tree gradually started moving down towards the heads of the two.

"Listen," said the captain. "They are singing like this, 'Friend, whatever threatens you' - a bullet went into the saddle the captain had laid in front of him - 'if you call me, I will help you.'"

Claren shot faster. There was a gap in the ring of the riders and one threw his arms in the air and fell off his horse. Now the singing of the Indians swelled with shrillness and the captain rushed ball after ball from the shotgun, calmly finishing the words of the song that the redskins sang, "Fearlessly enduring everything, I'll stand by your side."

There was confusion in the circles of the riders, as horses and men fell but the ring was closing ever tighter. Claren shot excitedly but the captain fired as if he doing target practice, with every shot finding its target.

Now the shots cracked in bursts under the trees. Wessel clawed his hands into the grass, trying to make out the guns from the captain's shots and the sound of Claren's rifle because the whipping, high tone of the German rifles could easily be distinguished. The Redskins were starting to shoot at evershorter intervals when one of the German rifles went silent and a short time later the other. Then the shooting stopped altogether and a wild jumble of voices was approaching. Wessel crept out of his hiding-place, as the redskins had dismounted and crowded together under the oaks, and springing up and running into the prairie to catch one of the horses, where there were none to be found.

After anxiously listening and keeping an eye out for a while, he circumvented the battlefield and found his way back to Austin. He had wandered all night through the prairie on burning feet, often sinking down and panting for breath, pain and worry after a few moments driving him on. Hunger and thirst gnawed at his body and the sharp grass struck wounds into his legs and arms.

Towards morning, he finally came upon the Colorado shining before him where he sought refreshment from a few sips of water. He had strayed to the right and now ran up the river towards the city, collapsing in the sheriff's office, after he had given the necessary information using the last of his strength. As soon as he regained consciousness, he set out with a squadron of dragoons to search the battlefield and pursue the Indians. They found the two dead, scalped and plundered, under the oak trees. The captain was riddled with nine bullets and Claren with thirteen as well as any number of arrow shots. They were hastily buried as vultures were already gathering on the nearest trees.

Wessel was then assigned five dragoons as cover for the journey to New Braunfels, the main group turning west and following in the footsteps of the Indians.

As night fell on one of the last October evenings, the merchant Eduard Wessel and his companions rode up the Vereinsberg to the "Sophienburg". From the dining room of Herr von

Wedemeyer on the market a light was shining as a folk song was echoing softly behind the riders. Over two or three deep basses floated the richness of a few girls voices'. The guard at the gate of "Sophienburg" accepted Wessel's message and woke the Commissioner-General.

A light appeared and Herr von Meusebach was quick on his feet, stepping onto the porch where he was startled to see Wessel climbing up the steps alone.

In front of the table, on which a high candlelight was burning stood the Commissioner-General with Wessel opposite him. In meager sentences the merchant reported the course of the ride up to the attack under the oak. Meusebach bit his lower lip and sank into the simple chair the carpenters had built for him. When Wessel had finally finished, they remained silent for a long time, the candle crackling as all sorts of insects buzzed in its glow.

"He was the best of them all," said the Commissioner-General. "Incorruptible, clean, never thinking of himself and giving everything for others. I can't imagine what'll happen now without him. And Claren — he would have become one to whom we could have entrusted our future without reserve, young, upright and firm, a man for Texas — we only have a few of his kind!"

The big clock in the corner showed the eleventh hour as the cuckoo rattled out from behind its door, crying out loudly eleven times into the painful silence. "I want to have Zink woken," the Commissioner-General interjected. "He needs to know everything because we'll have to figure out what to do right away." Herr von Meusebach stepped out into the darkness and shouted to the post.

During the night the news found its way down to New Braunfels and before dawn, most of them already knew what had happened in the captain's journey to Austin. People emerged from completed or partly built log cabins, straw huts or tents, speaking softly to each other. The captain had been all but certain that one day they would be standing where their hopes longed them to be, and they wonder what would happen now.

The leaders sat discussing in the great room of the Commissioner-General until well into the morning. Ervendberg had been brought in, as well as Julius von Coll, Beneh and Thomas Schwab.

"To me, the situation now looks like this," said the Commissioner-General, "The money is lost that the Society owes to the businessmen in Austin. This will have to be explicitly emphasized to those men, for in our situation, that shade of credit that we still have is indispensable. The Americans are already calling us 'a heap of beggars' which shows how we are judged. Koechert has meanwhile sent us the fourth, so far largest transport of people and those people certainly moved in like beggars. It must be looking bad in Carlshafen, if they were the best and yet many insecure people are amongst them. There are of course a number of decent families, people who seem to know what they want, despite their distress and hardship.

"So in the next few days I'll go on an expedition to try and reach the grant. If that doesn't work out, then at least I'd like to find a place where we can settle some of the people who burden us.

"First, I want to free New Braunfels from all the insecure persons. Herr von Coll will take over the guard as successor to Claren. Since we'll be penetrating ever deeper into Indian territory on our march, armed security must be particularly strong. You wanted to say something, Herr Zink?"

"Not really to the point itself but I must once express what has been pressing me for a long time." The others looked at the serious man expectantly. "Even if the purchase of the Fisher Grant is right, we only own it on paper and I'm afraid the area must first be wrung from to the Indians. We're too weak for an attack and will have to try by peaceful means to come to some agreement with the redskins even it necessitates some sacrifices. To me it seems wrong to attack them and to take revenge for the murder of our two friends, as Herr von Coll would have it, given our situation—despite how much we have the right to do so. We can only do that what's possible, and that's not very much."

So the expedition was agreed upon and Beneh and Coll were to take part as well as Herr von Meusebach.

The wagon train was prepared with zeal in the course of the next few days. The mood in the city changed as soon as the horror of the Indian raid had subsided. There were riots in which the Commissioner-General, being a representative of the Society, was violently attacked. The unreliable elements marched up to "Sophienburg" and demanded to speak to Herr von Meusebach. With bitter words they accused him of being to blame for the Society's faults and demanded quick help.

Herr von Meusebach openly informed them about the true situation, "We can't get any further and I'm not going to be pushed into rushing. In a few days we'll be starting an expedition to look for the grant. Anyone who doesn't like it here can join us but I reserve the final selection of the participants. Particularly those who've come here at the expense of the Society and who've found it unnecessary to work on the city lot assigned to them, should make themselves available."

"We want to go to the grant!" exclaimed some voices. "Better a terrible end than terror without end!"

"Fellow countrymen, be reasonable," replied Herr von Meusebach. "Many things have already been achieved, just turn around and look down. New Braunfels is growing but not out of grumbling and dissatisfaction. I'm determined to defend myself ruthlessly against those who refuse to knuckle down and undermine order. I say nothing new when I point out that there are a number of people amongst you who would've better stayed at home and who burden us more than they are useful!"

Before departure, the Commissioner-General still had to withstand a storm. One afternoon, three Austin merchants contacted him as they had learned about the proposed venture and had come to present some bills of exchange to the management. They could not have known the situation so Herr von Meusebach convinced them that they had tried for nothing.

"There's nothing to be done, gentlemen, the till is empty. If you intend to impound us, then you're cutting off your nose to spite your face because where there is nothing to collect, you too have lost what is justly yours. The best chance of seeing your claims satisfied is if you let us stay alive."

Despite their sour faces the Commissioner-General, particularly due to his eloquence, eventually managed to obtain a substantial loan from the Americans. How beaten they felt when they rode down the Vereinsberg again.

A few days later, about forty single men gathered in the market square of New Braunfels and moved towards the wagon train heading for the northwest into the Society's area. Additionally there were fifteen mounted horse guards armed to the teeth with Julius von Coll, as the successor to Claren, taking the lead, a troop that the Commissioner-General knew he could rely on. Everything that seemed necessary for the expedition—corn, wheat flour, spices, tools, implements, gifts for the Indians, tents and many other things as well as a cannon—had been carefully stowed within eight ox-wagons.

Zink had selected the best teams amongst the cattle. "Take care of the oxen," he told the stewards. "So far, we've lost a hundred and fifty head of cattle due to the carelessness and clumsiness of the wagoners—most of it in the prairie when the animals were grazing and couldn't be recaptured."

The Commissioner-General inspected the party again. "If somebody doesn't like it," he said afterwards to Coll, "then we'll make short work of it as the selection of the worthy is having to become more and more ruthless as conditions deteriorate."

Then they set of, the train slowly gaining altitude behind the city. Dry, stony soil was revealed by swards of grass and single groups of pole oaks standing still in the distance. In front of them, yellow and bare, stretched a meager plateau. Silently, the emigrants moved on into the unknown and only the cries and curses of the wagoners with their cracking whips broke the silence. The descent into a number of consecutive, gorge-rich rock valleys was dangerous and time-consuming leading to bruises, falls and abrasions in abundance.

As they came out on the other side of the valley every hand had to grab, push, and stare. Desolate loneliness received them on the drought-ridden plateau and the hard grass was scrawny and becoming increasingly rare. Very occasionally did they meet deer that were seeking their way on long treks to the few waterholes.

The Germans sought the way by compass into the distance and on clear days could make out straight bare mountain ridges far to the north. "Where's the grant? Maybe there's gold there? Where are the Indians? Will they dare attack us?" Such questions arose as they sat around the fires in the evening.

Then the wagon train crossed the narrow, fertile valley of the Sabine. Succulent grass grew on the black, muddy earth and in the river there were plenty of fish whilst two strips of forest lined the watercourse.

"Useless for larger settlements, despite all the fertility," said the Commissioner-General. "Maybe some farmers can settle here later."

The hunters scared away the wolves that were rummaging in the rotting debris and found abandoned camps of Indians with fresh traces of fire in the area. Marching security was therefore now redefined and the wings were brought in, the guard spreading ahead in a wide arc. Everybody was alert and on the alert.

For days they went through the headwaters of the Guadalupe over a bleak, ragged plateau, almost to the north, towards the Pedernales. They were on the watershed between Guadalupe and Colorado and finally descended into the valley of the river that felt like a green garden. There was a ford in the forest that served as a river crossing.

Waldbaer came flying back breathless after having ridden ahead the farthest. "Smoke is rising above the forest so I left the horse and tried to sneak up. Indians are camping on a grassy area on the hillside and I could count forty-six tents. Around the area are oaks, bushy alders and huge cedars. The slope behind the forest is fairly treeless and gives wide views to the east and west—there may be over a hundred redskins."

"We should've known that earlier," said the Commissioner-General as now we've got the river at our backs and it'd be better in front of us but nevertheless we won't go back. Come, Waldbaer, I want to see it."

With shotguns under their arms, the two of them stalked towards the Redskins' camp. Lying down behind a thick cedar, the Commissioner-General rested his binoculars on a root. "Now we've finally got them," he whispered. "Since we're weaker than they, we have to attempt a peaceful approach."

They slowly returned to the river where the party was excitedly and anxiously waiting. The Commissioner-General unpacked presents, red and blue woolen blankets, brass wire, calico and tobacco which five guards carried, Beneh accompanying them.

At the edge of the forest they leaned the shotguns ready for firing against some trees. Herr von Meusebach took a few steps out onto the grassed area and waved a white cloth. They all looked over at the Indian camp but nobody there seemed to notice anything. Finally the Commissioner-General shouted loudly, "Hello!" swinging the cloth back and forth. Now the redskins took up arms and converged at the exit of a camp track.

The Commissioner-General waved once again. Schmitz, his servant, approached him, seized the white cloth at the free ends and, stretching it tight, the two of them held it up high. After some time, three figures emerged from the horde of Indians and came slowly down to about the middle of the slope, stopping.

The Commissioner-General waved Beneh to his side and they slowly climbed up to the waiting men unarmed. As they were almost approaching, General Commissar Beneh whispered, "Look at that guy in the middle! His companions have coal-black hair, he himself is blond. What's this? An eagle feather in long, blond hair. Otherwise he looks like an Indian with deerskin trousers, bracelets and bare torso."

They stopped five paces away from the redskins, their hearts leaping in their mouths.

The Indians raised their right arms in greeting.

"Now we are missing the captain," said the Commissioner-General. "How should we start the debate now? Maybe they can speak English?"

"Gentlemen!" He began, looking into the blond Indian's blue eyes.

He made a gesture to cut off the speech and said, "It is not necessary, gentlemen, we can speak German and from your sign, I recognize that you come to us in peace. The valleys of the Llano and San Saba are the winter resting place of the Comanches. We share the area with a friendly tribe, the Wacos, and are here as a small hunting party under Chief Buffalo Hump.

The main people are camping a few days' journey northwest of here."

He paused to give the Commissioner-General the opportunity to speak. He stood rooted to the spot and stared fixedly at the brown, handsome man who had just spoken to him in the purest of German. Then he bowed as if in a distinguished salon and introduced himself, "Baron Friedrich von Meusebach, Commissioner-General of the Mainz Society for the Protection of German Immigrants in Texas."

The blond Indian slightly bowed his golden-brown body, replying, "von Kriewitzsch from Potsdam." He put his arm on the shoulder of his right companion. The Commissioner-General took a while to explain, "We are on the march to the Upper Colorado area, which the Society bought from Consul Fisher in Galveston."

"You're taking your chances," Kriewitzsch interrupted him, "I'd advise you not to push so hard. The country in the arc of the Colorado is Indian Territory, is fatherland and homeland to thousands and they'll not let themselves be driven off without a bitter fight. Your strength is not sufficient to obtain a victory. So do you want to sacrifice human lives meaninglessly? Make do with what is achievable. In your interest I'll conceal from the chief what you have just said. What message should I bring him?"

After a long consultation with Beneh, the Commissioner-General announced his answer: "Tell Chief Buffalo Hump that the Germans from New Braunfels are coming in peace. Their number in the city on the Comal River is growing larger and they need to search for a new urban area. The land at the Pedernales pleases them greatly and they asked to be able to settle there. They would pay a fair price and not be mean with gifts." Thus the fate of the wagon train to the grant was decided already, finding its end only halfway there.

"I'll make your request to the chief," replied the blonde Indian, and we'll see to it that you soon learn of our decisions." He bowed and went back up into the Indian camp with his two companions.

Down by the edge of the forest, the Commissioner-General's escort had emerged from amongst the trees, looking forward to his return. Julius von Coll still had his hands on his two pistols, as he was not one for negotiation and mediation. "Shoot 'n' go," he had said to his people—for him it had taken much too long. "Attack's the best defense. Besides, we've got to settle accounts with the tribe because of the Captain and Claren."

The Commissioner-General suddenly stopped and touched Beneh's sleeve. "Did I really see and hear that? A Herr von Kriewitzsch from Potsdam? The old Cooper with his leather stocking stories is an orphan boy in comparison! I almost want to ask you to pinch may arm so I can make sure I'm not dreaming. A Prussian Indian!"

He grabbed Beneh by the belt: "This is perhaps our greatest luck so far. The man has got to help us and he will, if he's got a spark of patriotism in his soul!"

Back at the river, the Germans had pushed the wagons together and built campfires. They squatted in front of them telling themselves atrocity stories about Indians. When the Commissioner-General returned, he briefly explained the situation to them and concluded with the words, "I hope they'll not keep us waiting too long."

He urgently pointed out the dangers that would face a further advance into the grant. "It seems to me to be tactically more important to secure the way to the Society area first through a chain of stations. The new town on the Pedernales can be easily taken from New Braunfels under supervision and its development can be monitored. You seem to disagree, Herr von Coll?"

"It's tingling in all my limbs because I'd like to hold the gun under the nose of that brown rabble. After all, we really don't need to beat about the bush with that bunch. Let's get on top of the guys—we'll hunt them down with our good rifles like chaff. I'd target this Potsdam oddball because he's not worth the trouble if he doesn't know which side he belongs to and I wouldn't want to throw away *my* good Prussian upbringing without a real reason."

The Commissioner-General replied, "I consider this path the most dangerous in our situation. You've got to imagine what these people are defending. Our law is written only on paper and rests on our rifles and cannons but they're defending their lives and their homeland. We'll certainly make more headway with skillful diplomacy but we'll keep our weapons in hand and nobody should be allowed to come too close. Think about what would be achieved by a victory that weakened us so much that we couldn't exploit it and if the negotiations go well, the second city will be founded here.

"Should we come to an agreement with the Indians, I'd ask you, Herr Beneh, to stay here and begin the work. I'll ride back to New Braunfels immediately with Coll and organize more supplies of people and material.

"I'll leave the guard with you here, only taking Waldbaer and Schmitz with me. We must try to exchange as much as possible with the Indians against our goods, especially food and tanned hides. Be economical and smart making sure that neither powder nor lead should be given to the redskins."

"Now we have to negotiate all over again for the land that the Society bought from Fisher—this time with the Indians," Waldbaer said to the guards by the fire.

The Commissioner-General had plenty of food distributed because he wanted to keep the people in a good mood. The fires had to be kept burning over night and the guards were doubled. A superficial sleep lay over the Germans. Restless, Ludwig von Coll roamed the woods, from post to post wondering why the Indians were waiting so long with their answer and if perhaps they were planning a raid.

In the light of the fire, one or the other had pulled his knife sharply over his thumbnail to test its sharpness and then put it back into his bootleg. Shivering, the people turned from their backs to their sides and back again, the night being cool and the dew soaking through their clothes.

At about eight o'clock the next morning, the blond Indian and his two companions were led by two guards to the Commissioner-General's tent bringing an invitation to visit the Indian camp.

An hour later, Herr von Meusebach set out with Beneh and a few others carrying gifts. They were received in front of the Kriewitzsch camp and led to a place surrounded by a row of leather tents. In the middle, twelve old redskins squatted on colorful blankets and skins in festive adornment together with Chief Buffalo Hump.

Kriewitzsch stepped forward and reported the arrival of the Germans. The Indians drew together and invited the Commissioner-General and Beneh to sit down in solemn silence. Then Chief Buffalo Hump was given the pipe of peace—a chunky head made of bone sitting on a long pipe. It went from mouth to mouth, each of them taking two or three drags as all faces were looking seriously at the Germans.

The Commissioner-General and Beneh had put on deerskin suits taken from the captain's estate and beautifully decorated dagger-handles shone forth from their broad leather belts.

After some time, Buffalo Hump made a light, inviting movement, and the Commissioner-General began his speech, which Kriewitzsch translated. Herr von Meusebach assured them that he would come with his people on the "white path", the path of peace. They were on a journey north, the purpose of which was to search for old Spanish silver mines. He was pleased to make the acquaintance of Chief Buffalo Hump, whose fame had already reached him from afar.

The Chief made a face. "The people are worried about the invasion of white men," he said through Kriewitzsch. "It's good that they come as friends. The way to the silver mines is far and they are buried in our hunting grounds, so there's no point in looking for them."

The Commissioner-General thanked the Chief replying, "Then we'll finish our expedition and ask only to let us buy land here so that we can establish a settlement."

The Indians looked at each other and were silent as mistrust stood like a wall between the two parties.

Kriewitzsch had been in New Braunfels, disguised as an American trader, already and had heard enough of the plans of the Society but he didn't tell the Indians that they hadn't been masters of their country for a long time. Had they have learned that, then the fate of the Germans would have been sealed.

The Commissioner-General now let his companions enter the circle and put down their presents in front of Buffalo Hump. The redskins followed each item with greedy eyes but none of their expressions betrayed the impression that things were making on them.

Slowly Buffalo Hump arose, thanking for the gifts and stating that the request of the Commissioner-General should now be discussed in the Council of Elders and he would send the decision to him in the white man's camp by the river. That was the end of the meeting.

"For heaven's sake! You can't pull the wool over the eyes of this irrefutable bunch!" cursed Herr von Meusebach on the way back. "But I think Kriewitzsch must be on our side, otherwise things might have turned out quite differently."

The next day the old chief announced his visit to the camp. The Commissioner-General ordered his men to come in and handed out all the reserve rifles to them. The fifty-five Germans stood in front of the edge of the forest at broad attention, the cannon in the middle, behind them a small fire flickering for ignition.

Herr von Meusebach, Coll and Beneh rode towards the Indians who were coming down the slope in a long line. The warriors rode on the right wing, to the left the women and children. All had blue-black hair, in which they had put feathers, wearing pearls, shells and bones to the neck and ears and whole bundles of thick brass rings clinking on their arms. The men wore buckskin trousers, adorned with colored leather or beaded and studded with glittering iron points. Everyone was wrapped in a red or blue woolen cloth under which contrasted with their brown-red painted skin.

They were armed with spears, bows and arrows and only a few had old flintlocks. On each left forearm hung a small, round shield, decorated with all sorts of colors and feathers. On some, the locks of hair from dead enemies were blowing about.

Buffalo Hump rode on the far right wing and on his head he wore fur and the horns of a buffalo. The Commissioner-General moved towards him and when they met, the chief leaned over to him, hugging him several times.

At a signal, the German squad at the edge of the forest lifted their rifles diagonally into the air, a salvo crashed into the blue sky, and immediately afterwards a shot thundered out of the cannon, echoing many times on the valley walls. The Indians' horses shied away and the redskins dragged them back, screeching and swinging their weapons and tearing down the slope. With a jerk they stopped close to the German front.

"That could have been dangerous," Waldbaer said later. "We didn't know at that moment whether it was a joke or serious and we were all pretty scared, which is what they'd probably intended!"

The Indians dismounted from their horses in a free spot by the river and settled in a wide circle, as instructed by the Commissioner-General. Women and children were returned to the forest with the individual animals as the men began to consult.

Buffalo Hump got Kriewistzsch to say that he was glad to welcome his white brother, the chief, Ma-be-quo-si-to-mu, that is, the chief with burning hair, in the land of the Comanches.

For lack of anything better, the commissioner-general handed round a half-length German tobacco pipe in a circle as a pipe of peace. Afterwards, Buffalo Hump declared that they were ready to allow the chief with burning hair to settle at the Pedernales. "We expect a thousand Spanish thaler as a price from the chieftain of the Germans, payable within two months," continued Kriewitzsch. "In addition, the people of the Comanches tribe should be allowed to trade with the Germans."

The Commissioner-General replied that he was happy to agree and invited his guests to a feast. There followed many embraces and endless protestations of mutual friendship as the solemn process came to an end.

Full of curiosity, the Indians ran through the German camp. Herr von Meusebach had a sack of rice cooked, which he had actually wanted to withhold as the most valuable possession of the expedition, and skewers were stuffed with fresh deer meat. A lively barter had already started to develop even before the meal had been prepared. The "squaws" sneaked around the camp, fingering and smelling everything that was foreign to them. They lifted wagon tarpaulins and crawled into the tents, dirty fingers messing up the supplies and lousy children crawling into every crack and cranny, nibbling and trying to steal so by the next morning quite a bit had gone missing.

Until dawn they feasted, promised friendships, dealed, lied and betrayed.

The Indians had their sights on rifles and ammunition but the Germans were wary. Their guns were stacked in pyramids together but Ludwig von Coll, who was against all the horse-trading, kept his weapons close.

"Anyone who dares to take a rifle gets his guts shot out," he said to Waldbaer and Schmitz, who were going up and down with unsecured guns. He also had the cannon fired several times, its mighty bang earning the extreme respect from the redskins.

The Commissioner-General was now standing with Kriewitzsch on the banks of the Pedernales listening to the life story of the man from Potsdam.

"What should I have done then," he said. "I had the choice of dying or putting the guns of the redskins in order. When I agreed, they broke my shackles and I got to work. Since then, eight years have passed. And flee? Where should I go without means, without good weapons? This people are feeling the pressure of the border, which is shifting further and further west. They can't stand by when from week to week the crowd of white men is growing, pushing the Indian back towards sunset, shooting up the game and making the ground arable. Many, especially a large number of Germans, have fallen victim to their revenge, many a scalp testifying to this. Now and then I managed to mitigate a fate but where they're superior they act without mercy.

"I was accepted into the tribe and enjoy the confidence of all chiefs as negotiator and scout. I'd like to follow your request and work for you as an employee of the Society but it might be better if I stayed with the Indians at the moment because then I can experience every decision of importance and can be as useful to you as anyone. My departure would only make people more suspicious and then you'd be in the dark in carrying out all your actions."

The Commissioner-General stroked his reddish beard thoughtfully as the last light disappeared on the water. All of a sudden everything came alive in the bushes on the shore and about twenty squaws suddenly jumped out like cats, grabbing the Commissioner-General and dragging him screaming to the water, laid him down, and held him there. Kriewitz was held by invisible hands on his feet and fell over. Hands were laid across his mouth and he was unable to move. At this point, an Indian woman drew water from the river with a pumpkin ladle and poured it over the Commissioner-General's head. He closed his eyes as a new fall of water poured onto his beard. Quick, brown hands then began to rub his head and beard and press. Curious women's eyes followed excitedly all during the rough washing. When the women saw that the water ran clean and clear from Meusebach's hair and they remained red-blond as before without losing a glimmer of their golden luster, they disappeared as fast as they had come.

Herr von Meusebach stood up, spluttering and spitting. His ceremonial three-corner hat with the white feather had been trampled in the turmoil and his tailcoat with its heavy, silver buttons had been soaked by the water. Kriewitzsch was also now able to rise as the unknown hands had released him, leaving the two looking at each other in astonishment.

Kriewitzsch was the first to laugh, "Herr Commissioner-General, aren't women the same everywhere? They couldn't resist their curiosity anymore and had to find out if your hair was real or dyed. Now they're satisfied and the haunting is over." Thus Herr von Meusebach remained for all future Ma-be-quo-si-to-mu, the chief with the burning hair. Only when the moon rose over the edge of the valley and its light cool and white spread itself under the trees, did Buffalo Hump and his people leave the German camp. Three times the cannon crashed behind them in farewell.

"Thank goodness, finally we're rid of the lousy party," Coll growled as soon as the third shot was out of the tube. "I wouldn't have thrown so many gifts to those bush thieves."

He said this a few times more as he sat together with Beneh in the tent of the Commissioner-General, who summed up the impression of the meeting with the Indians and expressed his satisfaction that they now had a reliable liaison man in Herr von Kriewitzsch.

"The day after tomorrow I'm riding back to New Braunfels," Meusebach continued. "Use every day to make progress here. Maybe we have prospects of still pushing forward to the grant. The march into the Society's territory remains our ultimate goal in spite of everything. Always remember Kriewitzsch—the man has to help us."

The next day Herr von Meusebach had six men move out with spades and hoes to gather samples of the ground and by noon he had staked out a vast tract of land as his personal property. "Now he's chosen the best for himself," people grumbled, "and we get what's left. The devil should get all the misfortune! Now we're sitting here in the jungle, with the Indians behind us and the old man rides back and is letting us sit in this wasteland with this young man Beneh."

The Commissioner-General acted as if he did not hear it and found some work to be done. "I'll say it again—no one is obliged to stay. If you don't like it—go. Perhaps reasons of economy will force us to take quite different measures in the future so that many will long for what now seems bitter and hard."

It was a difficult struggle that most of them had to wage with themselves when trying to come to terms with the harsh reality that was so unlike their dreams, desires, and yearnings.

The people who were to build the new city here were poorer and more dependent, ambivalent and less supportive than those in New Braunfels. Nevertheless, many of them gritted their teeth and began to clear the ground with courage and confidence. Others, however, crept through the day with a secret fiery glow in their eyes like repressed indignant rebels. They only did what they had to do and seemed to wait for the moment that would give them freedom from the tremendous pressure that this alien life had upon them. However, no one could escape the influence of the Commissioner-General and it seemed as if he were looking into the most hidden corners of every heart and felt the most secret emotions of hidden will.

Talking a lot was not his thing but what he did say hit the nail on the head and proved that he knew more than he showed. His decisions were quick-witted and always focused on the whole picture without any regard for the fate of individuals if necessary.

That was how most people experienced him but behind this outside was another human being. Perhaps he was not aware of his second nature and certainly nobody knew. He loved the adventure and that is why he had felt too restricted as a lawyer in

Prussia. In the midst of the sober considerations of a seemingly indomitable sense of duty, he suddenly embarked on a hunting daring that set everything on one card. Then the will to power paralyzed his cool reason and made the man jump around with people and circumstances as if they were just sand in his hands. Many hated and feared him whilst for others he was a haven of trust and security. On the one side, gluttons and drinkers were moaning about him, whilst for the others he was a model of frugality and self-effacement. He valued Zink for his skill and the sobriety of his decisions but he loved Julius von Coll, the daredevil, the indignant of passion, the wayward creative thinker. Between the waves of aspiring targets, he sank into the troughs of inner strife and powerlessness, until, like someone with a factitious disorder, he pulled himself up again with his reviving strength. Across the huge man there was a crack that always hurt and never allowed him to fully unfold the essential aspects of his character, and it made little difference whether it was day or night.

"And then I have another request, Herr Commissioner-General," Beneh said in the morning, before Herr von Meusebach rode back to New Braunfels. "Permit us to call the new town at Pedernales 'Fredericksburg' in honor of yourself."

Meusebach looked at him from the side and squinted. "Agreed, Herr Beneh—only I can only hope that nobody will have to regret it one day because premature praise is a delicate thing. I hope that my name doesn't perpetuate events that nobody thinks back on with joy."

Sitting up, Julius von Coll cracked the riding crop and the little troop set off. Waldbaer rode ahead as always whereas Schmitz held back a bit.

"I wish you a good start," cried Herr von Meusebach to the people who had lined up by the river. "Get to work, so everyone has a roof over their heads before the cold season starts and above all, always remain Germans no matter what!"

The ride lasted four days during which most of the time the Commissioner-General remained silent and gloomy. "Do you think, Coll, that this is going well?" He asked suddenly, as the horses crossed a stone-covered plateau. "The world will probably have to go a long way before plans as big as ours can happen. It often seems to me that it's all coming too soon."

At sunset on the fourth day they rode into New Braunfels. From the tavern of Herr von Wedemeyer one could hear roars and bellowing as croaking voices were yelling a German song. A clarinet squeaked and a dull shuffling in time and loud clapping revealed that dancing was taking place in the dining room.

The Commissioner-General straightened himself up and brought his horse to a halt. "Today isn't Sunday is it?" He hissed hard. "What's going on, why aren't people working? You're drinking brandy — where did you get that from?"

His riding whip in his hand, he leapt up the steps of the porch, forcing his way through the crowd in the dining room. Glassy eyes of men and women looked at him startled, as a gangway was made free. Two rows of colorfully gleaming bottles of schnapps were standing on the bar top. The riding whip swept them with one blow onto the floorboards. The landlord wanted to lean out from behind the bar and stop what had now fallen and splintered but the Commissioner-General grabbed the man by the collar, gave him a clap of his whip, snapping at him, "Man, where did you get that poison?"

Wedemeyer looked at him with puffy eyes. "Traders were here," he stuttered. "The poor people just want a…" The Commissioner-General interrupted him harshly, ordering the now sobered people, "Out with you! No penny shall be paid and as long as I've anything to say here, not a drop of schnapps comes back over that threshold!"

The tavern became empty as, grumbling and mumbling, the guests disappeared.

"Ah! These gents are already trying to push their way in with their business here — what are their names?" The Commissioner-General ruthlessly continued his interrogation.

Wedemeyer answered weakly, "There were three, Nußpicker, Kuhschmertz and Reinfall. They bought a load of liquor on credit"

"They'll never receive their money," Herr von Meusebach thundered. "And if they ever come back here, I'll shoot them to pieces!"

Meanwhile, Coll had ridden ahead to announce to Zink the return of the Commissioner-General and when he arrived, he was still excited from his experience in the pub. After a short welcome the engineer handed him a letter that couriers had brought from Carlshafen. Herr von Meusebach read and became pale.

He repeated aloud:

"Almost every day, ships arrive and bring people from Germany. There are already a thousand people in Carlshafen. According to reports, a few thousand are to follow before the spring."

He lowered the letter saying, "Did you understand that, Zink? A few thousand!"

The guard in front of the Sophienburg stopped and listened on the way from one end of the spacious house to the other. Nightbirds whirred past, their calls sounding like wailing. There was still light in the large room behind the porch as floorboards creaked under heavy men's boots. "What's his problem?" Thought the guard. The Commissioner-General was alone after dismissing Zink and the news from Carlshafen bore like a burden on his soul, the heavier it pressed the more he imagined what the coming months would bring.

"Who can accept responsibility for that before God and man?" asked Herr von Meusebach, staring into the flickering light of the candle. "Have they lost their marbles in Germany? Koechert didn't write anything about money coming with them. Only people, thousands of people! I see them coming like an army of worms threading its way over the rolling land, with hope in their eyes seeking New Germany. What do you reckon?"

He laughed hard, walking up and down, "Can I help them? With two hundred thousand dollars it would be easy but most are coming with nothing but a miserable bundle of worthless junk. We dare not focus on each person's need or each individual's yearning! What will become it all? The land is broad, its sky so high and cold that the loudest scream fades away and all becomes quiet again. Quiet! That which is against reason will be sacrificed and that which is too much will have to regain fit and proportion."

The light from the Commissioner-General's eyes seemed to fade as he stood at the window, putting his forehead against the cool glass and feeling it do him some good. He stared out into the night, searching for nothing. Then he turned around, blew out the candle and went into the next room where his cot was.

"At last," the guard thought. "I'd started to think that the man needs no rest at all but now he'll find sleep."

"Four o'clock," said the relief guard.

In the morning the Commissioner-General called the confidants together for a meeting. They all noticed how pale and sleepless Herr von Meusebach looked.

He introduced the men to the situation in short sentences. Behind all the clarity he was striving for, there was a certain shadow, as if he did not want to say it out loud. "Actually, we don't know anything definite. Koechert writes about a few thousand people who'll arrive over the next few months. That's all. One could just wait and see but he who waits too long can easily lose. They all know how we are. When, a few weeks ago, Messrs Swinford, Graham and Morris came over from Austin, each with a handful of bills of exchange, there were tough disputes. Finally, the suppliers felt the necessity of pulling out their revolvers and threatening me. I managed to postpone the redemption of the presented bills and to borrow a considerable amount on top. That says everything—so I intend to leave immediately to find ways to come to terms with the new situation —but it'll be hard, very difficult."

The men listened and tried to understand him but the last sentences remained unclear to them.

"Messrs. Zink and Coll will represent me in my absence. Herr Klappenbach will take over the commercial management and you, Herr Pfarrer," he turned to Ervendberg, who sat pale with narrowed lips at the bottom of the long table, "and you will probably be particularly busy over the next few months. I hope the old squad holds out because the shock troop is still the backbone of the enterprise. The future will put everything that has been achieved so far to the test and only if we meet the challenge will we be saved."

The Commissioner-General pausing and looking up toward the beamed ceiling of the conference room said, laying his hands over his eyes, "Yes, then everything will be saved. So I'm traveling," he continued, "in order to overcome the money worries, first to Galveston and then New Orleans."

In the courtyard of the Sophienburg, Zink said to Ervendberg, "I don't know what to think. Sometimes it seemed to me that he was saying goodbye forever and was arranging his estate beforehand."

From the afternoon until late in the evening the Commissioner-General composed a comprehensive report to Mainz.

Ruthlessly, he wrote, "So there is only one alternative, two hundred thousand dollars—or starving a few thousand people. That's all." With these words concluding the letter.

Then he grabbed the saddlebags, checked his rifle, prepared a good quantity of shooting supplies and put a bundle of papers into his pocket.

Waldbaer and Schmitz had hoped to accompany the Commissioner-General, but he had said nothing. Again, wandering up and down half the night in the great room, he spoke aloud to himself several times, the post between twelve and two o'clock at night understanding the words, "Nature will demand its right and will bring everything into balance again which has tried to prevent it."

Thereupon he threw himself fully dressed onto his cot. Rising up with the sun, he saddled and gave farewell greetings to Zink and Coll, and rode lonely down the hill, through the Guadalupe into the autumnal prairie.

Two weeks after Herr von Meusebach's departure, a party of creditors from Austin appeared and presented bundles of bills of exchange. These men were very determined.

Zink didn't have a choice but to pledge to them a large part of the land that the Society had secured as well as important supplies. He doggedly threw himself into his work, not allowing himself to think lest he should become scared by the confusion of the situation all over again.

One day Beneh came from Fredericksburg. "Help, Herr Zink! My people just don't want to carry on anymore. Such a mixed bunch has nothing in common that can carry and hold things together. There's partly a very bad pack that lolls in front of the forest in the grass, expecting the help of the Society and insisting on its rights. Only a few reasonable people are still working and the clearing work is only progressing slowly. It seems as if people want to destroy themselves through their stubbornness and insistence on principles."

He sat helplessly opposite Zink. "If I can't bring any help like better and more abundant food, medicines and money, then I'm useless. People want to go back to New Braunfels and I'm not sure how long I can rely on the guard. The party goes hunting and robbing ever further away, shooting away the powder and scaring away the game. Before the Indians had broken camp, Kriewitzsch was with me again warning me of the consequences of this behavior which makes bad blood among the redskins and won't be accepted for long because pointless poaching violates their code of hunting honor, challenging them to resist."

"If anyone should have the idea of coming back to New Braunfels, then he can't expect any favors here," said Zink. "Here in New Braunfels things are not progressing as we planned and since we admitted the American shopkeepers, a peculiar recklessness has come over a lot of people. They're buying all sorts of useless land with their last pennies. Liquor and wine are exchanged under the hand and drunk in secret while Ervendberg goes from person to person like a missionary. The cold season is coming and the wind and rain have already started, so the nerve fever is beginning to get at a lot of folks. The hospital tent is too small and Dr. med. Koester is both helpless and lazy whilst turning out to be a cunning businessman. He's running a good bakery with his father-in-law as well as a pharmacy and is in the process of starting up a tavern.

"Despite everything, Herr Beneh, whilst I believe in success, it'll only come about after a ruthless cleansing process. The thousands of new arrivals announced by Koechert will speed it up for sure."

Beneh rode anxiously back to Fredericksburg taking few supplies with him. He had received some money and was ordered to take all that Zink would send him in the near future together with the iron determination to ruthlessly prevail.

The Commissioner-General had crossed the prairie riding hard and had arrived in Galveston exhausted hoping it was still going to be possible to avert the worst. In the harbor he met a crowd of people as ship after ship came in, each dispensing new loads ashore. In between, Klaener walked around, trying to arrange and direct but the Germans continued to come up with the ideas, wishes and demands that the Society's program had awakened in them but nothing had changed after the return of the prince. They grumbled about any delay in the onward journey, insisting on their rights, so that Klaener had to do superhuman things to calm the people down.

Fisher remained gloating in the background, bought the Society's bills of exchange for peanuts and waited for the day when the decision to make or break was in his hands.

Despite all this, the Commissioner-General was able to raise new loans and, with the small amount of funds received from Germany, to satisfy the most burning demands of urgent creditors.

"Herr Klaener, if we were to take stock today, it would be a huge failure. We are Vabanque players and I catch myself since I've been here acting with a recklessness I've never known before, yet that is how one becomes. The people are not allowed to know anything about the true state of affairs—that would be murder."

By the end of the year, twenty-five foreign ships had arrived from Germany that were additionally packed with emigrants who wanted to go to the Promised Land without the help of the Society. Out of a hundred people sent to Texas via Mainz, only twenty-two had paid in full. The rest traveled at the expense of the state, the municipalities or organizations or were supported by the proceeds from collections on their behalf.

The old game of buccaneers and pirates started again. Ships, people and goods disappeared, the Americans became rich and the Germans became easy game in their helplessness.

The Commissioner-General was struck with wild indignation when he sought to reassure and apprehend the people. Since most of them were so poor that they could not live at their own expense, he had shacks and tents built to at least give them a roof over their heads. From the last money he bought a huge load of flour, which had been rejected by the Texas Army. "Now everything's been done that's humanly possible," he explained one day to Klaener, "the rest we must leave to Providence."

Then he traveled on to New Orleans and was again able to get a larger sum of money and to procure supplies. He let everything go to Galveston with the greatest haste and instructed Klaener to immediately forward goods and money to Carlshafen. Consumed and deathly tired, he sank onto his bed in the Grand Hotel. "Done, finished," he said to himself. "Just rest and relax. Now everything has to settle itself on its own accord, struggling through to everything that's possible!"

He left again in the afternoon of the next day and this time nobody knew his destination. He remained missing for more than seven months and nobody had a clue where he was.

Meanwhile, ship after ship was landing in Carlshafen.

"Wilcke, collect everything together that's still left from the summer and can still walk. Move out—we need space!"

Koechert urged him to hurry. "Doesn't it not look like the withdrawal of an army? So it seems that the prince couldn't manage to change anything and it's all breaking over us like a flood whilst Germany is being swept clean!"

Wilcke put a transport together in a hurry, as the situation demanded. The number of oxen wagons was much too small for the amount of people who were being sent on their way and the whole thing looked like a carnival procession. Wrapped in rags and towels, the children squatted closely together under the tarpaulins but there was hardly a family that did not leave a grave behind and a stately cemetery had grown in long rows around Luise Koechert's hill during the year.

"We're sending people out as if they were like fragile ice, not knowing if they are going to arrive on the other shore," thought Koechert.

Wilcke sat with Barbara Klappenbach in the storage barn the evening before the departure whilst the camp was sleeping, Koechert having gone out to leave the two alone.

"Come with me, Barbara!" said Ludwig Wilcke several times. "What do you even want to do here? We have to think of ourselves—we've a right to that, surely!"

Shaking her head, she looked into the candles flittering above the tall box.

"Come, sweetheart, we've sacrificed enough." He put his arm around her and pulled her close. "Above the Comal River stands the new city where we want to put down roots and build. It's certainly time and Koechert will let you go. In fact, he expects you to go, I know. And," he whispered in her ear, "I'm not able to look into the future with happiness — What do you think'll happen here when thousands are lying on the sand? - I feel sorry for Koechert but who thanks him? Is that what is happening here — and will still happen — worth so much that you're both willing to sacrifice yourselves?"

"Yes," she said softly. "Yes, Ludwig, it's worth it! And if you love me, you'd understand why I'm staying that — we've both got to get on with our work — you yours and I, mine."

A vague fear drove Wilcke to continue his courtship but Barbara remained firm.

"Fate has let us both subdue the worst so far," she said, stroking his forehead softly. "I saw many eyes in the hospital tent and witnessed the last glimpses from some of them. Of those who have recovered, some have stayed here and are now serving the well-being of all. Do I have the right to abandon them when something is brewing up which may be worse than anything before? You don't imagine that Koechert asked you to lead the wagon train for your own sake, surely? He placed a new task upon you and you have to get it done. Go, Ludwig, our time will come, but not until later and anyway, what would Koechert think of us?"

Wilcke flared up. "You always talk about him yet who's holding *him*? I want to get out of here but not without you. I want to see healthy, happy people again, I want to create something and no longer be the guardian of poor creatures who watch suspiciously from one day to the next with a loaded rifle in their hands."

She kissed him. "Maybe a life without distrust, being on the lookout and guns is not at all possible here. It seems to me it's the law of this country."

The candle flickered out and the two of them stayed there in the dark.

It was first, just before daybreak that Wilcke slammed the door behind him and stepped into the misty morning, beside him Barbara. The night had shown them their way.

The wagon train was already gathering in the camp and an hour later, the wagon chains were clattering through the gate in the parapet to the west with Wilcke riding at the head.

Two hundred and eighteen people already arrived on Christmas Eve of 1845 in Galveston, after a grueling passage on the three-master "Neptune", having been transferred without a stopover and brought to Carlshafen.

Among them was Cantor Blumberg with his wife and seven children from Kokozko in Kulm County. Blumberg's wife lay ill on a bundle of blankets and had, like most people, been ousted in wet clothes. The family had left home on August 19, at which time the Society of princes and noblemen had seemed to the cantor to be an instrument of God to lead poor people out of their misery. Now he found himself sitting dumb and dulled on the sand, suffering from the burden of responsibility he had taken upon himself.

Many found no accommodation—the round tents of the Society were already crammed full with sixteen people in some of them. When they slept, they had to squeeze together, wrapping their legs around each other. Koechert discovered that he had received twenty-two hundred people around Christmas time! At the end of the year there were still eight hundred to a thousand Germans in Galveston and a whole number of the animals that were to be supposed to pull the wagons had been used to feed them.

Quite a few sought to change their fate themselves as they set off, wading through mud and swamps to the nearest farms, but the farmers did not have a good opinion of the Germans and refused to offer them their rigs, even against exorbitant cartage fees. "No tracks are passable at this time of the year so what good are high cartage fees when the teams get sucked down in the swamps? When spring comes, we need our cattle ourselves for tilling the fields."

So, the days drifted away in hopeless monotony. Quarrels and strife were rife along the camp streets, there was knife-fighting and suicides terrifying the tent occupants.

"I see no other way," said Blumberg to some men who trusted one another, "we've got to break away from this community before it's too late, so I suggest we men move out and seek to lease land for ourselves and our families. Maybe Koechert'll be glad to gets rid of us!"

The others agreed with him and a few days later found them marching off with Blumberg, who took his eldest son Julius with him.

They got through to Victoria having been subjected to life-threatening marches that they only endured because each of them was driven forward by a sense of self-preservation. However, unacceptable leases, obvious fraud and bad soil that nobody would ever have wanted to buy, made it impossible to come to a deal and the men returned to Carlshafen, bitter and worn out.

Firewood became more and more scarce and the collecting gangs had to venture out further and further afield to find any.

Despite Koechert's strict prohibitions, stealing and swindling did not cease. A hearty bartering trade in those tiny bits and pieces which necessity leant value to developed, with many a piece of old family property, a chain, a ring, or a few silver spoons, finally changing hands for the sake of a quick buck. The teacher Wamel from Czarze, a friend of Blumberg, had lost his wife when the ship they were sailing on went down and he was now living with another woman from Hanover whose husband had died in the camp. She carried on an extortionate business with dubious food that nobody knew where it had come from.

Koechert, anxiously worried about the accounts, poured over the books, calculating and counting. With horror he had noticed that large quantities of corn had been gnawed to nothing by beetles and sacks of flour had become moldy.

After an unspeakably difficult ride, Waldbaer, Schmitz and Wessel from New Braunfels came over and reported the disappearance of the Commissioner-General.

"We hoped to find him in Carlshafen," said Wessel, "or at least to learn something about his stay. Where can he be?"

Koechert shook his head.

Quietly, the merchant continued: "The city's like a monster eating itself up. Zink can't cope anymore and the gravediggers are the ones with the most work right now. We met the last wagon train just behind the Guadalupe with Wilcke leading his starved horse by the bridle, walking along pale with feverish eyes and the rest staggering behind. The people in New Braunfels won't receive them well and will try to deport them immediately to Fredericksburg." The two looked at each other in understanding.

"Three thousand people are here now," said Koechert, shaken. "I'm often surprised that they endure and don't grow even wilder and become more brutal. There are always many among them who still hope and believe and there is something grand about this people that cannot be undermined."

The two of them listened as snatches from the sounds of a song drifted across the parapet.

"That's got to be girls and boys," said Koechert. "They're singing in spite of all the misery and are thus becoming my best helpers."

---

The arc of the sun was becoming higher and farther over the awakening land as early in the spring of 1846, the waning winter was fading out of the unknown plateaus and mountains of the interior. The sea stretched under the warming sun far and peaceful.

Koechert was standing with a group of men in front of the storage barn, putting his hand over his eyes and looking out into the blinding light, "Almost eight hundred have died in the last few months, Herr Altstaedter," he said to the tall man who was looking into the distance beside him. "It was almost a leisurely time when you drove the oxen around to buy food for the people and at that time, only hundreds had to be provided for. Around five thousand people have arrived here since autumn and I feel as if we've had to go through hell. There are no words to describe what distress and confusion transpired here on these sands." They looked down onto the crowds of people.

"What can we say about New Braunfels!" said Altstaedter "What we experienced on the way from there to Carlshafen was horrible. Look at us, Herr Koechert, we're now just eight men and two died on the way. The last remnant of will to live and the deep outrage from the city on the Comal River drove us away. We've saved so much strength and cash that we could dare returning to Germany and nothing shall be spared from their Lordships in Mainz—so help me God!"

Koechert looked at the eight men whose clothes were worn and shoes tattered, their scraggy white beards framing their emaciated faces in which a wild determination nonetheless burned.

"Come in, let's finish our indictment in the barn," said Koechert. He reached into the pocket of his coat and pulled out a letter. "Everything has conspired against us—I received this letter a fortnight ago from our agent Klaener."

They sat on boxes and sacks, Koechert reading, "It has become a fact that has been whispered for weeks—Texas and Mexico are at war. That changes our situation fundamentally. First of all, the Torrey brothers in Houston informed me that they could not comply with the contracts concluded with the Commissioner-General for the transport of our compatriots from Carlshafen to New Braunfels, preferring to suffer the damages they would have to pay if they withdrew from the contract. Herr von Meusebach had forced the prices down so far that it was no longer worthwhile, the transports for the Texas army being more lucrative.

"Shortly thereafter, the government issued a regulation about transport. Thereafter, all draft animals and wagons of the whole country have basically been seized and have to be made available to them as needed. Immediately I tried to get the necessary vehicles and teams released, but it was not possible and I hardly dare to imagine what this means.

"The same thing happened with food. All supplies have to be kept available for catering for the army and the government is buying whatever it can lay its hands on. Should it be at all possible to provide for our needs, it'll only be possible in a roundabout way and at prices far above the usual. If necessary, an attempt must be made to obtain food from the northern states via New Orleans but that too will be difficult. Moreover, there is always the possibility of their seizure by the state. I want to try everything but I can't give firm commitments due to the uncertainty of the situation.

"The city council of Galveston is increasingly putting pressure to bring the eight hundred people here to Carlshafen. Fifty are ill with fever, dysentery and scurvy and the city administration makes the point that the German immigrants jeopardize law and order and form a constant source of infectious diseases.

"Around three hundred people from the village of Steinbach in the Ore Mountains came with the last sailing ship, The Marn. Sure, they're able, good people but they were so poor, ragged and miserable that at first I didn't dare to take over the landing surety for them. They would have to be returned to Germany by ship but very few would have survived that. They begged and begged and finally, the poor people wailed at me so long that I deposited the surety. The captain had been furious when he realized the return load he'd be facing.

"Where's the Commissioner-General? Who should I settle decisive questions with in the future?"

Koechert put the letter to one side.

"This with the war, the transport and food sounds like a death sentence," said one of the men who wanted to travel back to Germany.

"I implore you, don't spare their Lordships in Mainz. We owe our misery to their paper plans, their money-making and their reckless hopes. Write down everything. Only now do I feel how dull I've become when it comes to remembering details.

"According to Barbara Klappenbach's findings, about twenty people died each day this week. Whole families have been wiped out and all regular nursing has ceased. I tried to stop the mass from sinking using persuasion and force and yet I didn't get through to them. Thousands have so far quietly disappeared and one can only guess what may have become of them"

A shadow fell through the door as a man in a long, brightly patched frock coat came in. Koechert took a few steps towards him. "Thank you, Mayor, that you have come to tell the men about the fate of your community." He pointed out the door, "Down there, to the left of the old hospital tent, is the rest of a community from Upper Hesse — and here's your mayor — now speak please, mayor."

"Yes, what's there to say? Our village was in the middle of the lands of Count Isenburg who wished to round off his possessions. So an influential man was offered a large sum if he could persuade the community to emigrate. We stood up against it but he managed to win a few troublemakers by giving them a Judas wage and who then helped him. Yet most remained firm because they didn't want to leave home.

"Now it was said, 'harass the fellows until they get totally fed up!' We were individually attacked and maltreated and it was literally raining threatening letters. Even our windows were smashed and they threatened to burn the farmhouses. Our appeals and complaints were all to no avail.

"In the end they had us where they wanted us and we sold house, yard and field to the count, entrusted the proceeds to the Mainz Society and set off to Texas. A third part of my people have already died but what will complaining change about it all now?"

Clenching his hands on his knees he remarked, "And the living, even though they are almost all related to each other are housed together like spiders in a pot, wanting to annihilate one other because each of them considers the other to be to blame for their fate. I begin to wonder if the old God is still alive." After a pause he added, "We want to try and send the strongest amongst us to New Braunfels at the end of the week, hoping that at least some must finally find their destination."

"So long as there's a God in heaven, this shan't be concealed from their Lordships in Mainz," cried Altstaedter, raising his fist threateningly.

"Please make sure to also note these recent facts", said Koechert excitedly, "the Mecklenburg government sent ten prisoners released from the Dreiberg Penitentiary under strict surveillance to Bremen with the three-master 'Dyl'. There were two robbers amongst them who had to serve a life sentence. The ship 'Franziska' brought the burglar Beelitz from Spandau. The Klinge family from Wolfenbuettel, a closed gang of thieves, caused a great deal of mischief in the camp. During the crossing they stole everything they could get their hands on and stirred the camp up so much that I had to have the eldest son shot. These are just a few cases. Try to get in touch with the press because, even if they keep their ears anxiously shut for a while, something has to slowly leak through and they'll listen. Only educating the public can prevent further mischief."

The merchant Altstaedter from Darmstadt sat down together with the other men. They wrote down everything about the suffering of the Germans in Texas, leaving out nothing. Then they set off with an empty barge taking them to Galveston whilst the eyes of those laying on the sand followed them full of longing and envy, musing if there was anything more which would bring more happiness than returning home.

Captain Buechel, the spokesman for a group of men, said the next day, "Herr Koechert, now the time has come. We've contacted the Government of Texas and want to form a German Voluntary Corps under my leadership. We're some three hundred men in all who've decided to join the Texan army. The liaison people came back today and the government undertakes to house, nourish and dress our families in empty barracks for the duration of the war.

"We'll be moving away in the next few days and the government's sending enough teams of horses from Houston to pick us up. Our decision is immovably firm and we think that in this way, the chances of being alive are a little better than if we were slowly decaying here on the sand. We only have one more question, what about our rights in the grant? Will we keep them?"

"Only the Commissioner-General can decide that," replied Koechert. "I've not communicated with him for some time but I promise to do everything I can for you."

Silently, the men turned around and due to the gravity of their desperate decision, there was little else to say.

A few days later a long wagon train stopped at the camp. The government was in a hurry because it urgently needed soldiers. To those who stayed behind, their departure seemed like a journey to happiness. There might have been some six hundred Germans who moved out to sacrifice themselves to the new homeland. Most of them succumbed as time and space devoured them and following generations hardly remembered them. The development of America stormed over it in rapid steps, where a few handfuls of alien mercenaries in comparison were as nothing.

The Cantor Lumberer had been able to lucratively sell his fields before leaving home and a handsome sum was still left. The strong thaler sat securely sewn in his waistcoat lining. Now he cut it open and put the coins in rows next to each other on the lid of a heavy box. "Mother, if we're lucky," he said, considering, "then the farmers in this remote area don't know anything about the seizure of the wagon train cattle. The money would be enough for two yoke oxen and I can then put our wagon together. The roads have become firmer in the meantime and so then we'll be off."

The sick woman raised her head and smiled. "The time will come—if I should live to see it!"

"See what a good idea it was that I disassembled and took our wagon with us! At the time, you didn't want to know about it. Today it's worth more than its weight in gold."

Lumberer was on the road for a few days and came back with a yoke of oxen for which had given almost all the money. The wagon had been put together, everything packed up and the cattle harnessed. The mother lay softly bedded in the front and wore a happy glow on her face.

"You want to dare it alone?" asked Koechert. "Take a gun with you and I'll give you some cartridges." Giving a bundle of letters to the Cantor to deliver to Coll and Zink, he continued, "And contact Coll about your claims, maybe he'll have some more money. My cash is almost gone. Happy travels!"

The gate in the parapet was open and no one was keeping watch. "Who is going to come here and do something to us?" The last post had stated. "There is nothing to be collected, only illness."

After Gonzales, Lumberer met with a rider and someone on foot. "We've come straight from Galveston," the rider said as they sat together by the fire. "My name is Soergel, I was a bookseller and I'm from Eisleben. I met Herr Scheller on the way. He wanted to make the way from Houston to New Braunfels on foot. Only Germans and Negroes walk, say the Americans. So I took him with me and we rode in turns. I was with two Germans before but since the going was too slow, they rode on without us."

The next day they met an American outfit. Scheller came to an agreement with the stranger, hiring him for eight dollars a month as a servant. "Better than nothing," he said as he bid farewell. "I haven't a penny and I'll send my wages to my wife. I can't do anything else for her."

It rained almost every day. Soergel often had to harness additional beasts to pull the sinking wagons out of the morass. Everywhere they found the horrific traces of people who had traveled the same path in front of them. After twenty-six days, Lumberer and his companions arrived in New Braunfels. He had to leave some of the baggage on the way, as the children, one after the other, contracted dysentery, having to be put into the wagons.

All reason seemed to have been obliterated in the city. The grousers and troublemakers were saying, "We want to move on to the grant! Where's the Commissioner-General? He'll have gone off and spent all our money or Indians have killed and robbed him. Maybe he's even sitting on the Riviera frittering away all that belongs to us! Leave the fields be, anyway, who should be left to reap the harvest if it carries on like this?"

Finished and semi-finished log cabins were sold off for peanuts. Except for a few, the men of the patrol troop had been carried off by the fever. Property passed from one hand to the other and work that had taken months was bartered away for a few sips of schnapps, making sure the taverns at the market did not go empty.

Zink had made some ticket money in order to yield to the crowd. It went from hand to hand at a fixed rate but the Americans did not bother with it in their shops and gave their wares at three to four times the price that one would pay in Germany.

A new innkeeper, who called himself Count von Donop, had opened and was making deals and close by, an incredibly fat cook, who used to work in a royal kitchen, opened a "prairie-dining-house", which was always well patronized. People ran about, crazy and arrogant in motley ragged clothes as if they were no longer of this world. Young boys clinked thaler-sized spurs onto their high boots with daggers, pistols and flashing knives being hidden behind fanciful belts. Course full beards proliferated on the pale faces and in the alternation from heat to cold they would threw garish blankets over their shoulders, whilst others were wearing brown, shaggy buffalo skin. Everyone swarmed as if in a fever of the happiness they wanted to have, only nobody knew where it was to be found yet enjoying its warmth. In comparison, what a contrast were the few industrious and conscientious who had remained faithful, who on the other hand managed to stay silent and dogged and who never lost sight of their goal.

The hospital barn was filling up more and more and it looked like an abandoned army camp in which the raiders and wounded had been left behind. The dead were poorly buried and wolves scraped out the corpses at night, polluting the air. "Let's enjoy life today," many shouted, "maybe we'll be dead tomorrow!"

Like an apostle, Ervendberg ventured into the wildest bedlam and sought his way to their souls. He went to the bar tables, to the gamblers, to the dancers and tried to save those that could be saved. No one came to the small wooden church on the main street with its empty window holes and for many hours he would be down on his knees in front of the altar wrestling with God for salvation and renewal.

However, the disaster continued as the plague found its way from the coast to the city and now raging. There was dancing in a wooden barn at the market where the sick, whose death was already in their limbs, roared around in desperate exuberance and became intoxicated. Weinreich sat on a raised place in the corner, his clarinet squeaking and making music that pierced the ear. The dancers panted in the heat, already staring with glassy eyes into the abyss waiting to devour them. A dance of death floundered across the planks of the room as Weinreich drank and howled with inner agony. He stared into the crowd of stomping dancers and, every now and then, he slapped the end of his clarinet on someone's shoulder and shouted, "You're the next one." at the same time naggingly laughing, "I'll bury you this night! Hey you—go and dance!"

The two Berliners had given up their position as gravediggers. Weinreich, with a few others, had become their successor for a high fee. "No, Hein, it's not for us, death has already kissed all of them. Let's dig—but no more holes for the dead.

We have to carry on as if we couldn't care less. We were willing to work but what did we get out of it—you know—a tiny house. Haven't you seen how our three chickens carry on with their rooster? Man, that's how we know why we can't blame ourselves. They should do what they want—just leave us in peace."

The two kept on digging and with every seed they put into the ground, they felt as if they were planting themselves into it.

"The Pastor's bringing someone in day after day", said Wilhelm Piesicke, "and the man still seems so quick-witted. What'll become of the children when he's not around to take care of them?"

Ervendberg collected the orphans together, spending days on the road and venturing out into the prairie alone to save the abandoned that he found along the way. He had taken up and looked after sixty of them by the end of the year, nursing and educating them during the following years until they were able to fend for themselves.

At the Sophienburg, the leading men were sitting filled with anxiety but very much alert. "That's the purifying process," Zink said, "and it has to prevail. The foam is scum boiling over leaving the good behind and we've got to concentrate on what's left. Thirty-two children have been born in New Braunfels so far and they and the mothers are our main concern. It was for this reason that a few days ago I had a man who was secretly sneaking up on the scarce supply of milk whipped out of the market. These children are our hope and we're purely the transition point, Coll. In the first instance, the stronger ones are standing upon our shoulders. Somewhere in the distance lies the grant and maybe they'll move into it one day, which makes us only the way and the tool to that end."

Lumberer entered the room where Zink, Coll, and Wessel were sitting. Wessel had returned with Schmitz and Waldbaer from Carlshafen, without any news about the Commissioner-General.

"He knew what was going to happen," said Coll, "and now I realize the meaning of many of his dark words of late."

"Gentlemen," began the trader, "I've allowed myself to be consoled until today. Despite the collapse down there, I have retained enough strength that I want to move on. You promised me a down payment on my balance with the Society and I can now buy a pair of oxen through the mediation of an American to enable me to continue to Fredericksburg which seems a safer place to me because I'm worried that New Braunfels could be included in the war zone."

"Do you think, Lumberer, that the Pedernales are better than here?"

"That's something I have to decide for myself. You promised me that money for the first of July and that's today—so now I want to collect it."

"That which I give you, I have to take from others."

"Then you shouldn't have promised anything. Money won't help many of them down there anyway."

He received thirty-three dollars for a second pair of oxen and left on July 2 for Fredericksburg. On July 14, he crossed the Pedernales only to find a terrible state of affairs.

The churned up and scratchy earth looked as if projectiles had plowed it over. The ground clearing had almost stopped and less than half-finished log cabins were scattered about. Whimpering and moaning sounded from the leaf and earthen huts and the whole place was contaminated. Wilcke's wagon train had carried the diseases of the coast into the interior and here there was no doctor or remedy. With puffed, glowing bodies, their mouths rotting with scurvy, sick people were perishing on the dry grass of the prairie as the living shared the property of the dead. Six hundred people were still waiting here, two hundred had already died and an ox-cart picked up the dead daily from huts and tents, driving them to a pit outside the city. Large troops of Indians were also making the area unsafe, their shrieking song sometimes to be heard from the huts.

Wilcke, Beneh, and Birkel held themselves determinably upright because they felt they were the responsible leaders in all this physical misery and mental attrition.

"How this will all end, I don't know," said Wilcke, when Lumberer asked for allocation of a parcel of land. "We'll be happy if today is not worse than yesterday. At some point this dying must come to an end. What do you know about Barbara Klappenbach? For weeks we've lost all contact with New

Braunfels and Carlshafen." he said, his burning, deep-set eyes looking at Lumberer.

And he then told what he knew about that brave girl.

"She's alive and she has to live," came from Wilcke's mouth. "Now everything's fine and I'm sure we'll survive it all."

Several times Lumberer held a worship service under the trees. He had a special way of expressing self-confidence and trust in the future to those who were despondent and weak and thus became a valuable helper to the leading men. Beneh ran the business, Wilcke surveyed the land and distributed it and Birkel acquired provisions.

Lumberer kept his family apart from the crowd, as he had in New Braunfels but he could not decide to start pushing his spade into the ground because a deep unrest was holding him back. Rolling on his bed sleeplessly, fighting with himself until he eventually saw clearly that his wife and children stood above everything and every step he had fought so far was for the sake of their wellbeing and their safety.

"Herr Beneh," he said one day, "I don't know if I came to Fredericksburg too early or too late but I am now determined to retreat to New Braunfels. Maybe one day I can completely break with the Society."

Wilcke and Beneh tried to talk the man into staying using all their powers of persuasion. "What effect do you think it'll have on the people when you leave us? Doesn't every clear-thinking person here have the task of setting an example against all the weakness and despondency through perseverance? Do stay and help us!"

However, Lumberer did not give in. "On who will we most surely rely upon one day, gentlemen? Only on the family. Just because I see that, I have to act accordingly because, here in a foreign land more than anywhere, the tight-knit family is the cornerstone of any structure."

He loaded the rest of his belongings together with his wife and children onto the wagon, harnessed the oxen and drove the ninety miles back to New Braunfels. Swinging the whip, he walked with firm steps, beside the ox-cart, as if he had never been anything but a settler on the Indian border. Behind all the hardships and all the wanderings, he clearly saw his destination, and he astutely assessed the commitment of strength and means he had to invest in order to carry it through. He was just the kind of man that this treacherous land needed.

As he drove into New Braunfels, he saw a cluster of people crowding its way up the hill to the Sophienburg. There was a smell of schnapps and threatening fists jutted over people's heads, pistols and knives flashing in the setting sun. The Palisade Gate was closed with the crowd jammed in front of it.

"Away with the name!" roared tired out, fragile voices. "It's our misfortune and misery! New Braunfels is done! Where are the men who are living at our expense? Hey, you cowards, you slave owners! Open up!!"

Kicks thundered at the gate that was then opened from the inside. Julius von Coll stepped out, unarmed. With his head held high he his eyes wandered over those in front. "What's going on?" he asked sharply and clearly.

"We demand that the city should no longer be called New Braunfels but 'Comal' from today," cried the spokesmen as the crowd hollered "Comal, Comal," in the background.

"So, that's what you want and you have no further worries? Turn around! Do you see the people out there in the fields? Why didn't they come with you? I'd rather talk to them about it than with you. For the time being it'll stay New Braunfels and anyone who doesn't like it can go. He won't be any great loss and if anyone wants to waste his time on such pathetic things for the sake of ranting and stirring up, then I won't give any food to those who can't leave it alone—that'll mean that there'll be more for those who want to work and move forward!"

He then stepped back and the door closed behind him, as the crowd remained staring disappointedly at the weather-beaten beams. Then off it went, "cheater! Killer! Cowards!" We want go to the grant and not rot here! We demand our rights!"

However, the gate remained closed and the crowd slowly crumbled apart and dispersed, leaving the taverns to go wild in the night.

Soergel took in Blumberg with his family and the two men spent a long time talking. The bookseller from Eisleben was a smart and confident man.

"Slowly the difficulties are easing," he said. "Finally, the diseases will ebb away in the countryside. Nature takes what are hers and everything balances out as death cleans up all weakness. People melt down to a number that is possible to support and I think we're gradually over the top of the mountain!"

## VII

"That's right, let in the sun and the scent of lime trees," said the pharmacist. "That'll do us good and one can certainly use it!"

The landlady from the Klosterkeller in Eisenach opened wide the colorful glass windows.

"What the times bring! Always something new, and afterwards it usually happens differently than you ever expected," grumbled the gaunt man to himself. "He always sat by the stove at that little table and I can still see him as if it were today. It's been a good two years now."

The landlady smoothed her white apron and asked, "Who do you mean, Herr Royal Apothecary?"

"Koechert, landlady, the student candidate Koechert from Stedtfeld. You don't hear anything good about Texas—who would have thought that? I'd like to know how the man is getting on."

"Always Texas, Texas and again Texas", sighed the landlady, "has anything else been talked about at the regular's table for the last two years? The men argue, getting red faces and worrying about things that don't really concern them. As far as I'm concerned..." She made an indifferent gesture as she put the beer mats in an orderly heap.

The apothecary had a stack of newspapers in front of him and was leafing through them searchingly as his eyes settled on something.

"This spring, steamboats happily made their way down the Rhine to Rotterdam with two hundred and sixty-five persons on board. Among them was a pastor with a considerable number of his parishioners. Joy was to be read on the faces of all passengers for they are heading for a happy future in Texas, having been promised mountains made of gold. A notarized document which has been written up in Baden secures them considerable property, tilled fields, meadows and beautiful forests are awaiting them and even places for them to live."

He flipped back and searched for the title: "From Someone Impartial on the Rhine."

"Hm, weird, despite everything, still all these fanfares."

Then he took his notebook out of his pocket and removed some newspaper clippings. "The German Adelsverein has not been lucky in its attempts to colonize the mountains of San Saba. A train of a hundred wagons was attacked by the savages on the way to this settlement and the German emigrants, though they fought desperately, were conquered by the superior force, leaving a lot of dead and wounded in the hands of the Indians." The pharmacist had written "Weserzeitung," in the margin.

The door opened. Carefully, striding out as between two filing boxes, the civil servant Weibezahl came in and greeted the apothecary. "What's the news from Texas?"

"Nothing good, my dear friend. All kinds of contradictions where the adverse reports outweigh the others. The newspapers don't dare to give details but it's enough for anyone who can read between the lines. Here, for example, 'Increasing numbers of emigrants are returning from Texas completely impoverished who want to sue the Mainz Society because they did not receive the land they were promised and for which they had made payments to the society, not even being able to recover deposited funds.'"

"Unbelievable," growled Weibezahl.

"Irrefutable just the same," replied the apothecary. "That was in the Cologne newspaper.

He laid out one clipping at a time before Weibezahl and picked from some apt phrase from each of them, "Already unhappy in the choice of the country whose climate does not suit... That the whole enterprise, after many hundreds of gullible Germans have been lured into an early grave or into the bitterest misery... and here, you listen to this, 'To the Society, the emigrant is like a commodity, to be loaded and transported on ships.'"

Weibezahl slammed his fist on the table and snarled excitedly in his dry voice, "Enough, nothing but evil rhetoric. I'm sorry that you believe such stuff—that such a thing can even be put into print!"

"I'm not finished yet," said the apothecary mockingly, '…miserably deceived by their vision, they will perish or return as ragged beggars.' Deutsche Allgemeine Zeitung. Enough? That'll surely be the truth and considering how cautiously our papers write, in reality things could be even worse."

"Stop!" Cried the retired civil servant Weibezahl with a red face. "How could something like that even be possible?" Violent sneezing shaking him.

"There are answers to that as well, you just have to be able to rhyme everything together," the apothecary continued.

His index finger skipped over the rows of notes.

"Here, if you please, 'Almost all the evils associated with the colonization of the Mainz Society can be regarded as a consequence of the delayed arrival and inadequacy of the funds indispensable to such a large enterprise. Herein lies the fault and guilt of this Society.' If you still don't understand then you can't be helped, Herr Civil Servant!"

"But that is…," roared Weibezahl.

From the door they heard the approach of a hefty babble of voices. The bookseller Jakobi was swinging a notebook through the air and shouting excitedly, "Be sensible, Herr Deputy Headmaster! If a man like this Constant dares to write a booklet against the Society he must be sure of it. You can't disprove with chitchat what the writer saw with his own eyes."

Schaefer swung his long pipe like a sword in defense, "To hell, let me get a word in. Any purchased scrawler can write poison and bile, and you'll believe it all unseen! I'd have thought you were more sensible, Herr Bookseller. I don't want to count the lawsuits that the Society'll hang around this cleancut gentleman's neck because of that lump of muck!" An asthmatic cough shook the excited man.

Behind them, the master plumber Sauermilch squeezed into the bar room. He was sweating with excitement and wiping his bald head with his green apron. "What is there to say," he gasped, "something like that! Unbelievable. Dear Lord, what may have become of Koechert and his wife?"

The three of them settled at the regulars' table and customarily greeted one another by beating their fists hard on the table. Jakobi put the booklet in front of him and churning inwardly read out a few sentences. "A noble intention was the at the root of things that mislead the practical realization, making many people unhappy, whilst those in the care of the Society are wandering aimlessly around the seashore. Colonization at large is a difficult thing and it cannot just consist of plans on paper. The masses were deceived by the semblance of conscientiousness and despite their ethics, the Society has brought in a lot of rascals, people who still have the strength to follow their own goals, gathering together the rest of their belongings and disappearing."

The further the bookseller read, the quieter it became at the table as any resistance against the credibility of the booklet was disappearing before the force of the facts.

"On the wagon train through the prairie, dead and dying people were thrown from the wagons." Jakobi looked up. No one said a word, scared eyes were pressing to read on. The landlady ran her eyes over the corner of her white apron when she heard "The day after, an American found a living child in the arms of its dead mother and he took it with him... Humans were bedded like cattle and were nourished with the remnants of ship's provisions."

The foam on the beer glasses that the landlady had set in front of the men had melted away, nobody even thinking about drinking. The flies could be heard buzzing around as the bookseller slammed the booklet shut.

"Who would've thought that?" The deputy pulled the page of the "Frankfurter Oberpostamtszeitung" on which the program of the Society was printed, out of his wallet, tearing it to shreds, repeating, "Who would've thought that?"

Many were asking themselves the same question in the German homeland at that time as the newspapers eagerly searched for news about Texas in letters that were passing from hand to hand coming from over the water describing the situation of the emigrants, whilst the most outrageous rumors were passing from ear to ear.

One had to be careful because the police were alert and acted where ever they could. The Society was suspicious of public opinion yet acting with indifference on the outside, despite the growing insecurity among a number of its members. A leading figure wrote in a letter: "It is clear we were not offering people a bed of roses so we had to expect some setbacks. I expected from the outset that there had to be some incurably dissatisfied persons amongst such a mixed public. So the national murmur cannot divert us from our task and if nothing else, something has been achieved — we have got rid of certain people forever.

"I suggest that one of the salaried men of the Society over in Texas should be instructed to write a pamphlet that would highlight and duly underscore what has actually been achieved. For a suitable sum it should be possible to find an official Texan department willing to authenticate it. However, my proposal must be quickly decided upon because some of those returning home are already causing great damage and disrupting our work with their fairy tales."

The news about Texas was beginning to leak ever denser and more persistently through to people from unknown sources. The pressure of authority and indifference were no longer enough to curb the rising tide and something had to happen.

The "Mainz Society for the Protection of German Immigrants in Texas" convened a General Assembly on July 10, 1846. Preparations for the big day were in motion in the castle garrison. Liebstoeckl was cleaning the brass rods that held the long, red runner and all door handles gleamed without a speck of dust anywhere. In the kitchen Haeberle the head cook was disappearing into clouds of steam and fragrance in his kitchen whilst the valet of His Highness, Sebastian Schmoller, stood before the high swing doors receiving their Lordships.

The hall on the first floor began to fill. The noblemen were speaking softly as there was something in the air suppressing free open speech. Before entering into the actual negotiations, the clerk Kangelmann was emphatically informed by the chairman of his commitment to secrecy and despite the summer heat, the windows of the hall remained firmly closed.

Count Charles of Castell opened the meeting. Firstly he gave a sober account of the state of affairs, closing with the sentences:

"The commercial virtues of Herr von Meusebach are nothing to brag about. He kept going on at us until the end of 1845, urging us to increase the current funding. The Finance Committee gave in to his relentlessness in two cases and added substantial sums to the regular remittances. Our repeated reminders of comprehensive accounting details have been treated with indifference to date. We therefore had to restrict his right of disposal and granted only twenty thousand thaler on a case-by-case basis. This delayed implementation but gave us the opportunity to keep the initiative in our hands and avoid any hasty expenditure.

"I don't know what might be preventing the Commissioner-General from maintaining commercial tidiness and order. He certainly has enough civil servants in the administration and the structure of the colony has been so well prepared here that he doesn't need to kill himself with work. It's also incomprehensible that in his last report, people are still not in the Society area, which is high time. After all, the circumstances aren't that extraordinary.

"I admit that the foundation of New Braunfels was necessary but it delayed the advance. But why not let the bulk of them go on? We thought of everything in our preparations and the Commissioner-General only needs to roll out bit for bit that which has been worked out here down to the last detail. After all, the main work was done by us! That shouldn't be forgotten. I would emphasize that I cannot imagine that at anytime a settlement undertaking was better prepared than ours. I want to emphatically point that out.

"Who among us would sit here with a good conscience if he didn't know that? The departure of further transports has been terminated during the summer and the next will first go in the fall. As a result, the Texas management have time to do everything the way it was planned here to be done.

"The lack of any further report since the end of last year is incomprehensible to me. To do something about it will be one of the most important items on the agenda. Instead, there are increasing rumors and newspaper articles and venal scribes are committed to denigrating our work in the public eye.

"Preventing this will be an important subject of further deliberations and it has often been that the more a good work is fulfilled, the greater the number of envious and sleazy ones appear. First posterity..."

The door opened quietly as Count Castell abruptly broke off the last sentence, all heads looking up. Sebastian Schmoller pushed his way through the crack, walked on tip toe around the horseshoe table and whispered something in the chairman's ear.

He became somewhat pale. "That's impossible! Tell the people I have no time and that they should come back tomorrow. Any further disruption from him has to be avoided!"

The valet bowed low and said, "Very well, as the Herr Count commands."

As if nothing had happened, the chairman once again began his last sentence: "Only posterity will appreciate how unselfishly and..."

There was considerable noise at the door as it was torn open and then slammed shut. An angry man's voice could be heard saying, "It just can't be — we have to speak to their Lordships!"

Schmoller's livery wedged itself backwards into the gap for a moment. He was heard whispering placatingly while the assembly pricked their ears.

"We want our rights!" Exclaimed the voice outside. "And anyone who has a clear conscience can listen to us without embarrassment!"

Whilst these words were being spoken Altstaedter rushed in followed by the rest of the Texas home-comers. "So we find their Lordships all assembled together — we couldn't have come at a better time!"

The Chairman shouted, his face red-hot with rage, "What do you want? Do not disturb us!"

"To tell the truth, nothing more than our rights, nothing more — plus the rights of all the dead and living who can't be here!"

Some of the noblemen jumped up, eyeing the intruders with disapproving glances wondering who were these men with their long, tangled hair and beards and yellow, sunken faces.

They were standing, legs astride, behind Altstaedter, allowing their eyes to wander accusingly across the table.

Prince Moritz von Nassau punched his fist into a pile of newspapers, calling into the oppressive silence, "Who are you, what do you want here?"

"You'll soon hear about it," answered Altstaedter coldly and firmly." I've come with my friends via Rotterdam on the most direct route from Texas. As you see us, tattered and penniless, we've emerged from those dying in great numbers and are fortunate enough to find the men who are to blame for it!" He laughed hollowly and made a long movement from left to right with his arm. "These are the ones," he said again, looking towards his companions.

"I'll have the police called," shouted the chairman.

"Please do," Altstaedter answered. "Then I'll say elsewhere what needs to be said. Nothing will stop us and we'll not be intimidated!"

The men around the horseshoe table stuck their heads together, talking excitedly. "Let the men talk," suggested Prince Frederick of Prussia.

Altstaedter did not await a decision but began speaking in a firm voice, "I won't go into the reasons that led you to start the Texas settlement project. Let's assume that it was really philanthropic—although some would say otherwise..."

The murmurs of the noblemen faded as they looked at Altstaedter with outraged expressions, listening unwillingly.

He continued, "None of you will claim that he knows the land over there that the Society's bought. None of your agents have ever seen it, not even Fisher and it's still in the possession of strong Indian tribes, despite the contract with this man. All your promises were exaggerated and fulfillment impossible. The plan for the whole thing was much too generous given the available means. As a result, far more people were shipped to Texas than could be accommodated in real terms, whilst setbacks hadn't been included in your calculations at all!

"You wanted to set up a German colony based on paper calculations but Texas can't be forced into a mold from the planner's desk because it works according to its own law. Some valiant men committed their lives in the indescribable need, preventing the worst but couldn't be pushed beyond the limits of their will and strength. You can't even guess what you have to thank these men for. It's only because of them if the German reputation in that foreign country hasn't been completely trampled under foot."

"Take it easy, sir," Prince Moritz von Nassau burst out indignantly, "You'll have to answer for your words!"

"With pleasure," cried Altstaedter, "truly with pleasure. Then everything will be revealed! I'm happy with every way that serves the truth and to you is not the only place I'll go!"

The chairman swung the bell. "Control yourself," he cried, "or I must deprive you of the word. I caution you! These present could certainly testify to what they have just heard!"

"That would be fine for me!" exclaimed Altstaedter, turning around, "Here are my witnesses! The truth is on the march and can't be stopped anymore. We owe it to those whose poverty and weakness forces them to stay in Texas and we don't come to avenge ourselves and cause a stir because that'd not improve things. We're only demanding justice and help!"

"Do you want to threaten us with this last sentence?" Asked the chairman mockingly. "Stop! Let them talk! Unheard of!" shouted the noblemen.

Altstaedter did not allow himself be put off. "Some gave us their last pennies so we could travel to Mainz. We *will* talk, if not here then elsewhere, even if it does make you feel uncomfortable. The abundance of misery we saw is so monstrous that nothing can silence us as it's all about the lives of several thousand people."

The air in the room weighed heavily upon everyone.

"In May, we set out from New Braunfels and went back the way we had come months before together with many others full of hope into the interior of Texas. We passed wagons with sick people, we found lone wanderers collapsed along a way lined with graves. Eaten by vultures to the bone and bleached by the sun, human remains lay in the tall grass of the prairie. Dead people were sitting by extinguished fires and we saw dying people rummaging through their possessions before their end, as though seeking to draw strength from the things they carried with them as a remnant of home and custom. Laundry, tools and kitchen utensils were scattered around, as this all no longer had value for anyone. Fever, dysentery and scurvy eventually also broke the toughest will. What may some have suffered before their last breath blew in the glowing breath of the prairie! All this, your Lordships, was not in your program and nobody knew anything about it before!"

It was sombre in the hall, Altstaedter's words opening up even the most arrogant hearts as he described the terrible fate of the German emigrants in bitter accusation whilst the assembled gloomily listened to him.

Concluding his speech and raising his voice he said, "It's too late now and won't help to point the finger. We need help! Send money and refrain from sending the rabble and scum! Many good German sorts were dragged down by the example of those that'd gone off the rails! Despite everything there are still individuals and whole families who're ready to sacrifice themselves full of energy over there and even, after everything bad and helpless has been lost, they'll carry the settlement into the future. The Society shouldn't tally the praise for this to their account because its plan is dead — now it only has obligations."

It took a long time before the chairman dared to break the onerous silence and in a low, inhibited voice finally saying, "From what we've just heard, it's necessary to fundamentally change the agenda."

Silently, the men assembled around the horseshoe table nodded.

The Texas men saw that their job was done here. Before they left the hall, Altstaedter exclaimed, "We will bring our claims against the Society before a proper court because it's important for anyone returning to know how the law stands for him and the Society."

The General Assembly of the Mainz Society decided on July 10, 1846 to send an agent via the quickest route to Texas. He should, equipped with appropriate funds, investigate the situation of the enterprise and supportively intervene. The decision described it as an important task of the representative to identify guilty and negligent persons in the administration, to sentence them and, if necessary, to dismiss them.

Zink and Julius von Coll sat on the veranda at the Sophienburg. It was Sunday and from the market the bell was calling to the church service.

"I believe that when this murderous summer's over, we'll be out of the woods—look at the fields out there! They're increasing all the time and on Sundays farmers can go to them and look at the fruit just like back home.

"I have feeling of certainty that we've passed the peak of our suffering and we've almost forgotten to keep asking each other the question that was so important, 'Where's the grant?' That's good because it took away our strength from doing the job here. Only in Fredericksburg are things still bad and Wilcke has to bear the whole burden because Beneh isn't equal to the circumstances. Yet even there, nature will speak the last word, leaving only those who are useful and fit behind."

After a while Coll said, "I see the development so far that a third of the people who came from Germany are dead or seriously ill. The second third broke away from the Society and disappeared—the majority of these will have gone down and only a few will have found suitable land, making it into something. The last third stayed here and will make their way through it all. These are just my guesses because there are still a few hundred people left in Carlshafen."

The bell below stopped ringing and the two of them looked over at the extensive sick camp. "What force is behind this Ervendberg!" Zink said, resuming the conversation. "He's pushed aside bigmouth Koester, taking over everything from him that he should have been doing, leaving the guy free to bake bread, hand out schnapps and extract the last penny from the rabble which goes around with him. And that pharmacy of Koester's is a junk shop. How happy Wilcke will be when he receives my letter with the comments from Koechert! Just imagine, Ludwig Wilcke has become a father! 'It's a strong boy, and the mother is fine,' wrote Koechert. 'Happy Barbara lies in a corner of the hut holding the child in her arms as all her charges crawl and teem around her, all the small fry which she wrested from death. Many have been recruited for the Texas army. Klaener has already provided part of his private property as collateral for loans to help us—without him we'd have starved to death.

"I've started to hold school. You need to see us and hear us, how we are writing, reading and singing. At the same time I feel something awaken in me that had been hidden as I begin to realize what these circumstances have made of me! As soon as the situation permits, I'll get the rest of the people who are still here on the march. Vices and debauchery of all kinds as well as the physical and mental inactivity are corroding attitudes and self-confidence. Nothing bodes well in the gloomy huts. Where's the Commissioner-General?' — I just remembered that from Koechert's letter."

"Yes, where *is* the Commissioner-General? What would he think about the election we're holding today after the church service?" Asked Coll.

"I could no longer evade the insistence of the Texas authorities in Austin," Zink replied, "and have organized everything so that I can answer to anyone. You know of course that they called for our city to set up a local government under Texas law, I suppose. Only men who've been here for at least six months will be eligible to vote, eliminating all the insecure political adventurers who've recently arrived. I refused to allow the occupation of the various offices with employees or officials of the Society since I want to keep Society and local administration clearly separate and I expect the community will survive the Society anyway.

"Since the Germans can't speak and write English, I nominated some of our best Texan fellow citizens for the most important posts. Judges, court clerks, sheriffs, magistrates, coroners and judges for guardianship and probate matters must be elected. This election will draw a clear line under the wild development so far and assigns us into the Texan state system. With that, New Germany is finally buried and we're once again under the law. This July 13, 1846 is a turning point in our fate — it makes us Texans."

July 15, 1846 had been exceptionally hot. The edge of the sky threatened thunderstorms but the storm did not break. New Braunfels was like a red-hot bell, dry and dull, thirsting for rain and coolness but the coming night brought no refreshment.

Zink was still sitting in the office, working. Outside, Waldbaer threw the gate shut, put the securing beam behind it and noisily slid the bolts into place. His was the watch from ten o'clock to midnight and his footsteps sounded hard on the well-trodden path behind the palisade wall.

The threatening thunderstorms slowly moved eastward, spitting yellow flames into the night sky. Sulfurous light twitched through the embrasures as the silence over the city was as heavy as lead.

Waldbaer stopped and listened, stopping suddenly he halted and drew his rifle as hoofbeats could be heard coming up the mountain. "Three to four horses," he thought. "The horses seem tired and thrashed out." He heard them stumble. "Come out watch!" his voice penetrated through the silence. The men crawled out of their bunks in the guardroom and took up their guns. Schmitz put a light to the big hurricane lamp and soon the six guardsmen were standing behind the gate armed with a rifle ready to shoot at the point where the riders had just stopped.

His hand on the gun in his belt, Zink had gotten up and was walking to the open window as he heard someone jump from a horse and hit the iron knocker hard against its base several times. Waldbaer took his time before pushing back the bolts.

"Open up for God's sake—we need help! Looks like you're scared out of your wits!" cried a rough, deep voice impatiently that sounded as familiar to everyone as a call from home. The locking beam was pushed to one side and the gate flew open.

Schmitz raised the lantern and Waldbaer stepped out. "Herr Commissioner-General!" He shouted in alarm, as if he had seen a ghost in the face before him. "Is that really you?" He grabbed Herr von Meusebach's hand as the lantern threw a yellow glow over the figures of the new arrivals. Behind the Commissioner-General two women were holding tired horses.

Zink hurried into the yard exclaiming, "Herr Commissioner-General—You're alive—Thank goodness!" The two movingly shook hands.

"Yes Zink, why are you so surprised? I've got to live because we've got to carry on—gosh, that *was* a hot day!" He was struggling to stand firmly, "Help the ladies of the horses!" He turned to the guards, who still couldn't understand that the supposedly dead man really stood before them.

The two women slipped out of their saddles and stepped into the light of the lantern. "Frau Elisabeth Stegner with Fräulein Cordula, her daughter, relatives of a friend," introduced the Commissioner-General. "They'll stay here until Stegner, who settled in Louisiana and has had some misfortune, has found something again."

Throughout the night, Zink was sitting with the Commissioner-General in the great room of the Sophienburg. The torment of eight months of difficulty burst from the depths of his heart as Herr von Meusebach recounted what he had been through.

"I don't want to justify myself, Herr Zink," he said, rather up tight, "but you should understand me. At first I thought it would be possible to fill our empty coffers with new loans. I chose all the cutthroats of this vast country to hawk money from them. I went out to New York but Fisher, the most dangerous of all bandits, did his work well and wherever I came, the seeds of his smear campaign had sprouted everywhere. I could barely get enough to even keep myself afloat. Fisher had deliberately destroyed the last remnant of prestige that the Mainz Society still possessed.

"Under such circumstances dealing with those thus incited, thawing the ice of mistrust by describing the sufferings of our compatriots took the last of my strength. In many cases I in fact achieved the opposite and they closed their minds and derided me. 'What's with such people?' mocked a money-man in St. Louis and he looked over past my shoulder and didn't even invite me to sit down. 'What do you want to do with thieves, whores, arsonists and bankrupts, with useless politicians, deserters and all the other scum? You won't even get a penny for that anywhere and we've got enough such dogs of our own!'

"There was nothing I could do and it was just the same with him as many others. I sold my valuables in order to live enduring every humiliation because I still hoped." He paused and with wide blue eyes looked at Zink, who was intently listening, his heart throbbing.

The Commissioner-General continued, "One day Fisher changed his tactics, having me followed and hounded until I ended up with the creditors on my back. The police were looking for me and a few times I only narrowly escaped debtor's prison. I was like a fly fidgeting in the web of the spider. Everywhere, 'Fisher, Fisher, Fisher!' was being screamed into my ears. I fled from farm to farm, friends and acquaintances hiding me. For a while, I was very close to the Nassau Farm and the pursuers lost my track but yellow fever seized me and in confused dreams I saw our people being poured into a mill that only surrendered the best."

He took wide strides as he walked back and forth in the room. Zink saw the furrows that grief and illness had grooved into the General Commissioner's face. Then Herr von Meusebach stopped and, sucking in deep breaths of the air that came in through the open window, remarked, "It smells different now, Zink—better, healthier, smelling of field and sweat, work and success but I know for certain that there were ashes and garbage, and it seemed to me in many a fever of the night as if I was being crucified for those down there, whether they were dead or alive. A presumptuous comparison, Zink but it was so. When I finally realized I could make no progress, I called upon the Society management for help in a flood of letters. From what I wrote to them they'd no longer be able to avoid the matter. I'm sure that the requested funds must arrive any day now and it was this confidence that gave me the strength to return. Whatever happens now it can't get any worse!" The Commissioner-General closed the window and pressed his hot forehead against the glass as he had done the night before his departure.

"Not once did you send us even one message, why?" Asked Zink. "It would have been much easier for us and for you."

"I wasn't allowed to, Zink!" cried the Commissioner-General, obviously in agony. "I wasn't allowed to because I had to leave the way open for you. That's the only way you could've sworn in an emergency any time that my stay and my fate were completely unknown to you."

Zink succinctly and clearly began his report on the past few months. Finally, when after several hours he had finished, the Commissioner-General took his hand and said firmly and warmly, "Thank you, Herr Zink, you certainly managed more than I did. The summer will pass and then death must finish its harvest and the living have won. After this cleansing we're one with the land for all times and it must now let us live as good Germans in Texas!"

Even before midnight, one of Waldbaer's guards had taken an hour's leave and had rushed down to the town to bring word of the return of the Commissioner-General to Thomas Schwab and some of the most faithful. Before daybreak it had flown from hut to hut and from camp to camp. In many hearts it raised courage and confidence but fear and guilt were aroused in many consciences, most thinking, "Now we're on the up and up and he'll do it,"

Herr von Meusebach immediately took over the management of the business. He had a notice posted on the trunk of the all-encompassing elm in the market square from which anyone could feel the fresh breeze that was now blowing down again from the Sophienburg:

German Countrymen,
From today on, the business of the Society will again be taken over by myself. We would like to sincerely thank all those who, despite the hardships, are committed to the good of the city and I call upon them to continue to help us.

The economic situation has not improved. Despite my cries for help not a penny has been forthcoming from Mainz in the last six months. Today, more than ever, we have to depend on ourselves and that is hard but it must be said so that no one is deceived. That is why I wish to make the following announcement:

1. Only those who work will be fed from the Society's supplies.

2. Anyone who does not immediately make his assigned land cultivable will be expropriated. The harvest in the coming year must make us independent of any outside supply.

3. The fencing of the plots of land are to be completed without delay so that the rearing of cattle for dairy produce and slaughter can be carried out to the extent that is in keeping with the size of our land.

4. The depletion of the forest belonging to the Society area has to stop immediately and in the future, wood assignments will

only be made through Herr Zink. He must receive an explanation of the purpose and scope of each timber claim.

5. Deliveries beyond the amount of wood due to an individual must either be paid for in cash or compensated for through community work.

6. As soon as the weather allows, the fleet of vehicles available to us will collect the people who are still in Carlshafen and there will be no reward for this.

7. I am resolved to intervene ruthlessly against all lascivious living with the help of the new community authorities. Joyfulness and entertainment should, according to our tradition, be carried out in a dignified and decent manner and for that reason I will have to close some dubious saloons.

8. Using all available labor, the Society plans to build a hospital and an orphanage as soon as possible and both facilities will be allocated the necessary land.

9. I recommend that all those who believe that they cannot submit to these stipulations should leave the Society's territory.

New Braunfels July 16, 1846.

von Meusebach<br>Commissioner-General.

That struck home but opinions varied. He who loved this life had to come to terms with the things that stood before them. Those feeling outrage and revolt kept to themselves.

Many hands got harder to work and only furtively did people wonder, "What will happen about the grant?" The fear of the Commissioner-General's energy and determination soon made things seem more concrete and more secure than they really were so things started to move forward. One blockhouse after another was finished and the development of the community, poor as it was, had already reached a certain constancy that could be inhibited by setbacks but could no longer be stopped.

The Commissioner-General was concerned about the conditions in Fredericksburg. Beneh had failed completely and Wilcke could not manage it on his own. The breakdown of the disposition in the city on the Pedernales had precariously advanced and intervention was now necessary. The medical doctor Schubert, an eccentric with strange healing methods, had come with Herr von Meusebach and he tried strange miraculous healing through the laying on of hands and mystical phrases. For many patients he was their last hope. It was said that he had tried to found a German settlement in Texas before the Society was founded and it should be known that his own compatriots had chased him away. Meusebach met him in Houston with the rest of his belongings and brought him to New Braunfels, appointing him at the end of July 1846 as director of Fredericksburg. Thus the Commissioner-General proved that he had little knowledge of human nature. On the other hand, Zink, after a few days of being with the man, did not have a good opinion of him and with great hesitation envisaged him going to the Pedernales.

The deadly heat of the summer subsided, slowly turning into autumn. The cemetery in New Braunfels had grown and the new hospital was still occupied to the last bed. Ervendberg continued to fight for every life and a young doctor, Dr. Keidel arrived from Carlshafen during the last days of August. He had managed to fight his way through the prairie with some young men to the Comal River and became a welcome helper to the pastor.

At the end of September, a messenger brought an urgent letter from Austin. When the Commissioner-General read its contents a happy smile flew across his face — the Society had made a new credit of seventy thousand dollars available to him. However, whilst reading it, two deep wrinkles formed over the strong nose in his forehead, "The hell, what's that all this about again?" and throwing the letter on the table he called to Zink.

"Here read this, what nonsense! What's the name of the man they're sending us? Kappes? As if we'd be helped by things like audits, commissions and inspections! What we need is just money but certainly no snoopers and babblers." He laughed scornfully, "What's in the letter? Privy Secretary with special powers? Truly, Zink, these people are really great at inventing titles and caveats and as far as I'm concerned, the Privy Secretary Kappes can go and get lost!"

On the same day, the special representative of the Mainz Society, Herr Kappes, landed in Galveston. Being a vain person in his mid-thirties, during the whole journey he had allowed himself to be carried away by the high feelings with which his important commission befuddled him.

"Captain," he had boasted one evening on the ship, "as true as I am sitting here, I'll muck those Augean stables out and won't spare anyone, as I wish to prove to their Lordships in Mainz how right they were when they sent me to Texas. The bubble will be burst because the management has failed miserably and now they blame us in Mainz but just wait, they'll be talking about Kappes for a long time afterwards for sure!" This pomp and circumstance made no impression on the captain as he blew a thick cloud of smoke out of his mouth and mused on his own thoughts.

Kappes was neither a farmer nor a merchant and he did not speak English, knowing not a single paragraph of American law. He was neither a soldier nor a technician but just a minion of the board in Mainz who was driven by vanity.

Soon after his landing, Herr Kappes heard all sorts of opinions about and impressions of the Commissioner-General. Since the speech that Herr von Meusebach had made to the creditors of the association before the prince's departure in New Orleans, he had become someone to be reckoned with for the businessmen crowd. Despite all the indebtedness and uncertainty of the whole undertaking, the Americans felt affection for the fearless daredevil. He was more akin to their kind and for many he just seemed to be in the wrong job. Even if they also blocked credit for the Society, many would have liked to personally help the commissioner-general.

The Privy Secretary listened but what he heard was not pleasing to him and he immediately realized that he would not be able to deal with Herr von Meusebach as he had bragged. Since he was too cowardly for honest action, he sided with the Commissioner-General's open and hidden enemies and sought to win them over for his dubious intentions.

"I *am* the Society," he cockily said to some merchants in Galveston. "Who hopes to settle his demands, must side with me because I'll be clearing up the mess and make the undertaking healthy."

He succeeded in bringing together a front against the Commissioner-General, also approaching Fisher, with the instinct of the hater. The two met in Houston like two foxes sitting opposite each other.

"That's clear," said Kappes, "if the grant isn't reached by the summer of 1847, the Society will lose it. I see right through the man and he's delaying the last foray into the colony until the crucial moment has passed wherewith of course your claims are lost, Herr Consul."

"Quite right, Herr Privy Secretary," smirked Fisher. "The contract grants me one-sixth of the area in the grant as personal property, and I don't feel like letting the dilatoriness of this man deprive me of my rights."

"In my opinion, it shouldn't have been so difficult to reach the Society's area. There was enough money and people to do it and we in Mainz really did not allow a lack of anything. Only mismanagement is to blame here for everything but I'll make the undertaking healthy, just wait."

"Bravo, Herr Privy Secretary, you are the man who has so far been missing so why weren't you sent sooner?"

Fisher proceeded according to plan and skillfully exploited Herr Kappes' pompous vanity to his advantage. He immediately recognized the reasons for which the Privy Secretary was approaching him.

"What do you intend to do first, Privy Secretary?" He flatteringly asked.

"There are many ways to Rome."

"But only one leads to New Braunfels," Fisher replied.

Kappes looked inquiringly at the consul who let him fidget for a while before he said with an amiable smile, "Maybe I can be of some help"

"Excellent, Herr Consul. I want to make you my special representative. You could travel ahead in an official position and settle the question of departure into the grant until my arrival with Meusebach. I have a lot of business to do on the coast which will delay me for a while so if you agree, I'll invest you immediately with the necessary powers and the injustice that the prince inflicted upon you when he dismissed you will now be made good. I authorize you fully in the use of your original rights."

"Too kind, Herr Privy Secretary. If you think I can be of use to you, please count on me."

Thus Fisher came back to New Braunfels. After the Commissioner-General had read the authorization, the two men looked at each other piercingly for a few moments.

"I don't think that Herr Kappes would have had a particularly good reception among the people here, quite apart from me so that's why he's sent you. Well, I have to acknowledge your position on the basis of the power of attorney and will appropriate quarters here in the administration building and you can eat with the Society officers at the common table. What you have to say to me please do so tomorrow, as I am rather busy today."

When Fisher looked out of the window a while later, the Commissioner-General was riding down the path to the city with two ladies. "The Commissioner-General is very certainly very busy," he thought. "It's going to be tough here."

Then he went out into the yard as Zink happened to run past him without greeting, taking over a transport of groceries that American merchants had delivered to the warehouse. Fisher tried to talk to him but Zink looked past him as if he were not there.

The next day Fisher had the first discussion with the Commissioner-General.

"So, what do you want, Herr Consul?"

Fisher called for immediate departure into the grant in far-flung remarks. He avoided talking about his rights and pretended that his efforts to get to the upper Colorado area had come only out of concern for the Germans.

Meusebach eyed the consul form Bremen sharply, "You'll not blame me Herr Fisher if I meet you with a good dose of mistrust. Through your business conduct you are to blame for the awful events of these two years, which is determining my attitude towards you. Admittedly, the concession expires on the date specified in the purchase contract but that'd still be *my* concern and not yours. Do you really think there's a reasonable person here who'd be responsible for the disaster that the settlement of the grant must bring with it? We've learnt the hard way enough already. Look over there. On the crest of the hillside is the cemetery where a few hundred dead are buried and a lot of that can be accounted to you."

"I thought you were tougher than that, Herr Commissioner. It was clear to every sober thinker that there would be sacrifices with an undertaking of this size and the move to the grant now demands the last one!"

The Commissioner-General looked hard at Fisher. "I know what it means to put aside the loss of human lives. You're sitting here as a businessman, hiding things from me which you cover over with philanthropic care. If we were sitting opposite each other as private persons, then I'd have to tell you all sorts of things. You've earned enough on the suffering of our compatriots and the fact that the prince threw you out of this enterprise is one of the few accomplishments of his that I acknowledge. For me, people of your sort on the whole are human traffickers and nothing more."

"Sir!" Snapped Fisher.

"No need to get worked up, Herr Consul! I respect you as representative of Herr Privy Secretary Kappes but I prefer to have people like you as enemies rather than friends. Just for the sake of clarity, before I make a general advance into the grant, an expedition would first have to explore whether it's worthwhile at all and whether we wouldn't do better to stay here. Your conduct of business, Herr Consul is not too different from that of Herr Bourgeois d'Orvanne. I have the honor!"

Although in speechless fury, Fisher held back. For days he did not have the opportunity to talk to Herr von Meusebach again but he had to do something so he sneaked up to the troublemakers in the city. Cleverly he knew how to fan the secretly smoldering glow to flames. Acting as a concerned honest man, he knew how to stir people up by pointing out the danger of losing the grant. The malicious agitator sat together with hotheads in the Count's tavern. A Herr Ivanowski took the word for those who as a beneficiary of the Society abhorred any regulated work. Fisher always gave the landlord sufficient money to ensure that the gathering was not lacking in schnapps.

They poked around in the private life of the Commissioner-General and puffed themselves up to act as moral judges "who are the two women, that he has with him?" It was said. "They are living at our expense. He must be held publicly accountable to the whole community and then scared away with shame and disgrace," some demanded.

"He's not worth it!" others cried. "Shoot him to pieces and then we'll be free!"

Fisher then deftly muffled and managed to extract from the confusion decisions that were to be handed over to the public as the "voice of the people".

---

"If you don't agree with my intentions, then you're free to resign your post because I'll turn Fredericksburg into a spiritual republic that'll faithfully respond to the promptings of the voices whose mouthpiece I am," said Dr. Schubert one day to Wilcke in unctuous tones.

"I'll not move one millimeter! I didn't get the job that holds me here from you but rather has it grown out of the fate of our compatriots and will be finished when it's so secured that I'm no longer needed. Herr Beneh allowed himself be pushed out but you'll not achieve that with me."

Schubert's enthusiasm and megalomania were taken to excessive limits.

Since the arrival of the miracle doctor much had changed in Fredericksburg. Like an apostle, the new director had come among the suffering people and preached to them that they needed to cleanse themselves in this world for a better existence in the hereafter. "Now I have appeared as a vessel of a higher will to mitigate your lot and only blind faith in me and my job can help you," he preached.

Dr. Schubert had received several thousand dollars out of the Society's last transfer from the Commissioner-General, which also went to his head. The man which had to date done little good for Texas thought that the money could never run out so he created a retinue of minions who worshipped him as long as they had an advantage from him.

People queued in front of Schubert's pharmacy every morning to receive his miraculous medicines that he secretly mixed. For some they worked well because they had nothing left except belief in the power of the new man. A strangely dazzling air of faith, hope, and poverty hovered over the fraught community.

"The Society is Satan," droned Schubert, "and out of its evil your misery will flow with this piece of earth which you call Fredericksburg destined to be a place of torment, cursed and damned as long as you stand upon it. Look west! Heaven has reserved a paradise for you that will make you happy because there lies the grant and God has chosen me to lead you!"

Eyes would glow when he talked like that, hearts beat faster and hope flew wistfully westward. Miracles were invented to prove Schubert's mission and many were infected by his mental illness. When Beneh came to New Braunfels and told about the mischief of the Fredericksburg director, the Commissioner-General immediately sent Dr. Keidel.

Schubert however denied him the use of the pharmacy, making any medical assistance impossible for him. "An envoy of Satan has come among us so keep out of his way!" Thus those who wanted to be sure of their benefits had to avoid Keidel.

In the morning of December 17, 1846, Dr. Schubert went west with fifteen people to fulfill his calling. Two light wagons hauled by mules carried the luggage. Cannon were included for which he had a large box of powder loaded. He took two Indians as guides who were intent on not bringing whites into their hunting grounds under any circumstances.

Granite and quartz mountains were crossed, going over bare, eerily quiet plateaus as Indian tracks multiplied. The days were warm, the nights cold and the loneliness was crushing. Often the cannon would be fired, their dull bang rolling alien over the strange earth to be once again even quieter.

One morning the two Indians had disappeared, taking the best horses. Dr. Schubert fired the cannon until the last grain of powder in the transparent air had turned to smoke. Then an inner voice told him he needed to return, so on January 1, 1847, the expedition arrived back in Fredericksburg.

After this strange undertaking, the halo with that Dr. Schubert had adorned himself with on his own volition began to slowly fade and Wilcke's influence increased once again.

At the same time, under the leadership of Fisher, disaster was brewing in New Braunfels. Almost as if agreed, Kappes appeared and everything was ready for a decisive blow. When the Privy Secretary was informed about the situation by Fisher, he attempted to be even more spiteful to Herr von Meusebach.

"Save yourself all the rest, Herr Kappes," said the Commissioner-General to him one day. "This winter and the next spring still and then we'll be living from our own bread!"

"I'm not deceived by your delaying and evasive talk," Kappes sharply retorted, "and I demand a detailed account of the financial situation."

"Just be calm young man," replied the Commissioner-General, "I refuse to do that point blank—you can only hold us back but you can't get the better of us."

"Commissioner-General, don't forget that I'm calling you to account as a representative of the Society and not as a private person."

"One is just as important to me as the other. I haven't been standing here for the sake of the Society for a long time and my only responsibility is to our people."

"Then I'll dismiss you!"

"I'll go when I want to and when it's time."

"I'll block the funds that are under my control immediately..."

"And upon the mountains of guilt that should be crushing their Lordships in Mainz load add yet another? So do what think you have to do." He laughed scornfully.

"Well, if you don't want it any other way I'll call the help of a Texas court"

"Perfect, Herr Kappes and I'll whip up our pack of Texas creditors who'll have you in debtors' jail for eternal life. Don't set it off because I can assure you of that already."

Herr von Meusebach let every attack glance off and became even cooler and superior. "Stop it, Herr Privy Secretary! Do what you want but leave me alone. There have always been venal persons who sought to hide a lack of conviction behind important words. I just don't want to be unnecessarily disturbed at my work." He turned and left.

On the same day Kappes had a secret conversation with the leader of the discontented, Herr Leopold von Ivanowski.

"Everything's ready," he said to him, "we just have to wait for the best time to strike. My people are burning to get hold of the tyrant. Of course I agree that Consul Fisher should be the successor and he deserves it. We can wait and see whether we shoot or hang Meusebach later after the verdict of a people's court. In any case, we have thirty rifles and an even larger number of pistols."

Christmas went by as northerly storms swept over New Braunfels, bringing cold nights in which a layer of ice as thick as a finger covered the puddles and ponds. Memories of the homeland wove delicate threads from person to person and most felt that the ground had become firmer under their feet and life had triumphed.

During the night of December 30, 1846, the ringleaders gathered in the Count's tavern to discuss the last measures for the strike. For a short time Fisher and Kappes also flitted in but before leaving the tavern through a back door, they handed Ivanowski a large sum of money that was turned into liquor and wine. After midnight, as courage rose, the loudest of the heroes signed a proclamation in advance designated by Ivanovsky to be posted on the trunk of the elm at the marketplace. It was determined that the crowd of conspirators would gather at the tavern after the signal from a horn at eight o'clock in the morning. From there, the storm on the Sophienburg would begin.

The rebels drank in increasingly wild enthusiasm, reaching a climax when Ivanowski laboriously climbed onto a table and read the text of the proclamation in a ranting voice:

"Citizens of New Braunfels!

"Today, on the last day of 1846, the year in which hundreds of our German compatriots fell victim to the poor administration of the Society for the Protection of German Immigrants...," he started, shaking from swallowing hard, "today I call you to shake off the shackles that are accompanying us into the new homeland and which daily come to the light of day as more oppressive and outrageous." He swayed thoughtfully from side to side and the large piece of paper slipped out of his hands, curling up. It was handed it up to him again and he smoothed it out, continuing, "All our compatriots in Germany are surprised at how we allow ourselves to be wickedly and fraudulently treated here by a single man named von Meusebach. All the citizens of Texas and every American laugh at the German servile mind which realizes clearly that the only plague is this Meusebach and yet doesn't dare to free itself by force."

An applause broke out and first when there was a break could Ivanovsky continue, "Forward! Let's end the old year by deposing and chasing away people who don't want the protection but the ruin of the immigrants. Let's call together,"

> Long live and may the Society live forever!
> But curse the human offender Meusebach!

A tremendous din arose, empty bottles flying against the walls and shattering as two men picked up Ivanovsky and carried him across the large room. A while later, the Count had to bring pen and ink as Ivanovsky had asked some of his confidants to put their names under the call, writing his own last.

"The Committee: C.W. Thomae, H. Bevenroth, Cr. Moesgen, P. Linnarz, Chr. Boeckel, C. Herber. Leopold von Ivanowsi."

The last of them staggered out of the tavern at four o'clock and went to their beds. When, on December 31, 1846, the hornist, after eight o'clock in the morning and shivering somewhat, nailed the proclamation to the elm and blew the agreed signal. He was surprised that none of the conspirators were on their feet. Brilliant trumpet sound pierced the morning mist as women and children came running and finally the first strikers arrived. As the sun came up Ivanovsky was nowhere to be seen.

After a while the crowd of curious people started to grow bigger and bigger, surrounding the heroes of the morning like a wall. At nine o'clock, Ivanovsky pulled Leopold out of bed. Startled, he looked at his watch, "Goodness gracious, almost an hour late!" He picked up his rifle, dagger and pistols and hurried to the meeting place. There, some of the conspirators had quietly disappeared again. Ivanovsky immediately took sight of the situation, passed a few liters of schnapps around and gave the order to ring the bell next to the church.

At the same time, the Commissioner-General was sitting at the Sophienburg with Fisher and Kappes at the breakfast table with nobody speaking a word. The two instigators laid tensely in wait, looking regularly at the clock. Kappes was pale and he felt every hair on his head whilst Fisher drummed his fingers nervously on the table top.

The sun was shining in the large middle room. A wonderful peace lay outside over the world as the bell sounded and the two looked at each other. "Finally," everyone thought. The Commissioner-General went over to the window where he saw a confused crowd of people, perhaps a hundred and fifty, the majority women and children, crowding their way up to the castle.

The bell rang wilder and Herr von Meusebach opened the window and asked back into the room, "What's going on?" but Kappes and Fisher just shrugged.

Down below, Ivanovsky jumped out of the mob and called on the women and children to turn back in case they could be shot. Weapons flashed in the sun and single shouts could already be clearly heard, "Murderers!" Shouted roaring voices. "Hang him up! Get him out, the bastard, the son of a bitch, the thief and robber! He wants to deprive us of the grant!"

Rifles were threateningly swung and hats waved, spurring them on. Ivanovsky had ordered not to fire before being attacked as the Commissioner-General had to be caught alive.

Meusebach turned around. His eyes glanced over the two at the table as he guessed their involvement.

Then he called out, "Guard!"

Waldbaer leaped over. "Herr Commissioner-General?"

"Open the left wing of the gate and let the people in. Do not shoot before the others start and the guard should hold back at the moment!"

Ivanovsky, his rifle under his arm, was the first to enter the wide yard and umped onto the veranda in front of the middle room. From the staircase he yelled to the following crowd, "He's sitting in the room, German compatriots, we've reached our goal. The days of the murderer Meusebach are numbered! We are the justice which shall find an end to its relentless journey!"

The crowd roared applause.

He leaned his rifle against one of the support beams that held the porch roof and demanded entry into the room.

Nothing moved within so he knocked harder. Meusebach's eyes were fixed on Kappes and Fisher as the fist outside thundered against the door. Fisher could no longer control himself and jumped up. The members of the committee had just come to the porch and Fisher talked to them persuasively for a while.

He entered the room again at the head of the committee. The Commissioner-General got up and looked at the men quietly and wordlessly and Kappes was deflated. At last the consul began, "The population of New Braunfels, represented here by these men, makes the following demands from you."

Meusebach looked at the deputation and said, "Herr Consul, you did not choose the very best for your cause. A nice city representation, I must say! Where is the mayor and why did the magistrate and other authorities not come? I know who's making themselves important out there. Tell me what do you want from me but be brief!"

Ivanowski sensed how the uproar of indignation was threatening to fizzle out with sober negotiations. Therefore he stomped his foot and shouted at the Commissioner-General, "Out there, the people's soul is seething and demanding its right!"

However, he could not change the situation and the rebels in the yard were shivering and the long wait was making them compliant. Four demands gradually emerged from the muddled speeches:

1. The grant may not expire. The immigrants should now receive individual allocations of their promised three hundred and sixty or one hundred and sixty acres of land in the Society's area.

2. An expedition must go forward into the grant as soon as possible and carry out a survey.

3. Anyone who for some reason, especially after the announcement of July 16, has been deprived of their claimable land in the urban area must receive it immediately.

4. Herr von Meusebach shall resign but continue until the arrival of a new Commissioner-General.

"I have nothing against you making these demands on me," said the Commissioner-General coolly.

Fisher hurried outside and read the demands to the rest of those still waiting. The people agreed, soon scattered and celebrated their victory in the tavern of the Count.

When Fisher had returned into the room, the Commissioner-General said sharply, "I emphasize that these remain only as demands whose fulfillment I reserve at my sole discretion!"

Kappes and Fisher were horrified to realize that they had done something stupid.

Smiling with a certain superiority, the Commissioner-General continued, "One claim could be fulfilled immediately and I will resign if Herr Kappes takes my place."

The eyes of the men of the committee pointed questioningly towards the Privy Secretary. "That is impossible—I have higher responsibilities and must reject the application," he said unctuously.

A few days later Fisher and Kappes left. They were going to seek other ways of eradicating Meusebach and achieving their goals.

So ended the "Storm on the Sophienburg" on December 31 1846.

---

"Now the time has come. I'm thinking of leaving on January 14." The commissioner looked down at the city as Zink was stooping over a drawing board.

"In case anything should happen to me, I'll leave the key for the box in my desk. There you'll find everything I have to say about the Society and myself. I notified the Government of Austin of the expedition to the grant but I didn't believe that so many young people would be registering to participate but the most able could be selected.

"Characteristic of the uproar of December 31 is the fact that none of those heroes has made themselves available and it's gone quiet where they're concerned.

"Please inform Herr Meriwether from Virginia that he may build a flour and sawmill on the Comal River at his own expense. It's sad that we were unable to bring the two mills which had been put up by the Society from Carlshafen to New Braunfels but the Society's property was always thrown away in an emergency before anything else. Then a letter from a Dr. Roemer has been received. The man is from the homeland, is currently in Austin and has heard of my intention to visit the Society's area and is now asking to join the wagon train. He is a scientist, geographer and geologist and his cooperation could be very useful to us so write to him to tell him to follow."

In those days, hardly anyone spoke of anything other than the wagon train to the grant. Once again the old dreams and hopes started to come to light.

The so-long-awaited paradise should lie in the northwest with unimaginable fertility and loveliness. Their eyes sparkled when the excited emigrants secretly and quietly talked about the joyous life that would await them there but many felt as if they were talking about something unattainable. They no longer viewed those withdrawing with envy and resentment but rather wished them well and a good homecoming.

The forty-man expedition in separate marching squads initially advanced to Fredericksburg from where it was to continue in a closed wagon train.

The Commissioner-General rode out from New Braunfels to Fredericksburg on January 20, 1847. There he checked people, animals and stocks for the last time. Some wealthy young men of education had also joined the adventurous train whilst the rest, well-armed people, were paid by the Society. The supplies had been put together with prudence and care with plenty of space for the gifts for the Indians.

The vanguard was led by the Commissioner-General himself, putting it together from old soldiers to whom Ludwig Wilcke, Beneh from Wehlar and a lieutenant von Plewe belonged. In the summer of 1846, the son of the Captain von Wrede who had been murdered by the Indians, arrived from Berlin with a lieutenant Zenner. They also joined the vanguard together with Schmitz and Waldbaer.

The expedition also included the two American surveyors Hovard and Tivg. They were particularly well armed for, as men seen as those who stole their land, they were more hated and persecuted by the Indians. The season demanded warm clothes so therefore a large supply of woolen blankets and buffalo skins were stowed in the wagons.

An impressive procession of cavalry, pack animals and wagons left Fredericksburg at the beginning of February 1847. The expedition headed northwest over barren heights covered with huge cactuses. Daily march progress was poor because of the difficulties of the terrain and the American horses were very sensitive. The most dangerous parts of the way had to be made passable with ax, shovel and hoe but finally they saw forest in the distance and a valley opening up before them. Oaks and mesquite trees sprang out of the ground, their tops pointing towards the steel-gray sky with a river gleaming through the trees.

"The Llano," said the Commissioner-General, "we are at the frontier of the grant but also in the hunting grounds of the Indians."

So they rested and the Commissioner-General had the camp fortified and reinforced guards deployed with a two-hour relief.

In the evening, six Comanche Indians rode into the forest, were stopped by the guard and demanded to speak with the chief with the burning hair. The Commissioner-General had an interpreter, the Mexican Lorenzo di Noza who asked the redskins what they wanted. Calm yet suspicious, they stated their enquiry, "We want to know what the white men are looking for."

Behind their words quivered great agitation and the spokesman betrayed himself once with the sentence, "We are ready to fight."

Herr von Meusebach assured them of the peaceful purpose of the journey and he was not ungenerous with gifts, suggesting that the Comanches make a solemn peace with him.

He invited the messengers to eat and they rushed like hungry predators at the supplies of the expedition. "These guys are starved and they don't seem to be doing well. We'll have to be careful," Wilcke said when he saw that.

On February 9, after a grueling march across sandstone and granite, the expedition climbed down into the valley of San Saba. They often came across rock crystals, some thinking that they were diamonds.

The Commissioner-General laughed when they showed him. "If they were really diamonds then the buccaneers of the whole world would have ransacked this wasteland long ago and we Germans would have come, as so often, too late."

A lovely hollow with wide meadows accommodated them and one of the men of the vanguard said, as they sat around the campfires, "What I've seen so far wasn't worth much. Barren highlands and bare mountains interspersed with a few narrow, more or less fertile valleys. If the blessing doesn't come soon, we can be glad we didn't bring our compatriots here. We should've taken Fisher with us to hold him responsible for his trade—right here on the spot."

The sun shone purple over the left valley wall of the San Saba and the Commissioner-General was looking at the turkeys that were stuck on the skewers. "You're right, Beneh," he said, "for larger settlements the country is inappropriate. Individual farmers would probably find enough usable soil but the wilderness between the rivers, the desolate vastness and the Indian danger —none would have it easy. Just now I thought that once I'm done with everything, then I could retreat into that silence to come back to myself out of sheer philanthropy."

Waldbaer whistled and called out, "Guard!"

They drove up and on the right edge of the valley five horsemen, doused by the embers of the setting sun, halted. The Commissioner-General blew the signal, the valley walls echoing brightly and the riders, waving their hats began to move as the dogs struck.

The Commissioner-General went to meet them and slowly the strangers groped their way down into the valley. They got off the horses and introduced themselves, "Dr. Roemeri, Major Neighbors with an assistant. In addition, the Delaware chief Jim Shaw as an interpreter with a man from his tribe."

"At last we have found you, Herr Commissioner-General," said Neighbors, pulling a letter from the saddlebag and handing it to Herr von Meusebach who immediately read it.

'The following reasons cause me to warn you against the entry into the Society's territory and its seizure. The border to Mexico is still in a state of war and it'd be possible for you to get between the fronts. The war has prevented the Indians from taking full advantage of their hunting grounds and in addition, military action against Mexico over large tracts of land has destroyed or displaced all the deer. The redskins are starving and may, as they see in the Germans invaders and land robbers, do everything in their power to annihilate you and your compatriots. Don't trust them!

'I'm unable to give you any protection, as all our forces are claimed by the war and so advise you to wait for a better time.

The Delaware chief Jim Shaw is accompanying Herr Neighbors and he is familiar with the situation and will give you information.'

That's what the Governor from Austin has written." The Commissioner-General looked up saying, "Thank you, Major, for taking the trouble to look for us." He shook his hand once more "And by the way, gentlemen, you are lucky—dinner is ready. Be our guests!"

Wilcke shared a tent with the Commissioner-General and before extinguishing the candle he said thoughtfully, "I don't know, Herr Baron, I don't like the whole story. The provision of the Texas government seems too generous for me to take it seriously."

"Why?"

"After what we've experienced since 1845, we're duty bound to be suspicious of everything here. Perhaps we could've made things easier for ourselves with a little more healthy mistrust as our basic attitude and that we didn't, proves how German we've been."

"And further?"

"The governor has an interest in us not reaching and settling the grant. He'd like it when the territory falls back to the state so that it then can be sold again—trust one of these huckster souls! As soon as they see that we're serious they're already there to scare us down to the marrow. I'd trust those people to work up the Indians against us."

The Commissioner-General pulled the buffalo skin over him and said. "Well, you don't need to see things so black as this. Just wait a bit and maybe everything will suddenly become easier than you think. So good night."

The men crept shivering out of their blankets the next morning as a heavy fog lay over the camp and the fires were being stoked busily. Sunbeams stabbed sharply into the gray ridge until they had found their way to the ground.

A white flag was fluttering on the top of a freestanding mountain and Waldbaer called the guard to be armed to and stand to attention.

The Commissioner-General putting his telescope to his eye, said, "Indians! The mountain's teeming with them as if a whole people were on their way. Blow the trumpet call!"

The horn sounded right across the valley.

"Individual groups are disengaging from the tangle and riding down to us!"

The Commissioner-General rode up with some companions to the redskins. At a hundred yards distance he had the rifles fire into the air and an answer came from the Indians' flintlocks. The redskins raced towards the Commissioner-General and his men at a gallop and hands stretched out from acquaintances, people of Buffalo Hump, toward the Germans who reciprocated. They then invited the Germans to visit them.

The Commissioner-General and his men followed the redskins, their rifles laid loaded over their saddles. "They don't seem to be feeling well, Beneh thought — the governor's right — the lads look hungry."

Neighbors said, "They live off horse and child theft, their raids usually going into Mexico, which the war has prevented. For high ransoms they return the abducted children to their relatives or sell them as slaves. We need to ask them for game and then we'll hear how they're getting on."

There must have been about six hundred warriors gathered in the camp plus an army of women and children but none of the old chiefs were there.

After the usual solemn greeting by a younger chief, Herr von Meusebach asked for meat.

"The white men have better guns," the chief explained. "Their powder is dry and stronger. The game has disappeared since the white men entered the hunting grounds of the Comanches and we don't have enough for ourselves."

A council was arranged for the next day and all the chief's answers were ambiguous and unclear.

"We've got to be careful," said the Commissioner-General as they rode back. "Under no circumstances should the fellows know our true intentions as they are touchy. I felt as though some were aspiring to our scalps."

Behind the Germans, the Indians flowed in waves down the slope on their skinny, swift horses, toward the camp in the valley where Herr von Meusebach had invited them. The expedition almost vanished in the hustle and bustle of the redskins as gluttonous, they plunged into all things edible.

The next morning, the best three horses were missing, among them the Commissioner-General's. Wilcke, packed to the brim with great treasures, rode up to the Indian camp and demanded the animals back. It was not easy to come to terms with the Indians because they stubbornly denied the robbery and only threats and gifts made the chief give in.

In the afternoon Herr von Meusebach rode to negotiations with a large entourage to the Indian camp. He told the redskins the same story as he did at the Pedernales, "We come on the white path and want to visit the old Spanish fort on the San Saba. Nearby are supposed to be silver mines and we want to see if that's true. So, depending on the outcome, it will become clear what the white men intend to do. This may be reported to the great chiefs, Buffalo Hump, Santa Anna, and Old Owl."

The young chief told them what he thought, "The people of the Comanches are alarmed by the incessant intrusion of white men. The San Saba Valley is our winter stay but more and more, the game is backing away. We're hungry and the war makes it almost impossible for us to get to Mexico. People are hard to keep under control so the white men should be careful and not dare too much."

The Commissioner-General knew how to dispel all the mistrust of the redskins and distributed a multitude of gifts.

The Indians affirmed under solemn assurances that they wanted to let the Germans move on unmolested. The Commissioner-General in his turn promised that after his return from the fort he would consult with the great chiefs and tell them what the outcome of the journey was.

The Spanish fort was, according to ancient reports, at the headwaters of the San Soba so on the trip there was an opportunity to explore the interior of the grant. One day a messenger from the great chiefs came to inquire about the status of the undertaking. The Commissioner-General told them that the Germans felt safe at peace with the Comanches and loaded him up with the last of the presents.

The terrain became more and more difficult. Axles broke and draft animals fell and had to be slaughtered. Their supplies were seriously depleted.

"Your expedition is too sluggish," said Major Neighbors to Wilcke as they had advanced but a few miles during the day. "There is too little food for the animals and they're starting to lose weight. We've not yet reached the destination and we'll have to go all the way back. I do not see a happy ending unless the Commissioner-General decides to change the undertaking and adapt it to suit the actual conditions."

Wilcke listened to these words with suspicion.

The Commissioner-General pondered for a long time when Ludwig Wilcke related Neighbors' worries. "If the man is honest, it's true what he says but if he's dishonest, he's right as well. I'll take it that he's honest," he finally said.

On February 14, the majority of the volunteers and the vehicles were sent back to Fredericksburg, Waldbaer taking the lead. Seventeen people continued on further. They were on horseback, apart from the two Mexican mule drivers. The traveling party intensified its vigilance so as not to be caught by surprise.

At one point they went over a bare plateau only for the wagon train to once again wind itself between jagged rocks. The horses suffered on the dangerous terrain, the mules coping with it better, and marching every day was an endurance test for humans and animals.

One evening the men, silent with weariness, lay on their blankets in a narrow rocky valley, the walls of which rose almost vertically, everyone giving their thoughts free rein.

"So this is the grant, the paradise of the Germans, the garden of the world, of which thousands dreamed and dreamed," mused the Commissioner-General. He felt the weight of disappointment that was making everyone sad and silent.

He straightened himself up, "Men," he called, "don't look at things on the dark side! Somebody say something! Come on Schmitz!"

The servant stood up, "Herr Commissioner-General, we need to find a way to make it easier for the animals as they are finding the burden very heavy. Do we have four barrels of wine? Put two of them into the round and get the mugs out, for a sip of wine will do us the world of good. Put wood on the fire because I want to see life crawl out of the trials and tribulation. Come on, let's sing a song!"

And as the men drank, the power of their singing started to grow. The old confidence came back to them and after the Commissioner-General had the last cups filled, they all stood up and sang at the top of their hearts Ernst Moritz Arndt's song, which had been banned in Prussia since 1841:

> *What is the German fatherland?*
> *At last give the name to this land!*
> *Where 'er the Teutonic tongue sounds,*
> *And God in heaven songs resounds,*
> *So shall it be!*
> *That, brave German, belongs to thee!*

The fort was reached on February 16. The valley of the San Saba arose softly from gorge and narrows onto a broad plateau. The fertile soil bore forests and meadows but wherever it merged into the plateau it became barren and stony.

The fort lay on a terrace above the left bank, the centuries had gnawed and crumbled it but still the bulky remains squatted upon the rocks.

"Europeans were living here a few hundred years ago but time has devoured everything that would remind us of what once was alive," Beneh said softly to Wilcke as they rode up.

The remains of the walls, eroded by wind and weather, rose some twenty feet in isolated places, silent and defiant. They went through the walls to find the rooms were divided like cells. Spanish soldiers had scratched their names on the walls and they could still be clearly read. The remains of a church could also be made out within the ring of fortifications but nowhere was there a trace of silver mines. The Commissioner-General had excavation carried out and the surroundings were searched step by step but without result. The wasteland was not going to elicit its secrets.

A narrow path lost itself above the fort in the mysterious, unexplored distance. "The Red Path, the Indians' warpath to Mexico," said Jim Shaw, the Delaware chief, sweeping his arm across from sunrise to sunset.

Dr. Roemer drew a broad, yellow spot onto the map that he had added to day by day. "All the major Texas rivers have their origins on this plateau. The fall of the land to the sea gives them their direction," he told the Commissioner-General.

On February 19, the return journey full of deprivation began. There was a lack of food and the animals dragged themselves forward, feebly and wearily. The men crashed out by the fire in the evening and everyone was disillusioned by the grant that only offered them all its poverty. One day Neighbors found a bee tree. An old, hollow oak was filled with delicious honeycombs and they broke up the floury wood, the honey spilling out towards them a golden yellow.

After crossing some of the smaller, fertile valleys, they came to the main camp of the Comanches with their three great chiefs. "Now the redskins can be reassured," said the Commissioner-General, who was riding with Dr. Roemer at the head of the wagon train. "We'll not be disputing this Dorado."

He called a halt and had the tents built up and the three great chiefs made their first visit to the German camp. After the experience of the journey, the wishes of the Commissioner-General had become modest when he sat down with the Indians for council. Major Neighbors read out the concerns of the emigrants and Herr von Meusebach asked for the lease of some land sections on the Llano and San Saba as they wanted to found individual German farms there. They were offered a thousand Spanish thaler, requiring that the surveyors should not be disrupted in their work.

After two days of negotiations, the Comanches accepted this offer. The Indians were given the right to barter with the establishments who promised to protect the Germans if they were attacked by other tribes. The Commissioner-General sacrificed the last sack of rice and the whole supply of deer meat that they had dried on the way for the feast.

The expedition arrived in Fredericksburg on March 7 accompanied by the Indians. The city was in the middle of a crisis with many cattle having starved to death over the winter and scurvy, dysentery and intermittent fever had demanded their victims. Dr. Schubert's willful administration had made everything even more muddled.

A few days before the arrival of the Commissioner-General, a wild shooting had broken out about a fight over a girl. The American Reynolds was thrown off the dance floor and he sought to avenge himself on his rival Martin from Frankfurt whose friends had driven him out. The American sneaked up to Martin's log cabin at night, lurked upon him and shot his friend Heimann in the dark thinking it was Martin. Thereupon he fled into the woods but bloodhounds and Indians found his tracks and he was caught. The outraged people locked him up with the dead man for two days and then strung him up.

"Dr. Schubert, it would have been your duty to stop this unworthy end and bring the man to a Texas court. We are beyond the wildest time of our development and I want to create order before I leave the service of the Society. The day must come when the community is freed from any paternalism of the Society. Since responsibility doesn't allow me half-baked solutions, I shall have to dismiss you, but if I can help you personally, I'll to do whatever I can."

The Commissioner-General was determined to use the last period of his administration to make New Braunfels and Fredericksburg as healthy and strong as circumstances allowed.

Leaving all his beneficiaries behind, Dr. Schubert left Fredericksburg a few days later.

"Since you, dear Wilcke, are settling on the Llano and want to make your home there with your wife and child, I can unfortunately no longer count on your help. Otherwise I would've asked you to take over the administration here. Maybe Coll will be willing to do so." said Herr von Meusebach, with melancholy in his voice.

He sat the whole long night in the administration building and worked over the report on the result of the foray into the grant to the noblemen in Mainz. In summary, he concluded:

"The territory is therefore not suitable for the settlement of large groups of people in closed communities. In the whole, vast country the size of a German kingdom, we found no consistent stretches of uniform, favorable soil. The distances between the few, really useful areas are too great and a regulated exchange of goods is therefore not possible.

"The Indians are always a threat to the small number of whites who are able to settle. All in all, the area doesn't live up to expectations and the Society has been cheated by Consul Henry Fisher.

"The two cities New Braunfels and Fredericksburg remain the only result of the enterprise and they must be the focus of all care in the future as they are the utmost that could be achieved by man and material under the given circumstances. Since conditions will continue to consolidate in the course of this year and my work will therefore become less and less, I ask for my dismissal. I'm intending to start a property at Comanche Spring."

As the Commissioner-General rode on to New Braunfels with his men, everyone was looking forward to returning. The city on the Comal had become their home, something that had become apparent to them whilst far away. House, hearth, family, friends, field and meadow drew them away from adventure with secret powers of their own.

"It'll probably be like this, Zink," said the Commissioner-General, as they sat together once again in the large central room of the Sophienburg, "there is no German luck in Texas but hopefully one day happy Germans! That, with New Germany we wanted the first, was a terrible mistake but if we reach the second, then the great sacrifice will take on a deep and eternal purpose."

# *Finale*

The spring of 1847 enticed the Germans from their houses and huts early in the morning. The sun poured its invigorating light over the Texas west and they began to farm in the fields, sowing and planting with sprightly courage. Now no one was in doubt about what was required of them.

Under pressure from the German public, the men in Mainz had made a significant sum of money available. The food was getting better and life becoming safer. Earth, sun and man had come together. There were still sick, despondent and helpless people but the healthy and the determined knew that they had won. The power of the new home rose from forests and furrows, from gardens, workshops and living rooms. It strengthened their hearts and directed their will.

Hermann Koechert in Carlshafen received sufficient funds so he had oxen, cows, and wagons bought for him in the northern states and now one wagon train after the other went off to New Braunfels and Fredericksburg. The camp emptied itself and it became still in the harbor at the blue sea.

American entrepreneurs founded the port of Indianola in the neighborhood. They scented business because they knew that the Germans had prevailed and they knew that the Society would be extinguished like a light but the power of the Germans would grow and become indispensable for the development of the young state. Thus they secured the gate into the future.

Once again in the summer, a horde of young intellectuals came across the sea. They wanted to rescue, help and fundamentally rebuild because in their opinion, no one had been able and worthy to actually found New Germany. They had come together in Darmstadt, Dr. von Herff, the son of the Hessian Minister of State, had led the party. Based on the teachings of the Hessian pastor Weidig, they wanted to lay the seed for a better world on a communist basis and show the bunglers in Texas the causes of their painful experience. However, this enterprise came to a speedy end as the young men, forced by the constraints of reality, abandoned their theories, here and there finding a piece of land that they silently worked with their hands.

The successor of Herr von Meusebach, forestry candidate Spieß from Darmstadt, arrived with them. His head was also full of the fog of mighty plans and he was soon mixed up through excessive zeal in misguided dealings and after an inglorious shootout on the Nassau Farm, he soon disappeared in the vast country without a trace.

In the summer, when the camp was almost empty, Koechert harnessed the last two ox wagons for Barbara Klappenbach. Under the protection of some of the men, she was finally able to make the trip to the man she loved and for whom she now wanted to become a housewife. She took thirty-two orphans with her to whom she had previously been a mother, plus her own son Ludwig, who was already starting to walk.

Hermann Koechert escorted her a good stretch, only returning to the desolate camp in the evening. His heart was about to burst with pain— from beginning to end of the adventure he had never had time to think about himself. Poorer than he had come, he now stood under the dark night sky, lonely and puzzled. He went up to Luise's grave and found that it was almost leveled, the loose sand sieving away after each time it was banked up. Behind it long rows rippled, hump upon hump, the victims of the struggle of the Germans for a new home.

A stranger had left a gnarled stick in the hut that was Luise's and his little souvenir from his homeland together with his own few possessions, were all that the school-board candidate Hermann Koechert from Stedtfeld near Eisenach took with him out of the camp the next morning. He became a soldier, then worked as a servant, played the organ and the flute, was a cotton picker and a cargo coachman. On the way to California he wrote his last letter home, which was a strange piece of writing that his family did not know how to handle. At the end it stated:

"Maybe humanity is destined to live out the four seasons of its existence in different parts of the world. Asia was the cradle of the human race, Europe saw the desire, the strength and the exuberance of her youth, in America, the fullness and wisdom of masculine seniority developed and after millennia, aged humanity heats its cold, trembling limbs in Africa's sun, finally sinking as dust into dust."

The light of the Mainz Society for the Protection of German Immigrants was snuffed out in 1852 with the vigorous help of its Texas creditors. It liquidated and lost everything as paper and ink were subdued to reality.

In 1848, the Stiehler Hand Atlas showed a large area in yellow print on the map of Texas. It said, "German Colony of the Mainz Society" but in the next issue, this entry was missing. Yet the names of the two German cities of New Braunfels and Fredericksburg have since been found in every major atlas as well as many others such as Weimar, New Ulm, Dresden, Castell, Leiningen, Metz, Minden, Berlin.

The Germans in Texas have never forgotten their descent, not even in the storms of the World War. They cultivate German art, read their own German newspapers and with a burning heart share in the fate of their fatherland.

If this story helps to tie the bonds hither and yonder, then it shall not have been written down in vain.

## List of Illustrations

Fig. 1: Survey Map drawn by H. Wilke. Mit Erlaubnis: https://www.raremaps.com/gallery/detail/32972?view=print.

Fig. 2: Carl Friedrich Wilhelm Emich Fürst zu Leiningen. By Josef Kriehuber (1800 -1876) [Public domain], via Wikimedia Commons.

Fig. 3: Sam Houston in 1861. By Mathew Brady - http://old-photos.blogspot.com/2009/07/general-sam-houston.html, Public Domain, https://commons.wikimedia.org/w/index.php?curid=7697111.

Fig. 5: Friedrich Ludwig Weidig. By unknown - http://www.xlibris.de/Autoren/Buechner/Buechner-Bilder/16g.jpg, Gemeinfrei, https://commons.wikimedia.org/w/index.php?curid=5082886.

Fig. 6: Carl Prinz zu Solms-Braunfels (1812-1875). By unknown - Privatbesitz von Aldina de Zavala (Texas), German Wikipedia, Public Domain, https://commons.wikimedia.org/w/index.php?curid=969353.

Fig. 4: The Stamp of the „Mainz Adelsvereins". Public Domain, https://commons.wikimedia.org/w/index.php?curid=2901212.

Fig. 7: St Louis in 1846, Painted by Henry Lewis (1819–1904) - Own work by QuartierLatin1968, 2011-05-27, Public Domain, https://commons.wikimedia.org/w/index.php?curid=15393386

Fig. 8: Germans on the way to New Braunfels. Bundesarchiv, Bild 137-005007 / CC-BY-SA 3.0 [CC BY-SA 3.0 de (http://creativecommons.org/licenses/by-sa/3.0/de/deed.en)], via Wikimedia Commons.

Fig. 9: *The farmhouse of Nicolaus Zink near Comfort, in which he died in 1887.. Von Unbekannt-http://www.rootsweb.com/~txkendal/mark.htm, Gemeinfrei, https://commons.wikimedia.org/w/index.php?curid=706954*

Fig. 10: *Costume designs for Samiel and Caspar in the original production of "Der Freischütz" ("The Marksman") - Opera by Carl Maria von Weber. Stürmer - User scan of Sadie, Stanley, ed. (1992). The New Grove Dictionary of Opera, 2: 297. London: Macmillan. ISBN 9781561592289. Credit: Kunstbibliothek, Staatliche Museen, Berlin. https://commons.wikimedia.org/wiki/File:Costume_designs_for_Samiel_and_Caspar_in_%27Der_Freisch%C3%BCtz%27_1821_-_NGO2p297.jpg*

Fig. 11: *March Route. Adapted by the author.*

Fig. 12: *Georg Jochim Jacob Friedrich A. Klappenbach, 1860's. http://sophienburg.com/blog/wp-content/uploads/ats_20130504_klappenbach.jpg*

# Notes

*(All notes have been based on information from Wikipedia unless otherwise stated)*

1 The Mainzer **Adelsverein** at Biebrich am Rhein (Verein zum Schutze Deutscher Einwanderer in Texas, "Society for the Protection of German Immigrants in Texas"), better known as the Mainzer Adelsverein ("Nobility Society of Mainz"), organized on April 20, 1842, was a colonial attempt to establish a new Germany within the borders of Texas.

The Adelsverein was organized on April 20, 1842, by twenty-one German noblemen at Biebrich on the Rhine. They gathered at the castle of the German Duke of Nassau, the future Adolphe, Grand Duke of Luxembourg, who was named Protector of the Society. In Germany, the society was referred to as Mainzer Adelsverein after the city of Mainz where it was officially registered. The society represented a significant effort to establish a new Germany on Texas soil through organized mass emigration. The land for the emigrants was to be purchased by the Adelsverein or secured through land grants from the Republic of Texas.

On January 9, 1843, Count Ludwig Joseph von Boos-Waldeck bought the 4,428-acre Nassau Plantation in Fayette County Texas for $0.75 an acre and named it after the Duke of Nassau. Twenty-five slaves were bought to work the property, which initially was considered as the primary base for arriving German immigrants. When Prince Carl of Solms-Braunfels inspected the plantation in 1844 he recommended the Verein divest itself of the property, rather than be associated with slavery. Gustav Dresel, Special Business Agent for the Adelsverein, sold Nassau plantation on July 28, 1848, to Otto von Roeder [Ed: Otto was a great uncle of the author of this edition]. Von Roeder had been the first settler in Shelby, Texas, in 1841, a year before the Adelsverein was founded in Germany, and three years before the Adelsverein sent its first colonists to Texas. Von Roeder had emigrated to Texas from Westphalia in the 1830's and was not affiliated with the Adelsverein's colonization efforts. The community of Shelby had been named for David Shelby, one of the Old Three Hundred under Stephen F. Austin. Shelby became the home of many Adelsverein colonists in 1845, but it was not founded by the organization. Because many of its German settlers spoke Latin, Shelby is

# Notes

*(All notes have been based on information from Wikipedia unless otherwise stated)*

believed to be part of the Latin Settlement communities populated in Texas at that time.

Prince Carl was appointed commissioner general by the Adelsverein in May 1844 to lead its colony in Texas. Each head of household was required to deposit 600 gulden (300 gulden for a single person) with the Adelsverein to cover transportation and housing at the colony and as credit to draw upon until they made their first harvest. The first Adelsverein-sponsored immigrants arrived in Galveston in July 1844. They traveled from Galveston to Indianola in December 1844, then moved inland to land grants acquired by the Adelsverein near Comal Springs. Prince Solms named the first colony New Braunfels in honor of his homeland.

Henry Francis Fisher and Burchard Miller sold their 1842 land grant to the Adelsverein on June 22, 1844. This grant was intended to provide for more settlements in Texas.

After Prince Solms returned to Germany, John O. Meusebach was appointed the second commissioner general of the Adelsverein in April 1845. He founded the first settlement on the outskirts of the land grant, and named it Fredericksburg, in honor of Adelsverein member Prince Frederick of Prussia. The land grant was located in Comanche territory, and to colonize, Meusebach first negotiated a treaty between the Adelsverein and the Penateka Comanche.

A separate agreement was made with the Darmstadt Forty, to settle socialist colonies within the land grant.

In 1853, due to a large amount of debt, Adelsverein ended its colonization campaign in Texas.

2   Carl, Prince of Leiningen, KG (Carl Friedrich Wilhelm Emich; 12 September 1804 – 13 November 1856) was the third Prince of Leiningen and maternal half-brother of Queen Victoria. Leiningen served as a Bavarian lieutenant general, before he briefly played an important role in German politics as the first Prime Minister of the Provisorische Zentralgewalt government formed by the Frankfurt Parliament in 1848.

    On 20 April 1842, he and 20 other noblemen gathered at Biebrich

# Notes

*(All notes have been based on information from Wikipedia unless otherwise stated)*

Palace, where they established the Adelsverein to organize the settlement of German emigrants in Texas; Carl was elected president of the society.

3  Ed.: On July 3 and Juli 6, 1842 two land grants were allocated to **Alexander Bourgeois d'Orvanne** and Armand Ducos to be settled by 1,700 Families on den Uvalde, Frio und Medina Rivers. On April 7, 1844, after all efforts at colonization proved fruitless, Bourgeois und Ducos sold their grants to the Adelsverein on the condition that Alexander Bourgeois d'Orvanne was appointed Colonial Director.

4  **Ernest II, Duke of Saxe-Coburg and Gotha** Ernest II (German: Ernst August Karl Johann Leopold Alexander Eduard; June 21, 1818 – August 22, 1893) was the sovereign duke of the Duchy of Saxe-Coburg and Gotha from January 29, 1844 to his death. He was born in Coburg; his father Ernest III, Duke of Saxe-Coburg-Saalfeld, became Duke Ernest I of Saxe-Coburg and Gotha in 1826 through an exchange of territories.

A supporter of a unified Germany, Ernest watched the various political movements with great interest. While he initially was a great and outspoken proponent of German liberalism, he surprised many by switching sides and supporting the more conservative (and eventually victorious) Prussians during the Austro-Prussian and Franco-Prussian Wars and subsequent unification of Germany. His support of the conservatives came at a price however, and he was no longer viewed as the possible leader of a political movement. According to historian Charlotte Zeepvat, Ernest became "increasingly lost in a whirl of private amusements which earned only contempt from outside".

Ernest and his only full sibling, his younger brother Prince Albert (consort to Queen Victoria of the United Kingdom), were raised as though twins. They became closer upon the separation and divorce of their parents as well as the eventual death of their mother, Princess Louise of Saxe-Gotha-Altenburg. Their relationship experienced phases of closeness as well as minor arguments as they grew older. After Albert's death in 1861, Ernest published anony-

# Notes

*(All notes have been based on information from Wikipedia unless otherwise stated)*

mous pamphlets against various members of the British royal family. However, he accepted Albert's second son Prince Alfred, Duke of Edinburgh, as his heir-presumptive. Upon Ernest's death at Reinhardsbrunn, Alfred succeeded to the ducal throne.

5 **Prince Carl (Carl) of Solms-Braunfels** (July 27, 1812–November 13, 1875), was a German prince and military officer in both the Austrian army and in the cavalry of the Grand Duchy of Hesse. As Commissioner-General of the Adelsverein (Adelsverein), he spearheaded the establishment of colonies of German immigrants in Texas. Prince Solms named New Braunfels, Texas in honor of his homeland.

Prince Friedrich Wilhelm Carl Ludwig Georg Alfred Alexander of Solms-Braunfels was born in Neustrelitz. His father was Prince Friedrick Wilhelm of Solms-Braunfels, second husband of Princess Frederica of Mecklenburg-Strelitz, who bore thirteen children during the course of her three marriages.

6 **Samuel Houston** (March 2, 1793 – July 26, 1863) was an American soldier and politician. An important leader of the Texas Revolution, Houston served as the first and third president of the Republic of Texas, and was one of the first two individuals to represent Texas in the United States Senate. He also served as the sixth governor of Tennessee and the seventh governor of Texas, the only American to be elected governor of two different states in the United States.

Houston settled in Texas in 1832. After the Battle of Gonzales, Houston helped organize Texas' provisional government and was selected as the top-ranking official in the Texian Army. He led the Texian Army to victory at the Battle of San Jacinto, the decisive battle in Texas' war for independence against Mexico. After the war, Houston won election in the 1836 Texas presidential election. He left office due to term limits in 1838, but won election to another term in the 1841 Texas presidential election. Houston played a key role in the annexation of Texas by the United States in 1845, and in 1846, he was elected to represent Texas in the United States Senate. He joined the Democratic Party and supported President James K. Polk's prosecution of the Mexican–American War.

# Notes

*(All notes have been based on information from Wikipedia unless otherwise stated)*

7   **Bernhard II. Erich Freund Duke of Sachsen-Meiningen** (Duke Bernhard Erich Freund (Freund = "Friend of His Subjects") born. December 17, 1800 died December 3, 1882 was the Duke of Sachsen - Meiningen from 1803 until 1866. (wikipedia.de).

8   **Friedrich Ludwig Weidig** (February 15, 1791–February 23, 1837) was a German Protestant theologian, pastor, activist, teacher and journalist. Initially working as a teacher in Butzbach, he then spent a short time as a pastor in Ober-Gleen, a district of Gießen. In what is now Hesse and the Middle Rhine, he was one of the main figures of the Vormärz and a pioneer of the 1848 Revolution.

Weidig was born in the Oberkleen district, Langgöns, northwest of Wetterau. The son of a chief forester and his wife, her maiden name being Liebknecht. He went to Butzbach in 1803 to go to school. During his theological studies in the Ludoviciana in Gießen he was a member of the 'fränkischen Landsmannschaft'. In 1812 he became headmaster at the boys' school in Butzbach. Following Friedrich Ludwig Jahn's example, Weidig taught his pupils drill and physical exercise and in 1814 founded a parade ground on the Schrenzer, a north-eastern foothill of the Taunus—later historians and biographers thus called him the "father of Hessian drill".

From 1818 Weidig was monitored by the authorities for his political activities in teaching, preaching and in private—he was one of the liberal democrats who aspired to establish Germany as a unified democratic nation state. In 1832 he thus travelled to south-west Germany and helped in the preparations for the Hambach Festival.

In 1833 Weidig was arrested for the first time, but in 1834 he still published four illegal issues of "Leuchter und Beleuchter für Hessen (oder der Hessen Notwehr)". The same year saw his first meeting with Georg Büchner, with whom he worked on a manuscript that Weidig then published against Büchner's wishes as "Hessischen Landboten". Weidig and his students also organised the printing and distribution of illegal pamphlets.

On 5 April 1834 Weidig was suspended from his teaching post and demoted to a small village called Ober-Gleen, now in Kirtorf, im Vo-

# Notes

*(All notes have been based on information from Wikipedia unless otherwise stated)*

gelsberg. When the "Hessischen Landboten" project was betrayed in summer 1834, Büchner fled to Straßburg but Weidig refused to emigrate to Switzerland with his family. Soon afterwards he was arrested in the Klosterkaserne barracks in Friedberg and in June 1835 put under house arrest in Darmstadt, where on 23 February 1837 he committed suicide after two years' questioning and physical abuse by state investigators, including Konrad Georgi, a known alcoholic. Ill and desperate, he had written letters to his wife from prison that were retained by his questioners "for state-political reasons" for many years after his death. His friends noted on his gravestone that he was a freedom fighter, but this was bricked up by the authorities.

9 **Carl Georg Büchner** (October 17, 1813-February 19, 1837) was a German dramatist and writer of poetry and prose, considered part of the Young Germany movement. He was also a revolutionary and the brother of physician and philosopher Ludwig Büchner. His literary achievements, though few in number, are generally held in great esteem in Germany and it is widely believed that, had it not been for his early death, he might have joined such central German literary figures as Johann Wolfgang von Goethe and Friedrich Schiller at the summit of their profession.

10 **Count Ludwig Joseph von Boos-Waldeck** (November 26, 1798–October 1, 1880) was a German noble who promoted the settling of Texas by Germans.

Boos-Waldeck was born in Koblenz as the son of Count Clemens von Boos zu Waldeck (1773-1842) and Freiin Johanna von Bibra (1774-1856). He descended from a line of Rhenish knights and nobles dating back to the 13th century. Boos-Waldeck married about 1827 Freiin Henriette von Wessenberg-Ampringen (1807-1856), the daughter of Johann Freiherr von Wessenberg-Ampringen (1773-1858). He was the uncle of the composer Victor von Boos zu Waldeck (1840-1916).

In April 1842 Boos-Waldeck and a few other nobles met at Biebrich on the Rhine, near Mainz, to organize a society that they called the Adelsverein (Adelsverein), to promote German immigration to

# Notes

*(All notes have been based on information from Wikipedia unless otherwise stated)*

Texas. In 1843 Boos-Waldeck bought and developed the Nassau Plantation near Round Top, Texas on behalf of the Adelsverein. In addition to his native German, he spoke Spanish and English when Texas came under Mexican and U.S. rule. He died in Aschaffenburg, Kingdom of Bavaria.

11 **Carl Friedrich Christian Graf zu Castell-Castell** (born December 8, 1801 at Castell Castle near Würzburg, Unterfranken, Bavaria, died March 2, 1850 in Wiesbaden, Hessen) was co-founder, Vice president und Managing Director of the "Mainz Adelsverein" as well as Duke Nassau Colonel in the War Ministry. (from wikipedia.de)

12 Ed: **Hermann Koechert** Ed: I can find no record of a person with this name so I assume that Scheffel created this character who seems to resemble himself somewhat because he also was dismissed from his post as a teacher in 1933 for political reasons.

13 **Emanationism** is an idea in the cosmology or cosmogony of certain religious or philosophical systems. Emanation, from the Latin emanare meaning "to flow from" or "to pour forth or out of", is the mode by which all things are derived from the first reality, or principle. All things are derived from the first reality or perfect God by steps of degradation to lesser degrees of the first reality or God, and at every step the emanating beings are less pure, less perfect, less divine. Emanationism is a transcendent principle from which everything is derived, and is opposed to both creationism (wherein the universe is created by a sentient God who is separate from creation) and materialism (which posits no underlying subjective and/or ontological nature behind phenomena being immanent).

14 Klemens Wenzel Nepomuk Lothar, **Prince of Metternich-Winneburg zu Beilstein** (May 15, 1773-June, 11 1859) was an Austrian diplomat who was at the center of European affairs for four decades as the Austrian Empire's foreign minister from 1809 and Chancellor from 1821 until the liberal Revolutions of 1848 forced his resignation.

A traditional conservative, Metternich was keen to maintain the balance of power, in particular by resisting Russian territorial ambitions

# Notes

*(All notes have been based on information from Wikipedia unless otherwise stated)*

in Central Europe and lands belonging to the Ottoman Empire. He disliked liberalism and strove to prevent the breakup of the Austrian Empire, for example, by crushing nationalist revolts in Austrian north Italy. At home, he pursued a similar policy, using censorship and a wide-ranging spy network to suppress unrest. Metternich has been both praised and heavily criticized for the policies he pursued. His supporters pointed out that he presided over the "Age of Metternich", when international diplomacy helped prevent major wars in Europe. His qualities as a diplomat were commended, some noting that his achievements were considerable in light of the weakness of his negotiating position. Meanwhile, his detractors argued that he could have done much to secure Austria's future, and he was deemed as a stumbling block to reforms in Austria.

15 **The *Wandering Jew*** is a mythical immortal man whose legend began to spread in Europe in the 13th century. The original legend concerns a Jew who taunted Jesus on the way to the Crucifixion and was then cursed to walk the earth until the Second Coming. The exact nature of the wanderer's indiscretion varies in different versions of the tale, as do aspects of his character; sometimes he is said to be a shoemaker or other tradesman, while sometimes he is the doorman at Pontius Pilate's estate.

There are clear echoes of the *Wandering Jew* in Wagner's The Flying Dutchman, whose plot line is adapted from a story by Heinrich Heine in which the Dutchman is referred to as 'the Wandering Jew of the ocean'.

16 This obviously refers to **Henry Francis Fisher** (1805–1867) who was a notable German Texan. Born in Kassel, Hesse, in 1837 or early 1838 he came to Houston, Texas, where he served as Hanseatic (Bremen) consul to Texas. He became interested in the exploration and colonization of the San Saba, Texas area and in 1839 was acting treasurer of the San Saba Company that was later reorganized as the San Saba Colonization Company. He was a key party in the Fisher–Miller Land Grant. He spoke German and additionally Spanish and English when Texas came under Mexican and U.S. rules.

# Notes

*(All notes have been based on information from Wikipedia unless otherwise stated)*

17 **Nicolaus Zink** (1812–1887) was the founder of Sisterdale, Texas, and builder of the fort Zinkenburg. Under the direction of Prince Carl of Solms-Braunfels, Zink led a caravan of new settlers from Indianola to New Braunfels. He laid out the town and divided the original allotted farm acreage. In 1984, the Zink house in Welfare, Texas, was designed a Recorded Texas Historic Landmark, marker 3595.

For four months, December 1844 to March 1845, Zink oversaw the settling of the colonists who arrived at Indianola, renamed Carlshafen in honor of Prince Carl of Solms-Braunfels. The colonists rode covered wagons, pushcarts, and walked, as Zink led them to New Braunfels, arriving on March 21, 1845. The first structure in their new home was a fort named Zinkenburg, in honor of the man who brought them from Indianola. Zink laid out the townsite and adjoining acreage. Zink Street in New Braunfels is named after him. In return for his labors, Zink was given 25 acres in New Braunfels and 100 acres of farmland. He subdivided the farm acreage and sold it in tracts. By 1846, Zink was bringing new colonists and merchandise from Houston to New Braunfels.

In 1847, Zink divorced Louise. By 1850, he was married to Elisabeth Mangold. They sold their Sisterdale home and acreage to Eduard Degener and moved to Barons Creek near Fredericksburg to start a gristmill. On June 4, 1866, Zink married Sara Agnes Williams.

In 1853, Zink was living in Comfort, which had opened to German settlements in 1852.

Zink acquired land on the Kendall County settlement of Welfare in 1868 and built a limestone house there. He died in Welfare on November 3, 1887, and is buried in an unmarked grave on the property.

18 **Friedrich Wilhelm von Wrede** (1786-1845) on October 24, 1845, when returning from Austin to New Braunfels, von Wrede und Oscar von Claren were killed and scalped by Indians at a place known as Live Oak Spring, approximately ten to twelve miles from Austin.

19 **Ludwig Wilke** (1818-1893) was earlier a Lieutenant in der Prussian Army and already had lived in Texas with his family by the time Solms' arrived.

# Notes

*(All notes have been based on information from Wikipedia unless otherwise stated)*

20 **Louis Cachand Ervendberg** (1809–1863?) held his first church service with the Germans in Texas in Houston on Dezember 22, 1839. He was also pastor in Industrie, Cat Spring, Biegel, La Grange und Columbus. Ervendberg was invited by Prince Carl von Solms-Braunfels to serve the Adelsverein's immigrants who he accompanied from Indianola to the area of today's New Braunfels. (Ed.)

21 **Carlshafen or Karlshafen** is the previous name (1844–1849) of the today, deserted town Indianola (Texas).

22 Dr. **Koester** was born in Frankfurt in 1817.

23 According to a story by Myra Lee Adams Goff, **Johann Jakob von Coll**, was born in Wiesbaden in 1814. In 1852 von Coll owned a saloon on the market place in New Braunfels. A farmer named Voelker came in complaining about the Adelsverein, calling it a criminal society. Von Coll collected his pistol from his room and as he returned, Voelker attacked him with a knife, drew Coll's Pistol und shot him.

24 **Oscar von Claren** (1812–1845).

25 The **Comanche** became the dominant tribe on the southern Great Plains in the 18th and 19th centuries. They are often characterized as "Lords of the Plains" and, reflecting their erstwhile prominence, they presided over a large area called Comancheria that came to include large portions of present-day Texas, Colorado, New Mexico, Oklahoma and Kansas.

Comanche power depended on bison, horses, trading, and raiding. The Comanche hunted the bison of the Great Plains for food and skins; their adoption of the horse from Spanish colonists in New Mexico made them more mobile; they traded with the Spanish, French, Americans and neighboring Native-American peoples; and (most famously) they waged war on and raided European settlements as well as other Native Americans. They took captives from weaker tribes during warfare, using them as slaves or selling them to the Spanish and (later) Mexican settlers. They also took thousands of captives from the Spanish, Mexican, and American settlers and incorporated them into Comanche society.

26 A Blue Norther, also known as a **Texas Norther**, is a fast moving

# *Notes*

*(All notes have been based on information from Wikipedia unless otherwise stated)*

cold front marked by a rapid drop in temperature, strong winds, and dark blue or "black" skies. The cold front originates from the north, hence the "norther,", and can send temperatures plummeting by 20 or 30 degrees in merely minutes.

The Midwest lacks any natural geographic barriers to protect itself from frigid winter air masses that originate in the arctic. Multiple times per year conditions will become favorable to push severe cold fronts as far south as Texas, bringing sleet and snow and causing the windchill to plunge into the teens. Depending on the time of year, high temperatures that immediately precede a Texas Norther can reach 85°F or even 90°F under bright sunlight in nearly-calm conditions before the cold front approaches. However, most Blue Northers don't advance as far south as Mexico, and even the most severe examples typically reach their apex midway through Texas. For example, cities in North Texas, like Dallas, experience drastically more Blue Northers than cities along the Gulf of Mexico, like Houston. As a city is struck by a Blue Norther, its temperatures can be 30 to 50 degrees colder than neighboring cities that are only a few miles away that have not yet been struck. Blue Northers can be dangerous due to their volatile temperature swings that catch some people unprepared.

27 **San Antonio** is the oldest city in Texas. The area was first discovered by a Spanish expedition in 1691. Der Name can be traced back to Saint Anthony of Padua, on whose feast day the missionaries made a halt. In 1718 the Franciscans founded it as a Mission and colonial outpost and the city became the first chartered civil settlement in present-day Texas in 1731. The area was still part of the Spanish Empire, and later of the Mexican Republic.

In a series of battles, the Texian Army succeeded in forcing Mexican soldiers out of the settlement areas east of San Antonio that were dominated by Americans. Under the leadership of Ben Milam, in the Battle of Bexar, December 1835, Texian forces captured San Antonio from forces commanded by General Martin Perfecto de Cos, Santa Anna's brother-in-law. In the spring of 1836, Santa Anna marched on

# Notes

*(All notes have been based on information from Wikipedia unless otherwise stated)*

San Antonio. A volunteer force under the command of James C. Neill occupied and fortified the deserted mission.

Upon his departure, the joint command of William Barrett Travis and James Bowie were left in charge of defending the old mission. The Battle of the Alamo took place from February 23 to March 6, 1836. The outnumbered Texian force was ultimately defeated, with all of the Alamo defenders killed. These men were seen as "martyrs" for the cause of Texas freedom and "Remember the Alamo" became a rallying cry in the Texian Army's eventual success at defeating Santa Anna's army.

In 1845, the United States finally decided to annex Texas and include it as a state in the Union. This led to the Mexican–American War. Though the U.S. ultimately won, the war was devastating to San Antonio. By its end, the population of the city had been reduced by almost two-thirds, to 800 inhabitants. Bolstered by migrants and immigrants, by 1860 at the start of the American Civil War, San Antonio had grown to a city of 15,000 people.

28 **Juan Martin de Veramendi** (December 17, 1778–1833).

29 **Georg Friedrich August Klappenbach** was Bürgermeister (Mayor) in Anklam in 1844. (http://www.anklam.de/Rathaus/Bürgermeister/alle-Bürgermeister).

30 The **Cunard Line** is a British–American cruise line based at Carnival House at Southampton, England, operated by Carnival UK and owned by Carnival Corporation & plc. Since 2011, Cunard and its three ships have been registered in Hamilton, Bermuda.

In 1839, Samuel Cunard, a Halifax, Nova Scotia, shipowner, was awarded the first British transatlantic steamship mail contract, and the next year formed the British and North American Royal Mail Steam-Packet Company together with Robert Napier, the famous Scottish steamship engine designer and builder, to operate the line's four pioneer paddle steamers on the Liverpool–Halifax–Boston route. For most of the next 30 years, Cunard held the Blue Riband for the fastest Atlantic voyage. However, in the 1870s Cunard fell behind its rivals, the White Star Line and the Inman Line. To meet this

# Notes

*(All notes have been based on information from Wikipedia unless otherwise stated)*

competition, in 1879 the firm was reorganized as the Cunard Steamship Company, Ltd, to raise capital.

www.ingramcontent.com/pod-product-compliance
Lightning Source LLC
LaVergne TN
LVHW032008070526
838202LV00059B/6342